RETROSPECTIVE

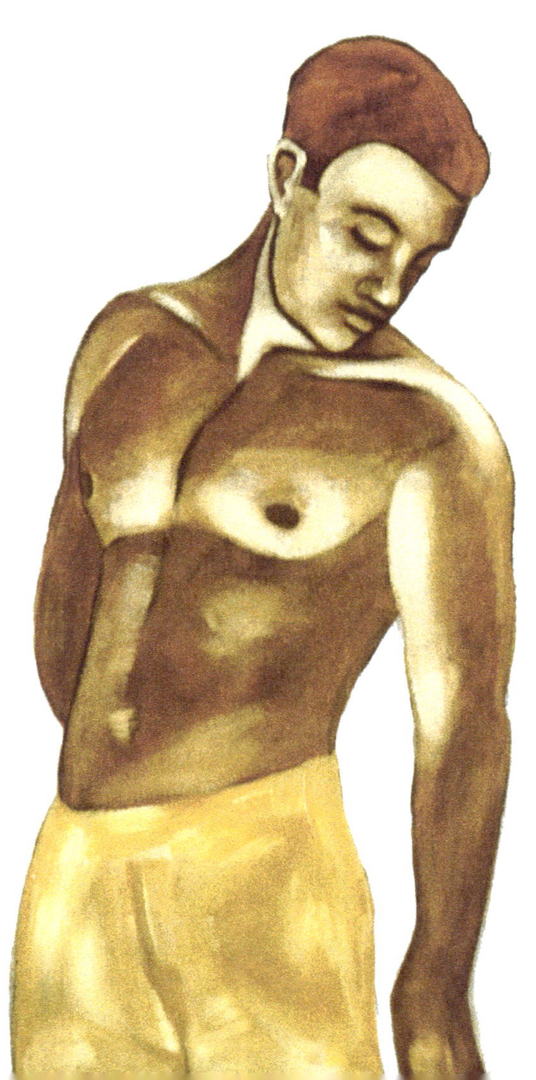

RETROSPECTIVE

Michael Tice

introduction by
Philip Mullen

bd
nyc

for Ramon

Retrospective

Published by bd-studios.com in New York City, 2017
© 2013, 2017 Michael Tice
Introduction © 2013, 2017 Philip Mullen

This book was originally published in hardcover by bd-studios.com in 2013.
New Lit Salon Press also published an ebook version at the same time.

Art Direction and Design by luke kurtis

ISBN 978-0-9890266-0-4 (hardcover)
ISBN 978-0-9992078-1-9 (paperback)

Table of Contents

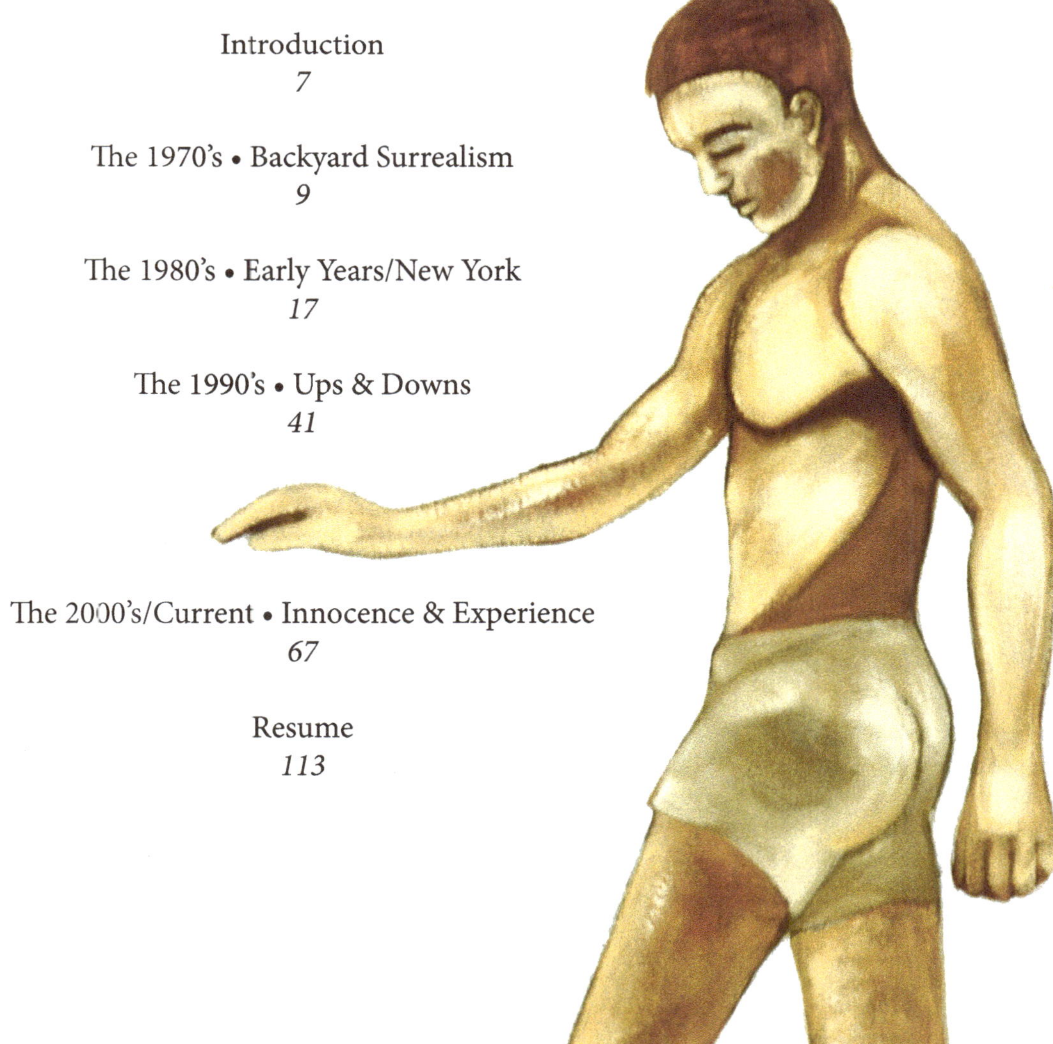

Introduction

I first met Michael Tice in 1973. As an art professor at University of South Carolina, I taught Mike advanced drawing. The class met in the basement of the library school. Being separate from the usual Art Department facilities, we could use the space at most any time. This made for an exceptional collegiality. Mike could be depended upon to show up and when he did he really showed up. One day Mike did a beautiful, large drawing during class. His skill with the medium was distracting, as other students could hardly work that day for watching him. When class ended, he painted solid white over the piece. His classmates went wild. Why would he destroy a drawing they would have cherished and protected?

Even in those early days, Mike already knew that he wanted to develop his art and understood to do so meant not considering it too precious. His approach and talent allowed him to develop a strong technical foundation. Along with these skills he had a faith in his work that somehow let him believe that what went on in his life and fantasies would actually engage others. There he was a college student doing art work about something as seemingly innocent as his childhood bike and his fellow students were absorbed in it.

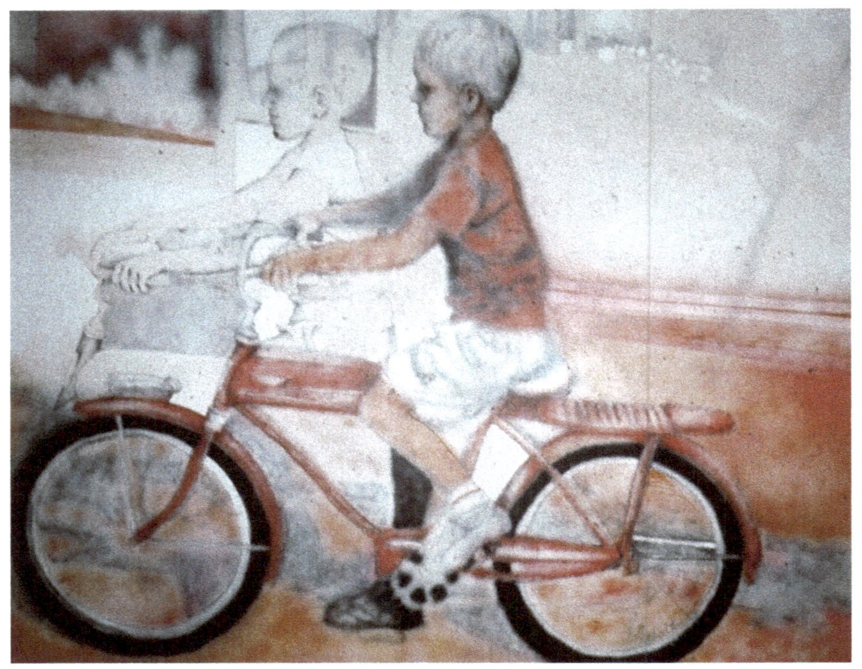

Mike's Bike, 1973
Ink, acrylic, & pencil on masonite, 48" x 60"

Mike had established two precedents that would serve him well during his career: trust in his own life for subject matter and dedication to his work without considering it too dear. In the 1980s and 90s he introduced more adult experiences into his work and allowed his technical skill, which he could be confident in, to recede. Since the turn of the century Mike has revisited, with the understanding of maturity, many of his old subjects.

With a career spanning over four decades, Mike Tice has created a body of work based on his own inner workings. His confidence and vision has allowed him to create art that simultaneously reflects the innocence of childhood and the experience of maturity. Looking through the pages of this book one can easily become as enraptured by Mike's work as his classmates were back in 1973, but for more complex reasons. *Retrospective* is about the journey from then to now.

Philip Mullen
Professor Emeritus of Art
University of South Carolina

1970's

BACKYARD SURREALISM

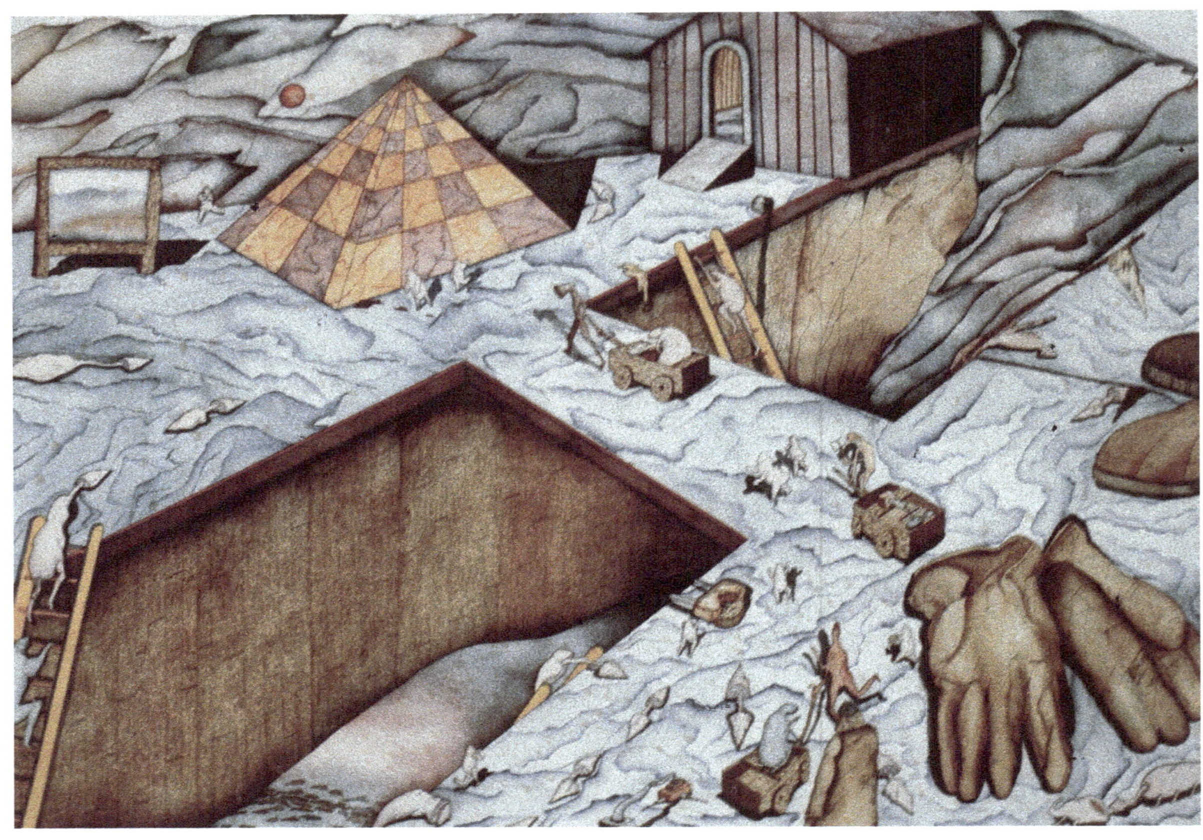

ABOVE

Country Expedition, 1979
Ink & watercolor on paper, 22" x 30"
Private Collection, New Hampshire

OPPOSITE

Life at the Laundromat, 1979
Ink & watercolor on paper, 36" x 26"
Private Collection, New York

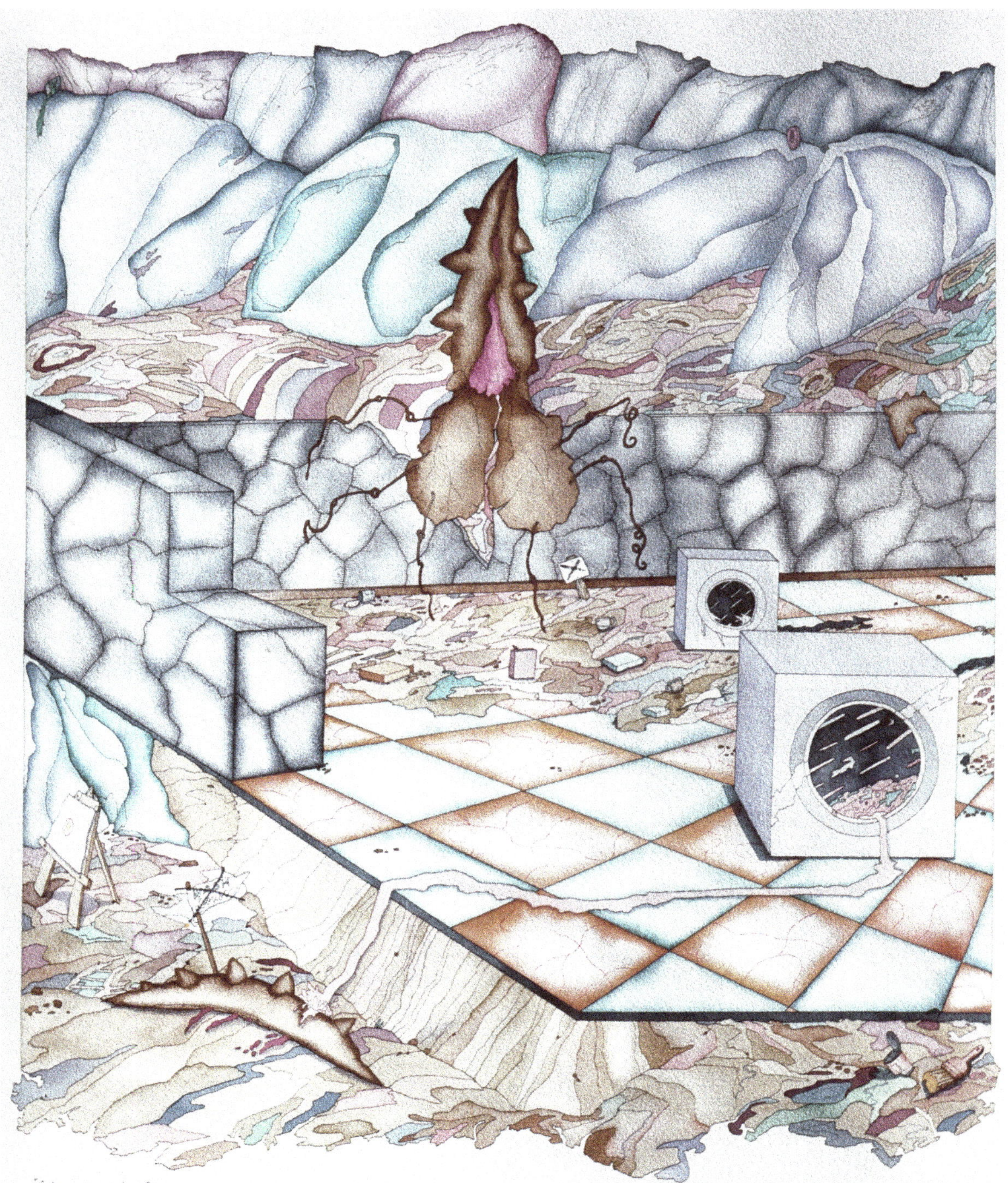

HURRY ON DOWN TO OUR LAUNDROMAT (for your mind) and try our brain-washing
USED BRAINS
Meanwhile, back at the wrench... uh, I mean the laundromat.... each
it's like finding "GOLD."
WHAT ELSE CAN DO IT? (SKY'S A LIMIT)
to be the "End of the Trail" for some folks.
we're all Humdrough, right?
Yeah, I think all that. Relax. Go to a mirror and See Yourself.
Michael Tice 1978

Ship of Fools, 1979
Ink & watercolor on paper, 22" x 30"
Greenville County Museum of Art, Greenville, SC

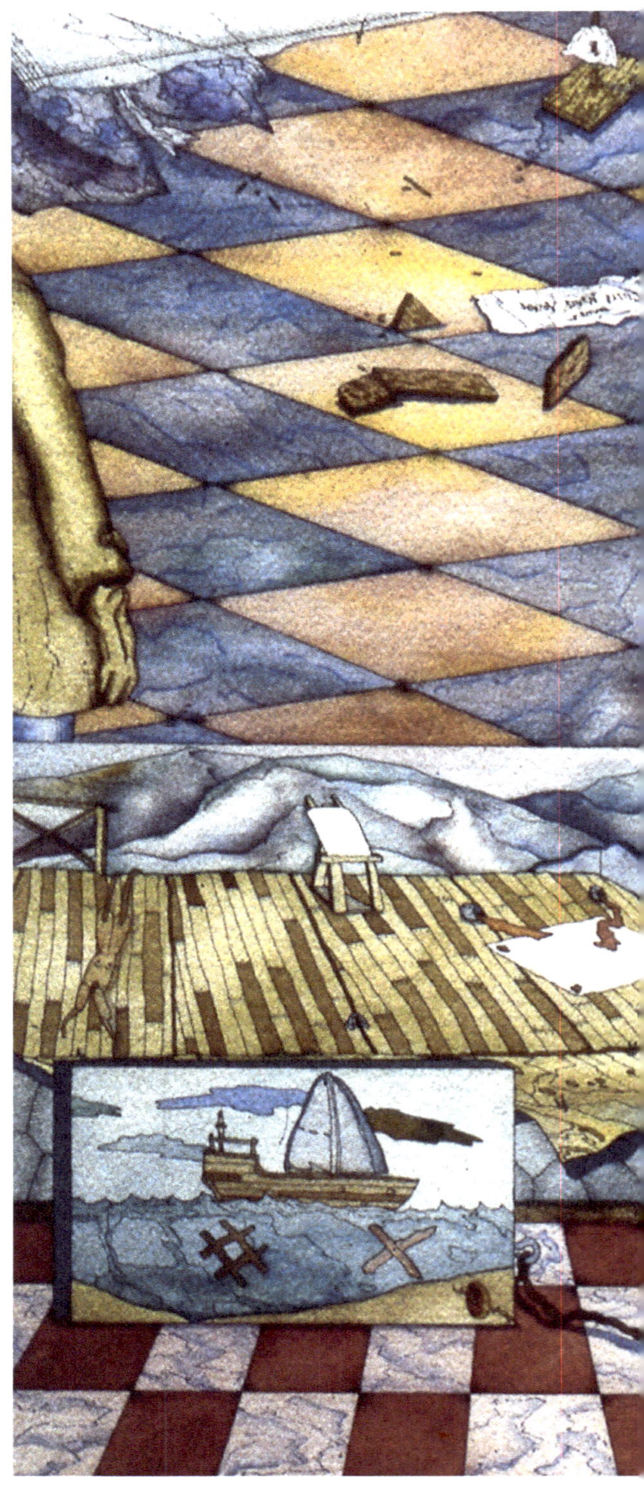

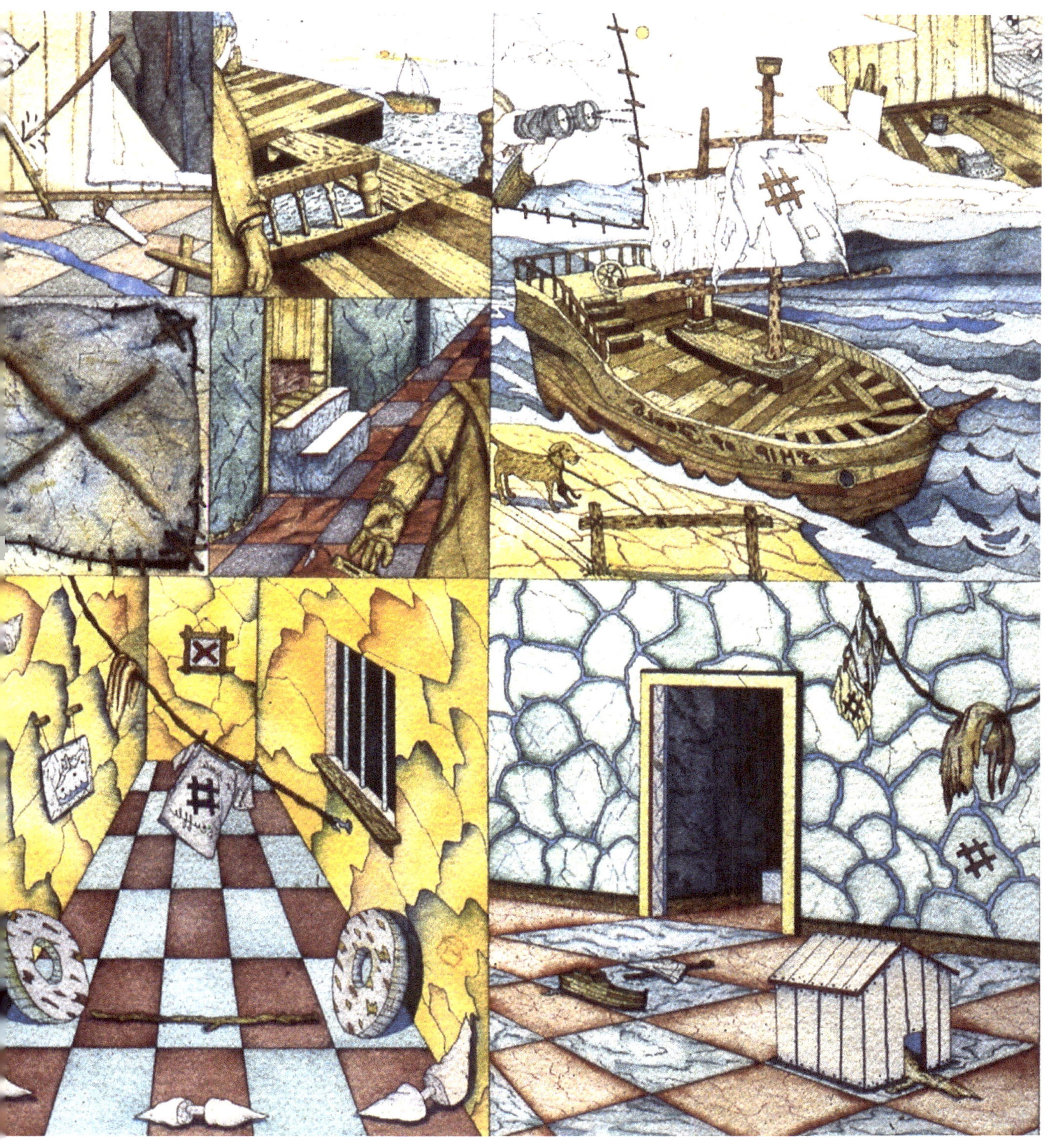

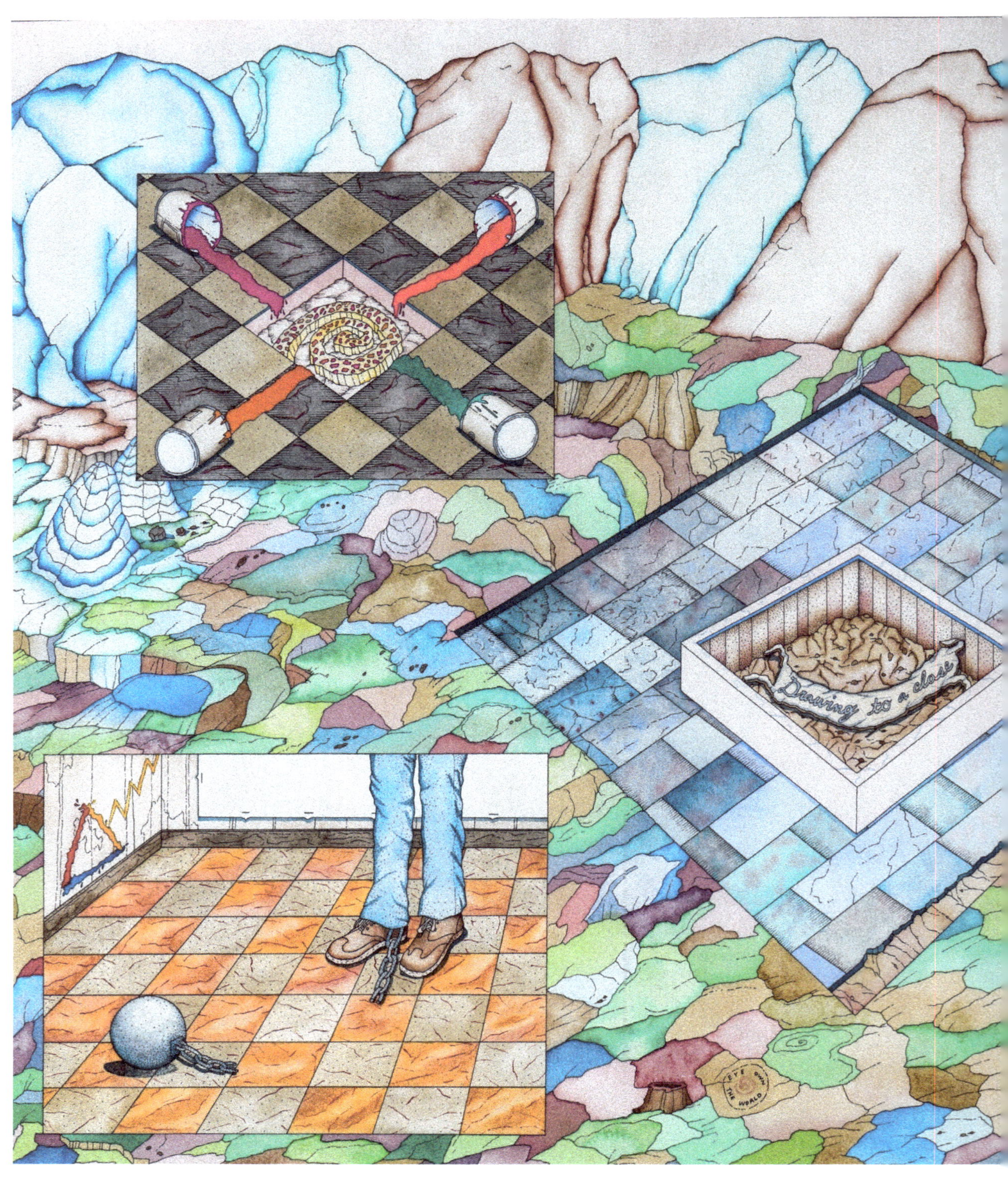
Drawing to a close

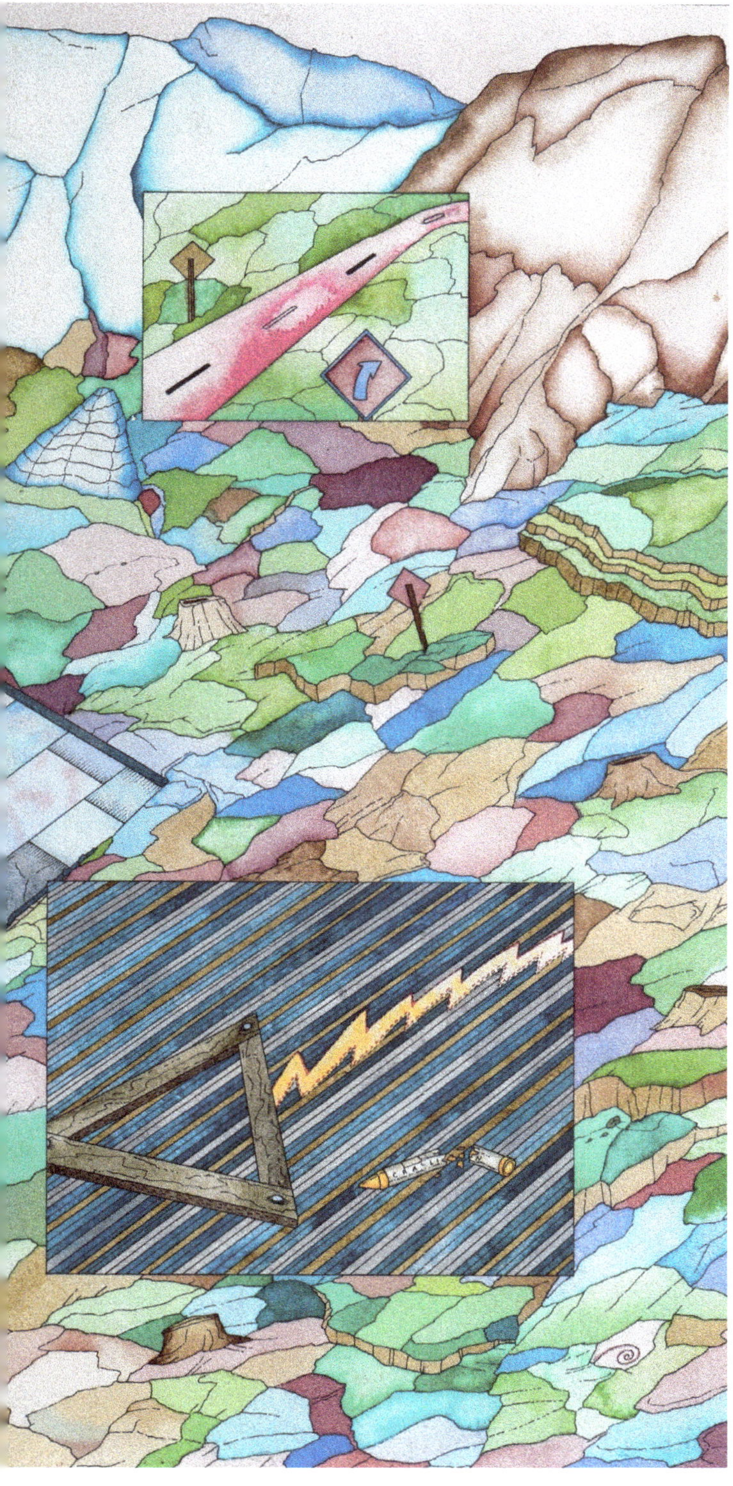

Eye Get A Kick Out of View, 1977
Ink & watercolor on paper, 26" x 36"

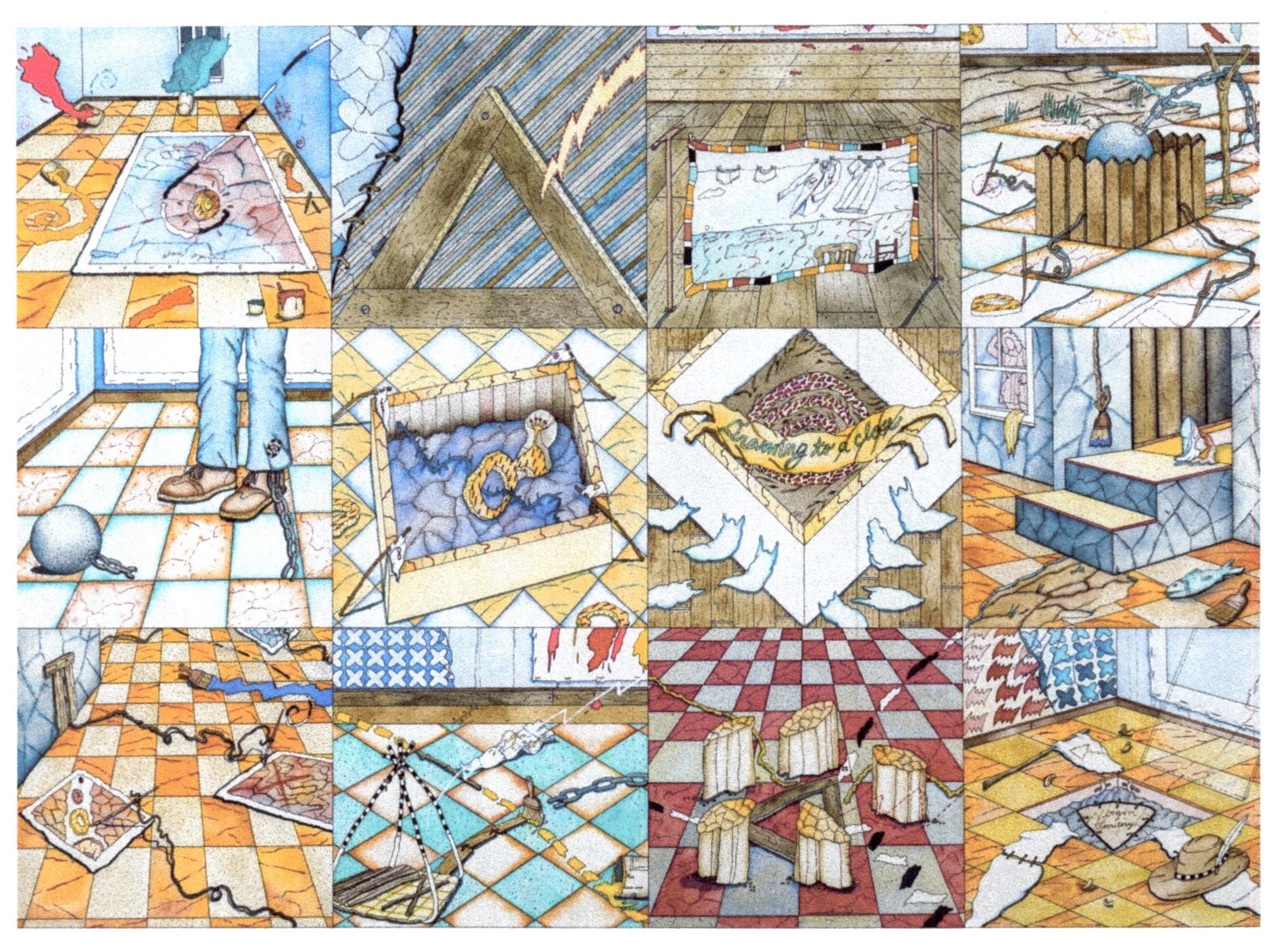

Spur of the Moment, 1977
Ink & watercolor on paper, 26" x 36"

16

1980's

EARLY YEARS / NEW YORK

A Story Without a Name, I, 1980
Ink & watercolor on paper, 22" x 30"

FOLLOWING

Little Peace, Little Wars, 1982
Watercolor on paper, 26" x 40"

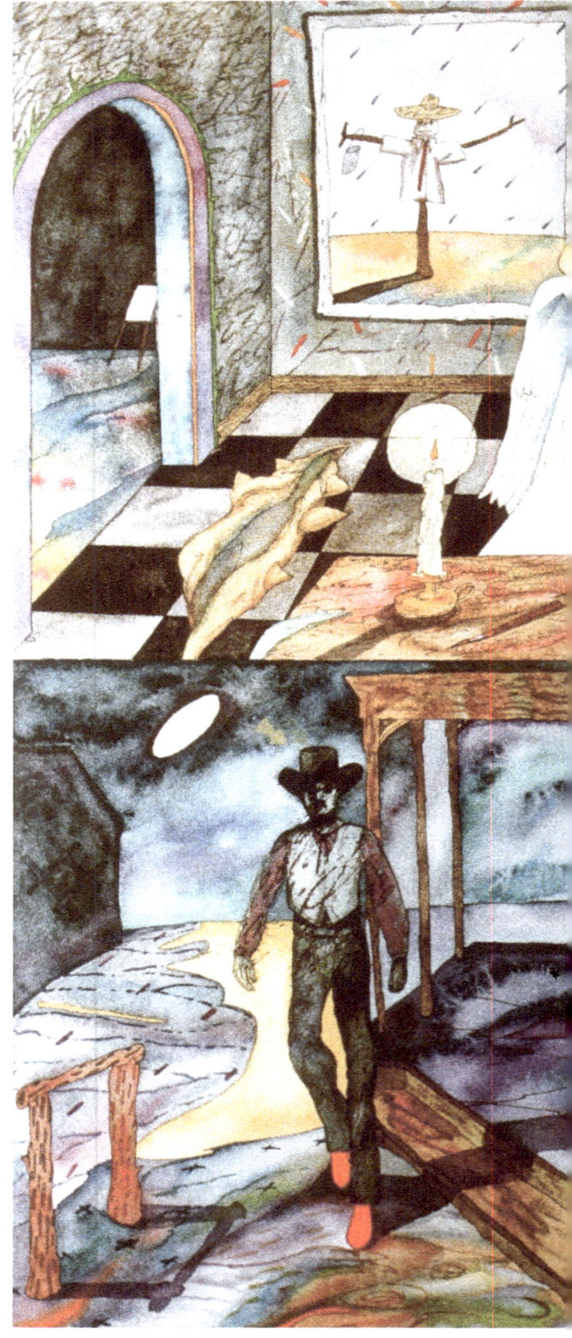

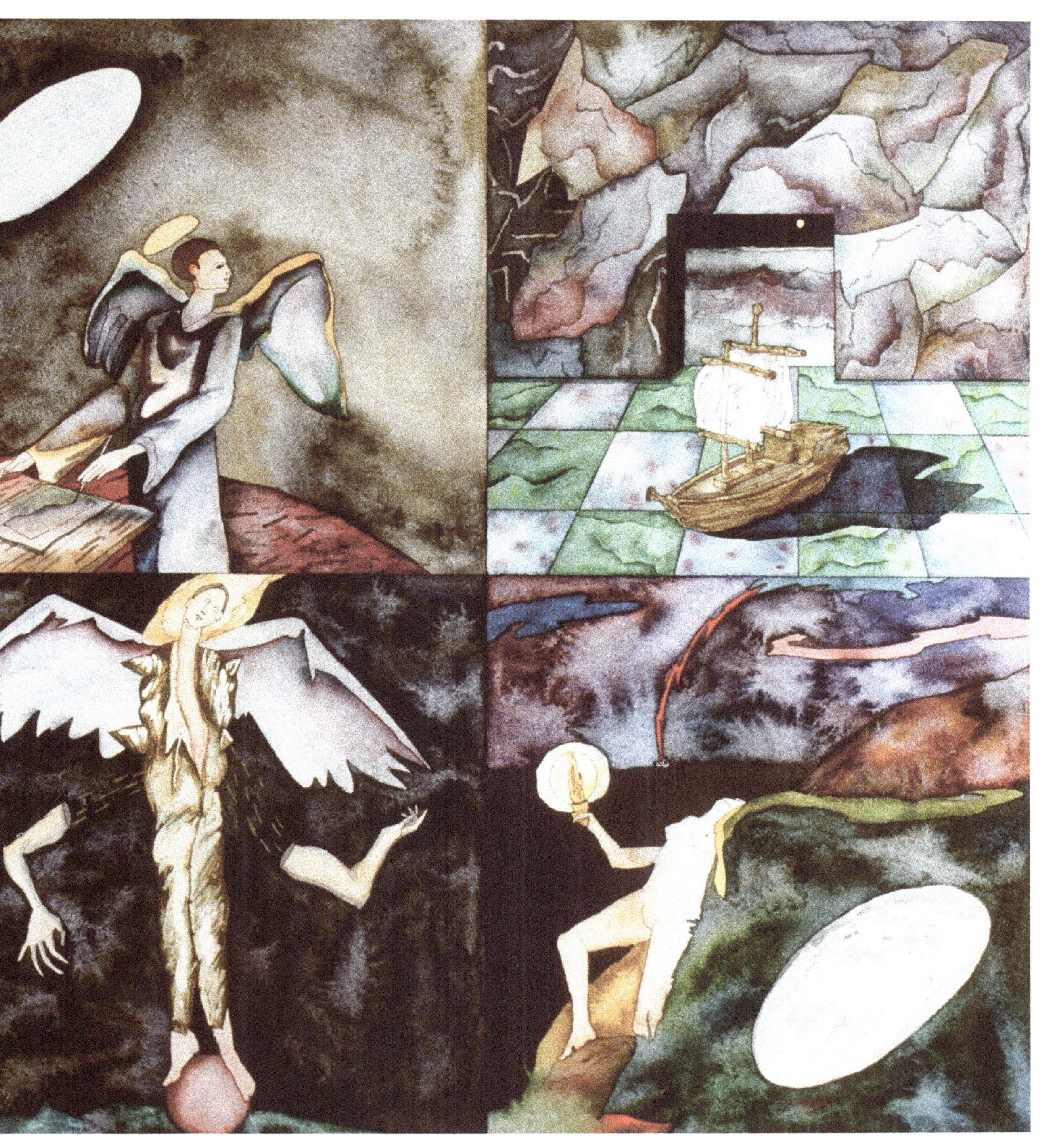

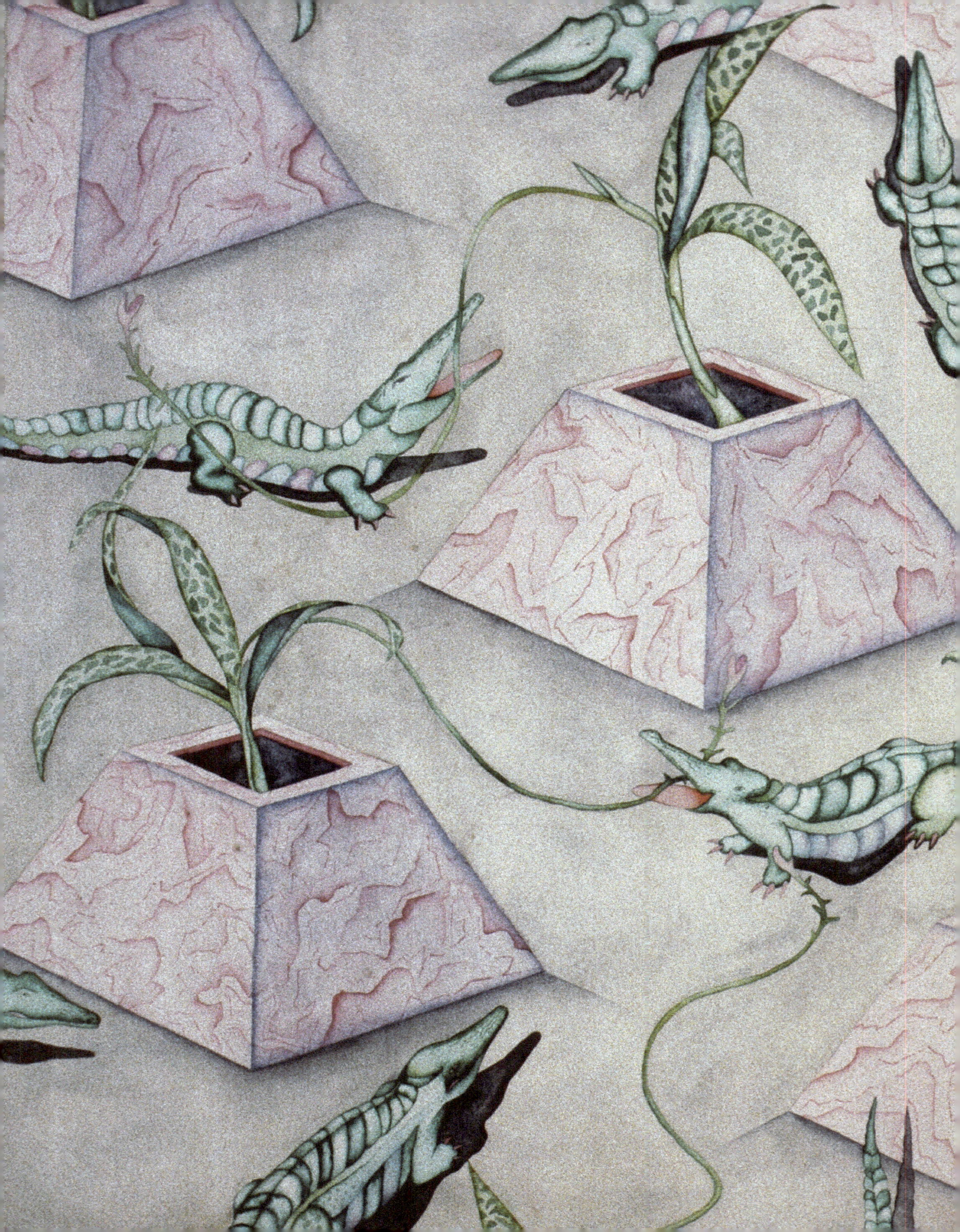

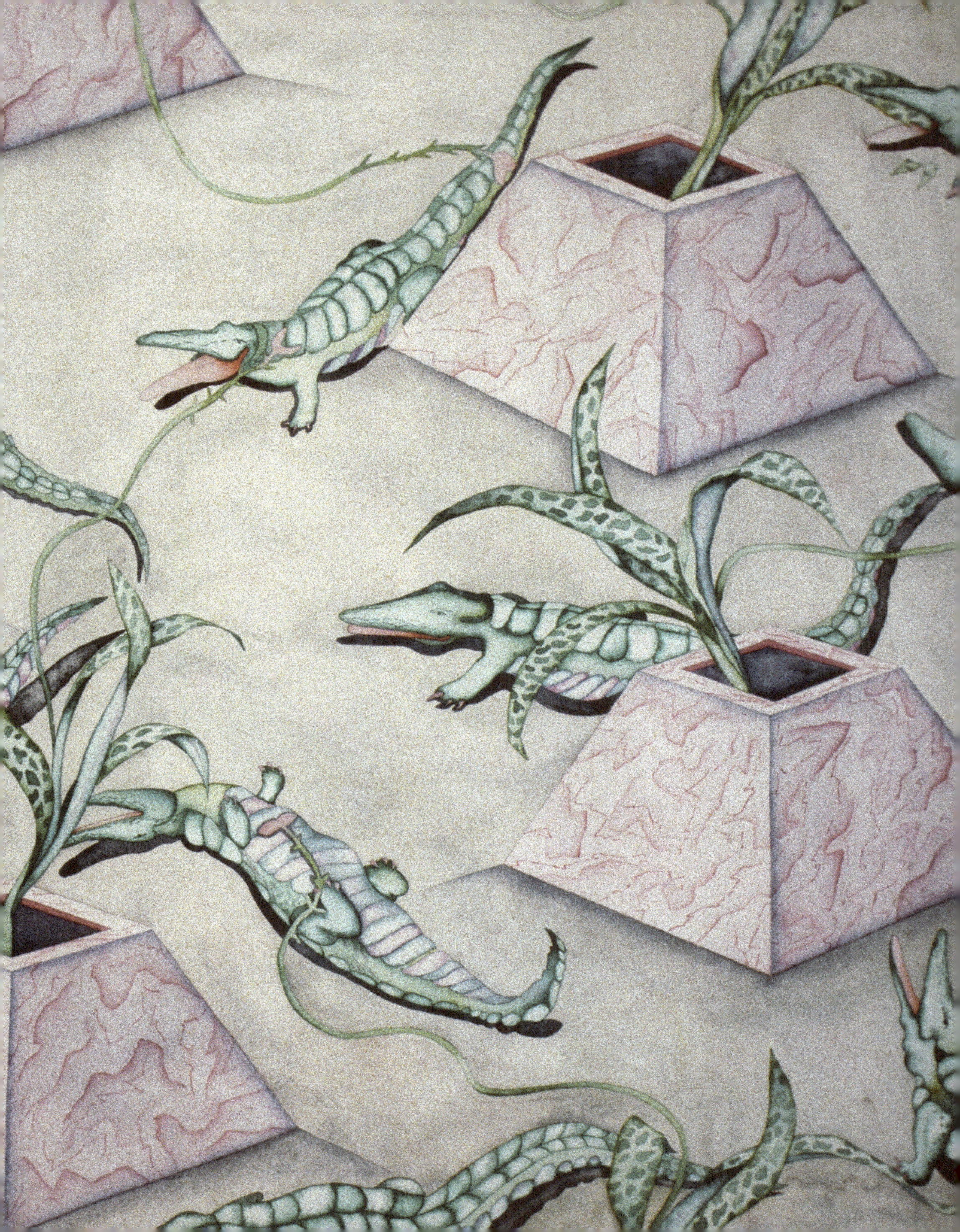

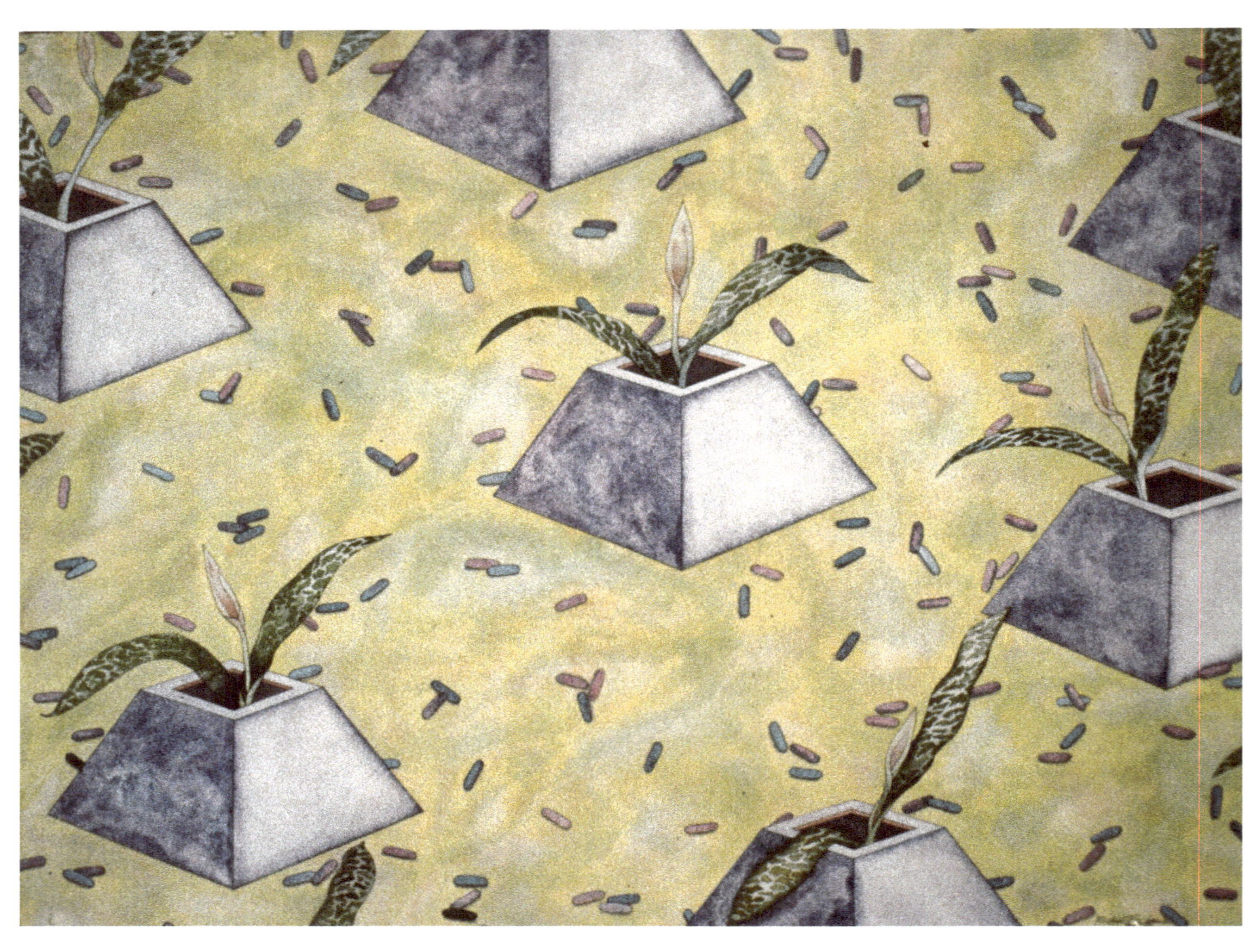

New Pleasures, 1982
Ink & watercolor on paper, 22" x 30"
Miller Brewing Company, Edenton, NC

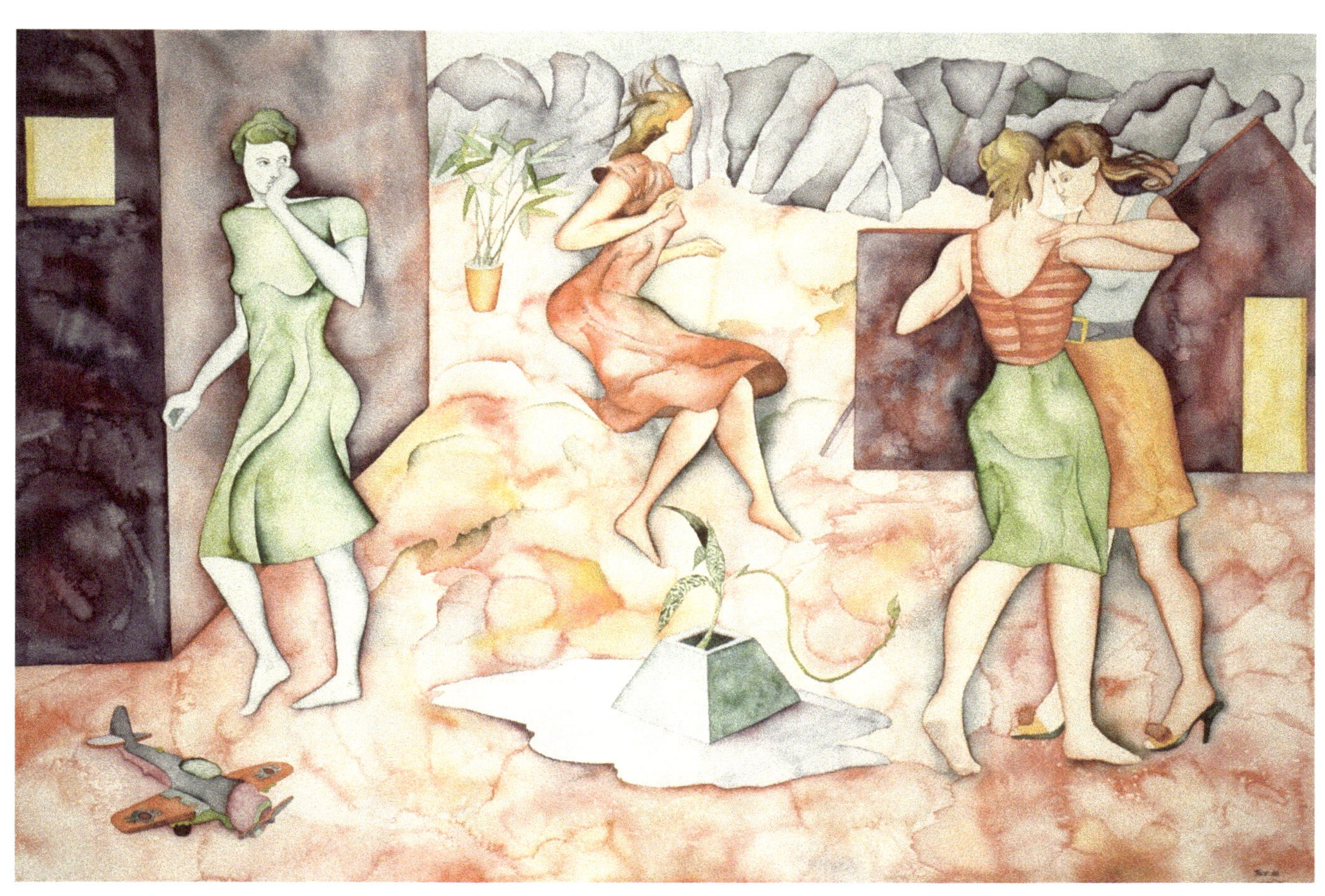

Everything Happens At Once, 1985
Watercolor on paper, 40" x 60"

FOLLOWING

The True Light and A Sure Haven, 1982
Ink & watercolor on paper, 26" x 40"
Private Collection, Hong Kong

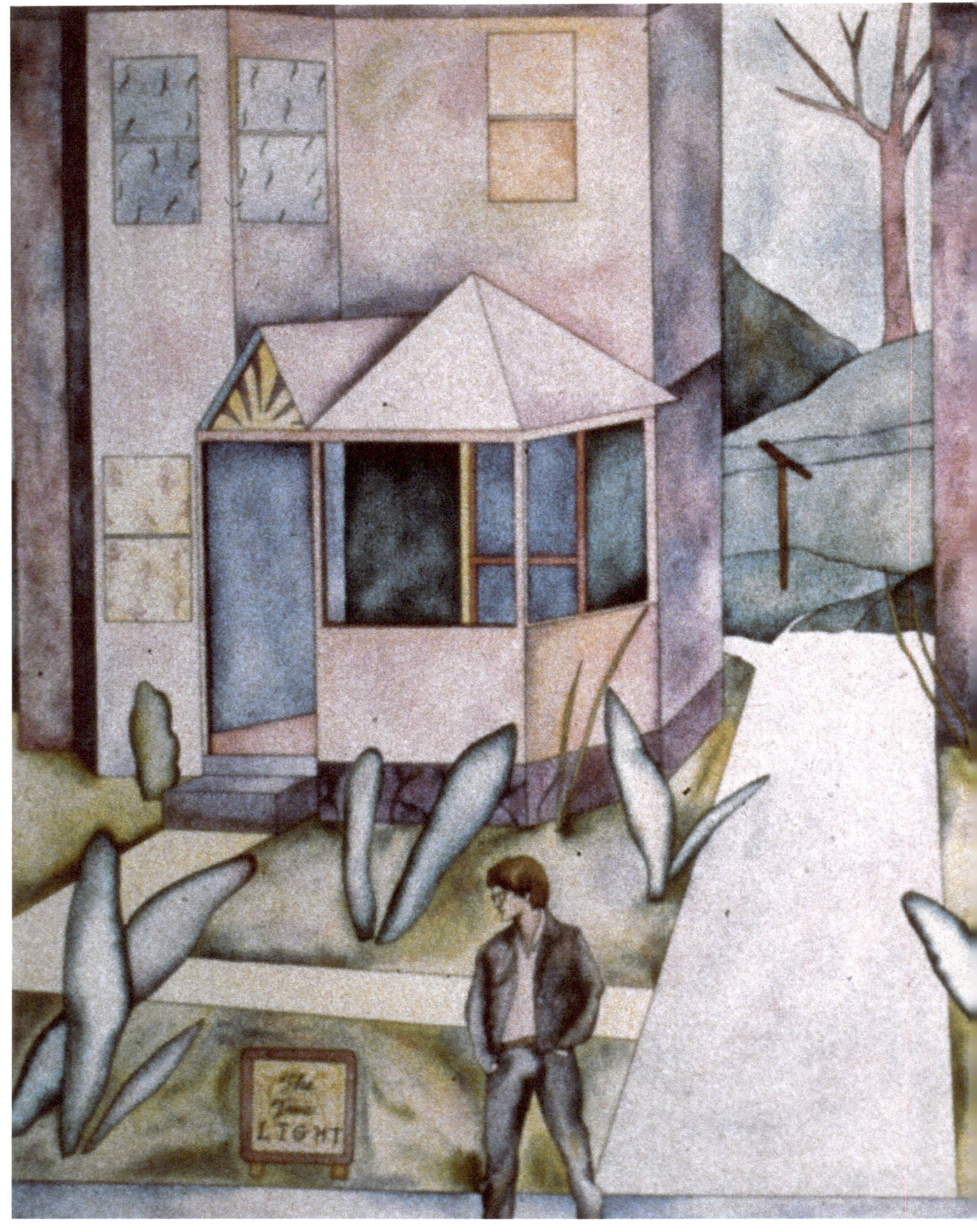

24

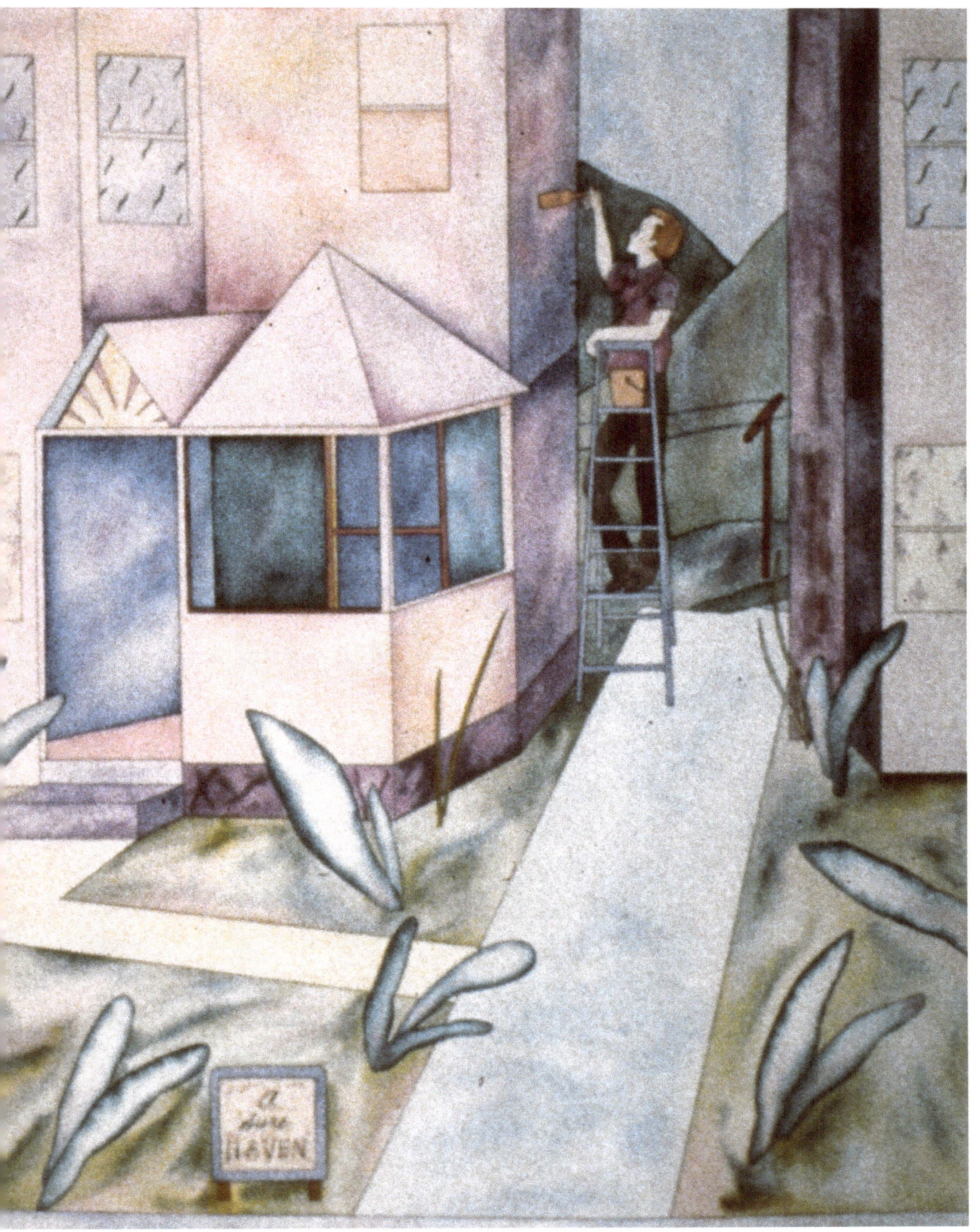
a Safe
HAVEN

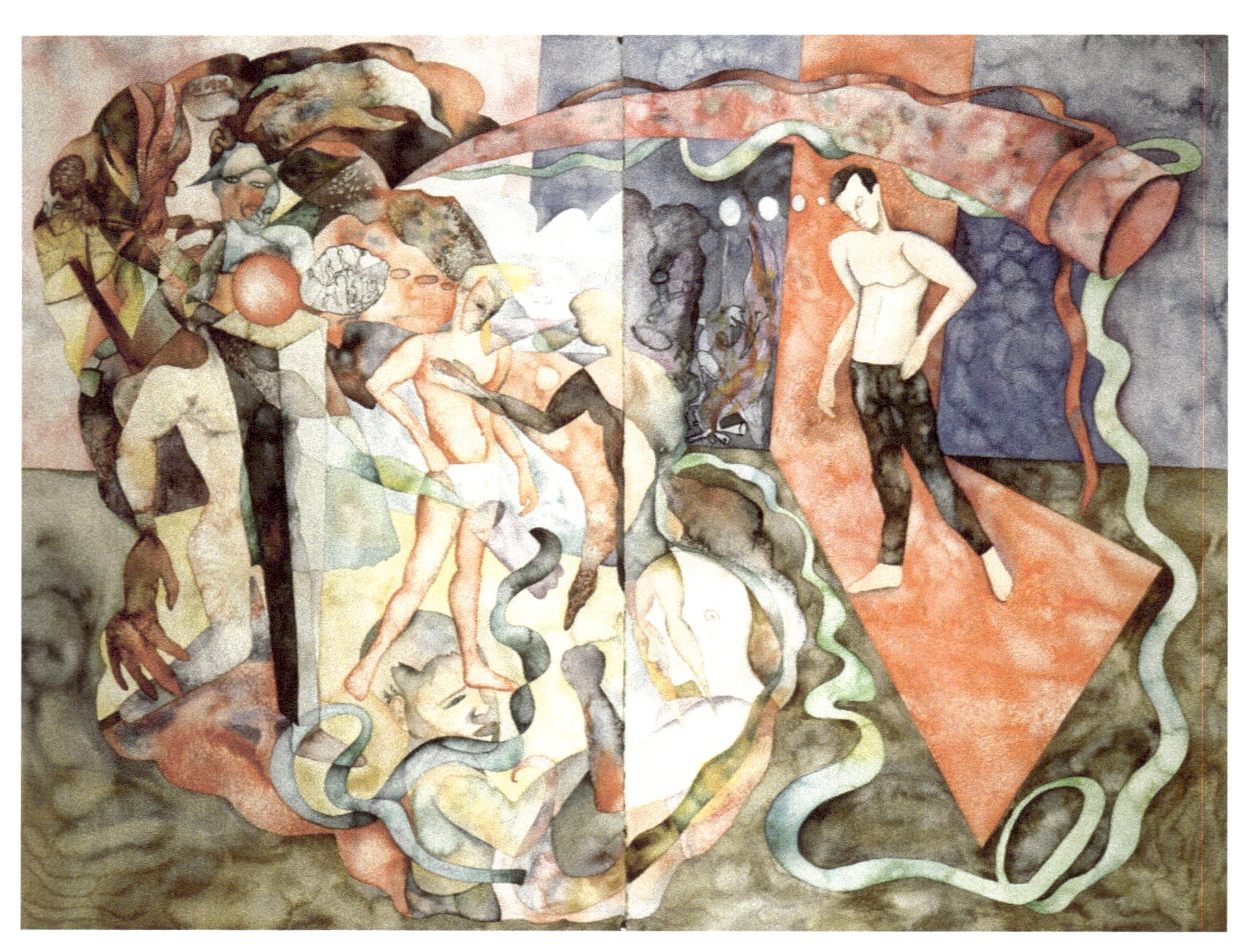

Untitled, 1985
Watercolor on paper, 60" x 80"
Private Collection, Hong Kong

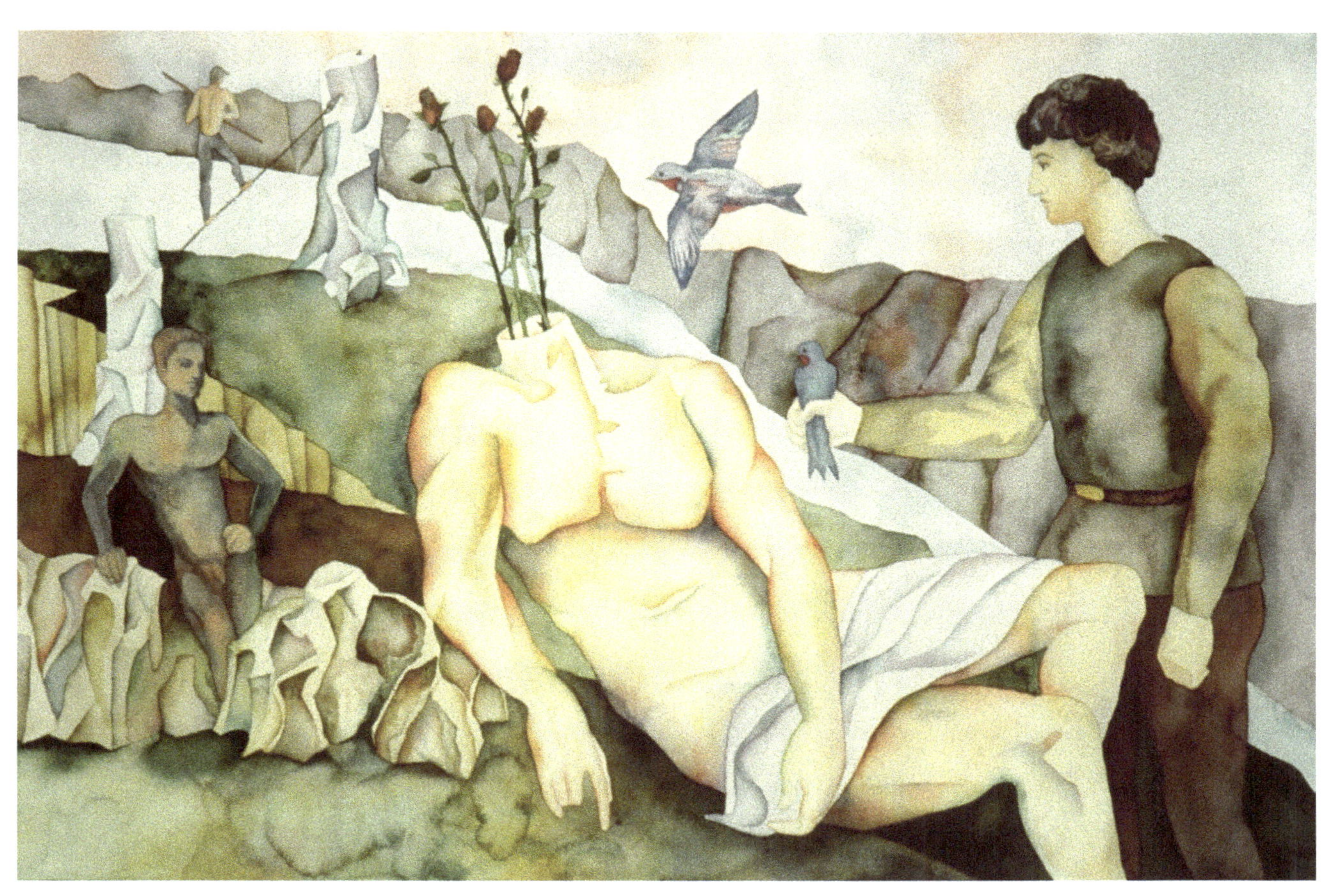

Untitled, 1987
Watercolor on paper, 28" x 40"

FOLLOWING

Balancing Bodies and Voices, 1984
Oil on paper, 26" x 40"

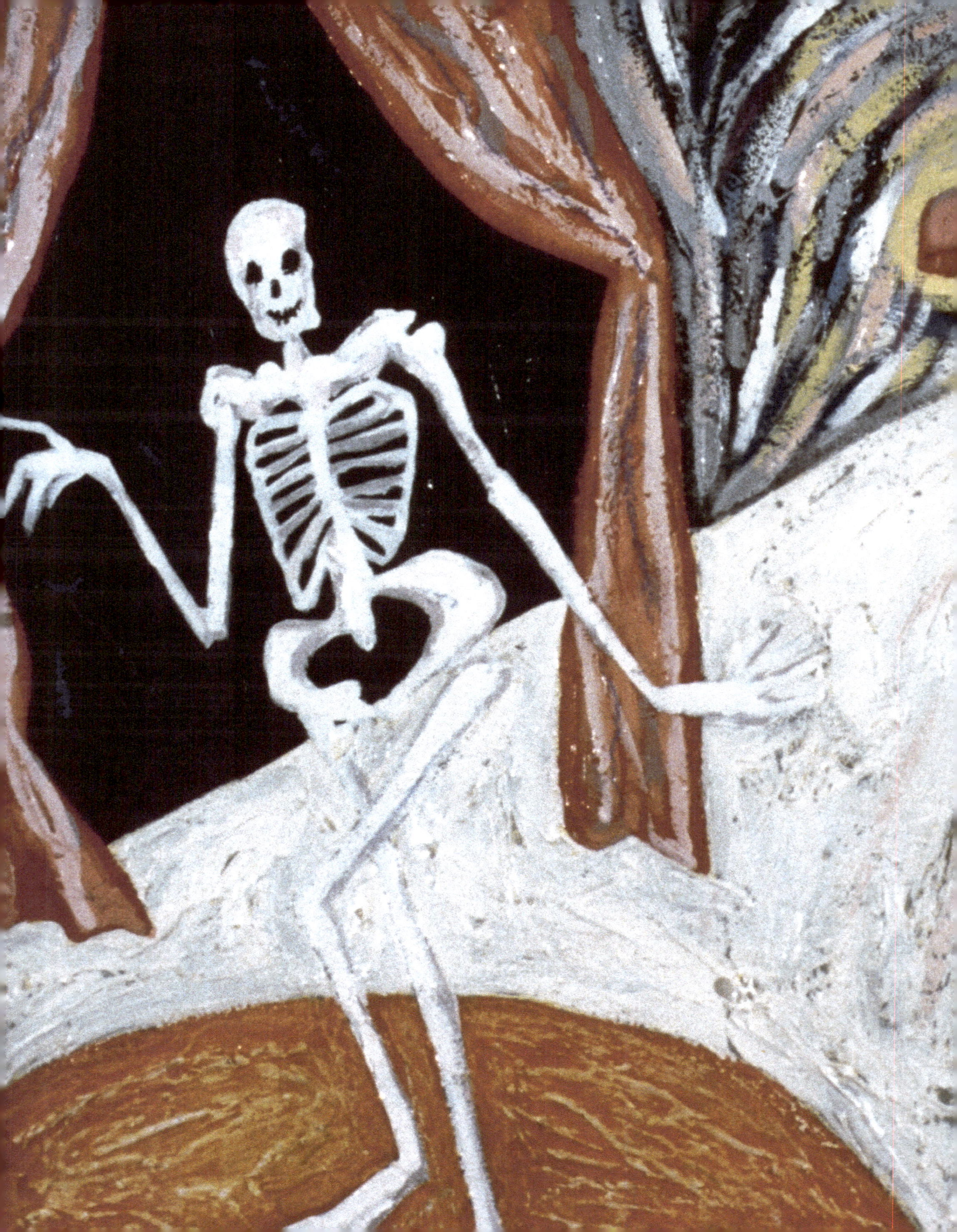

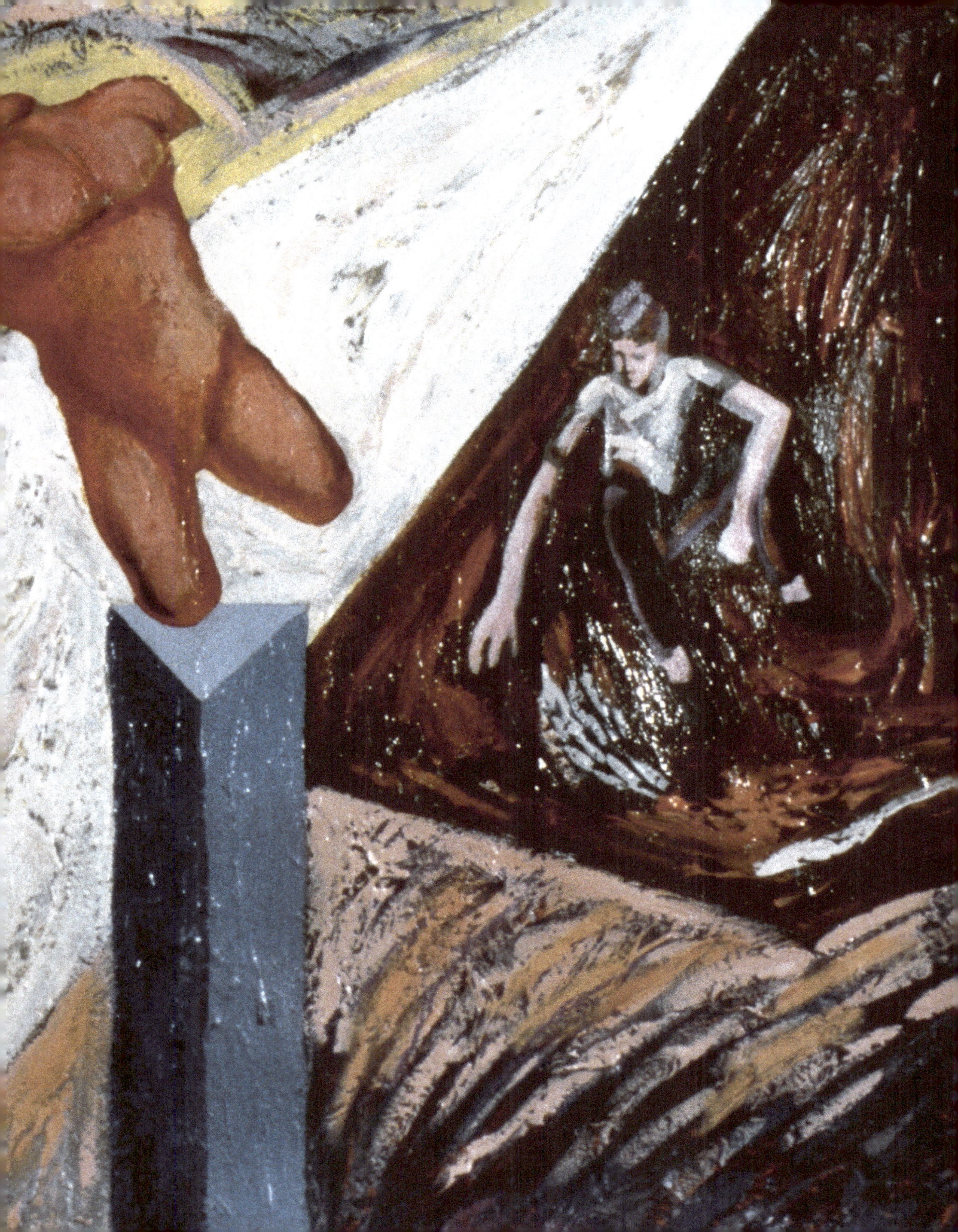

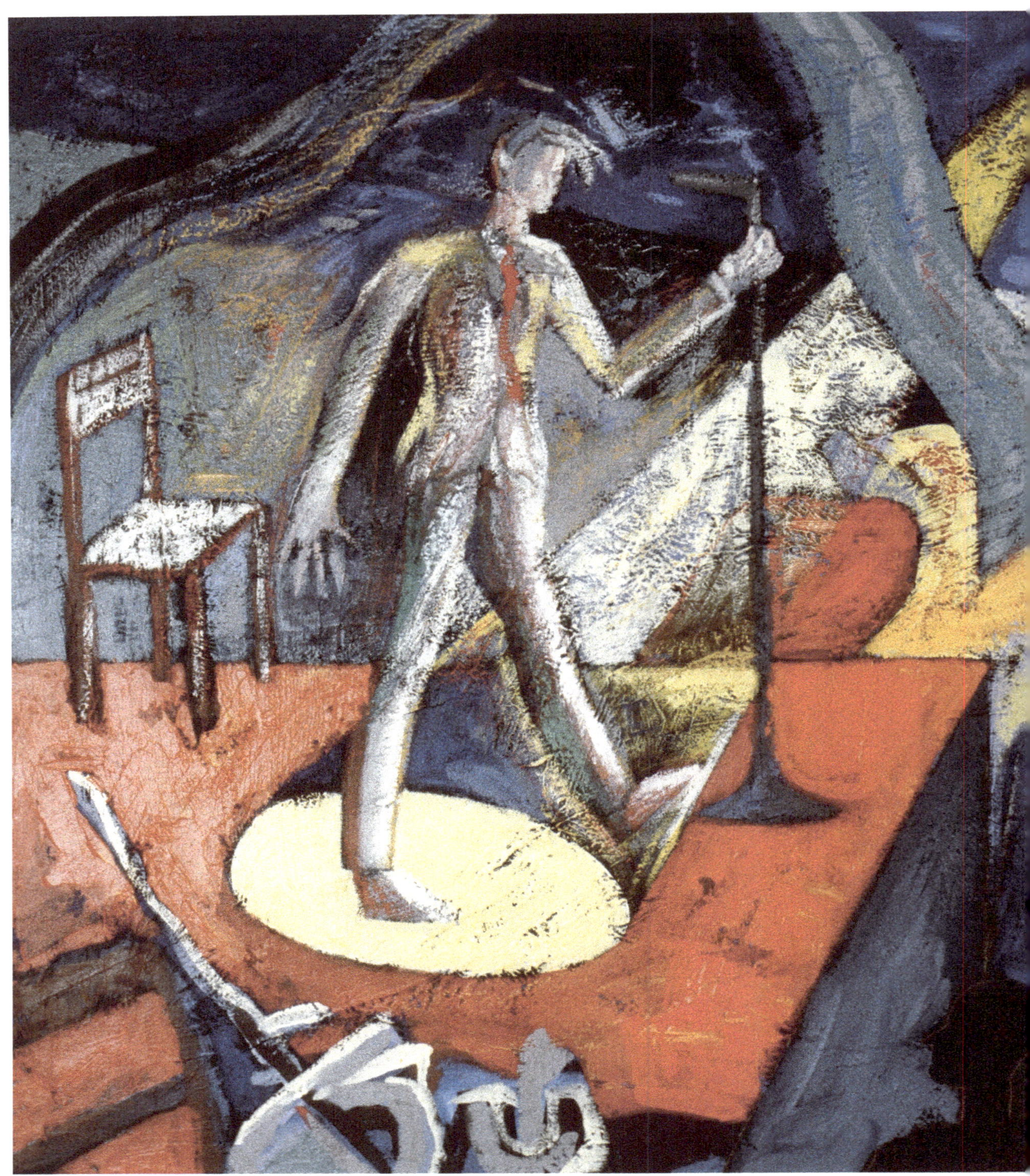

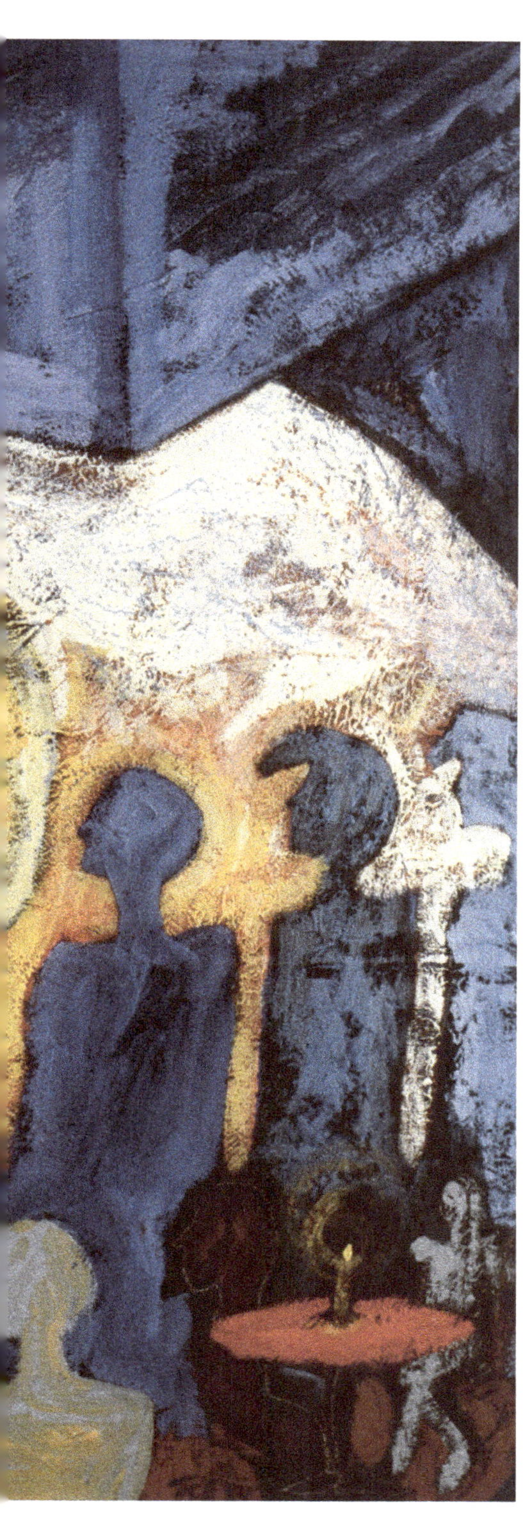

Nightclub, 1984
Oil on canvas, 24" x 30"

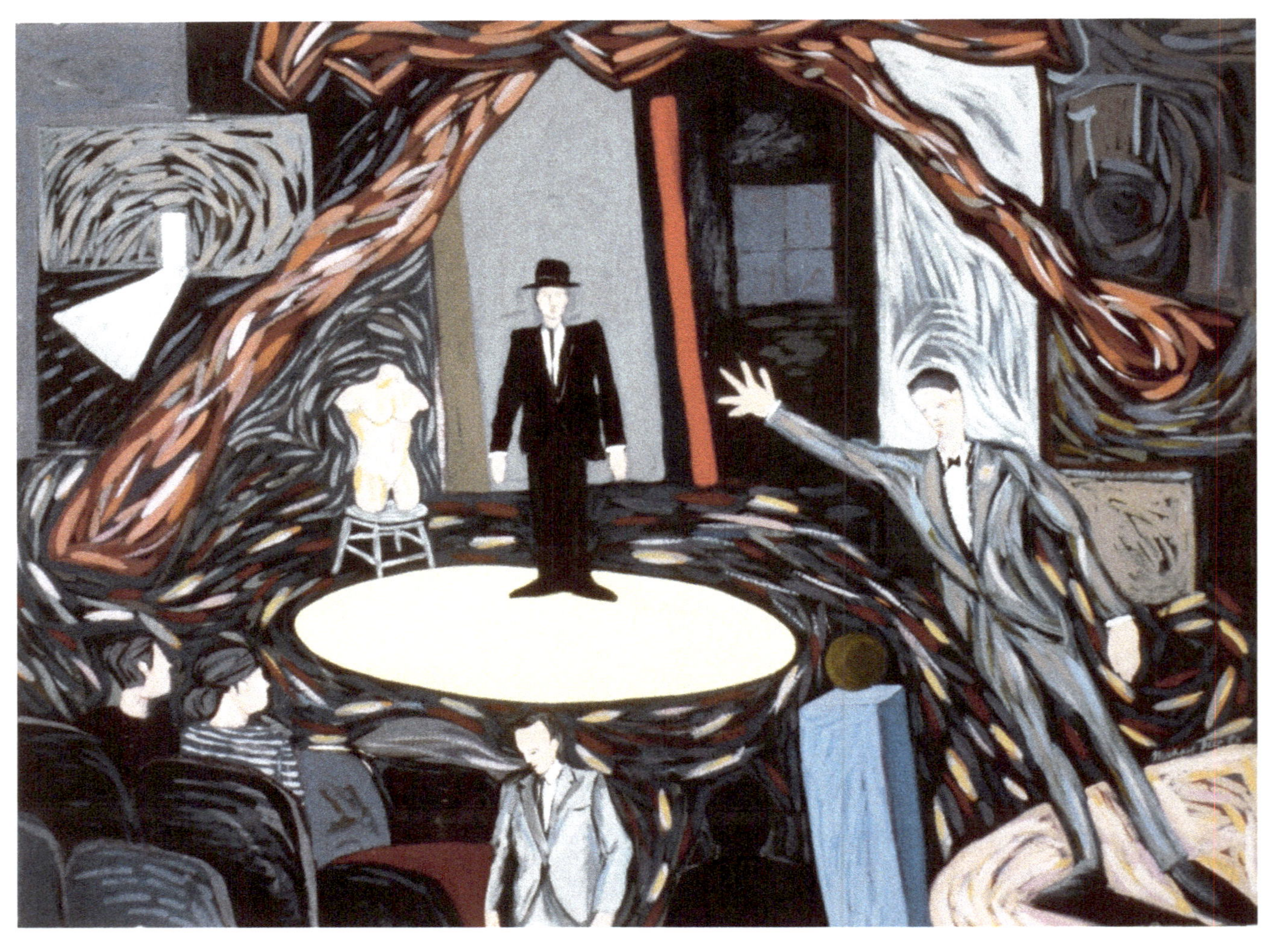

Telling Stories, Defining His Fears, 1983
Acrylic on paper, 36" x 40"

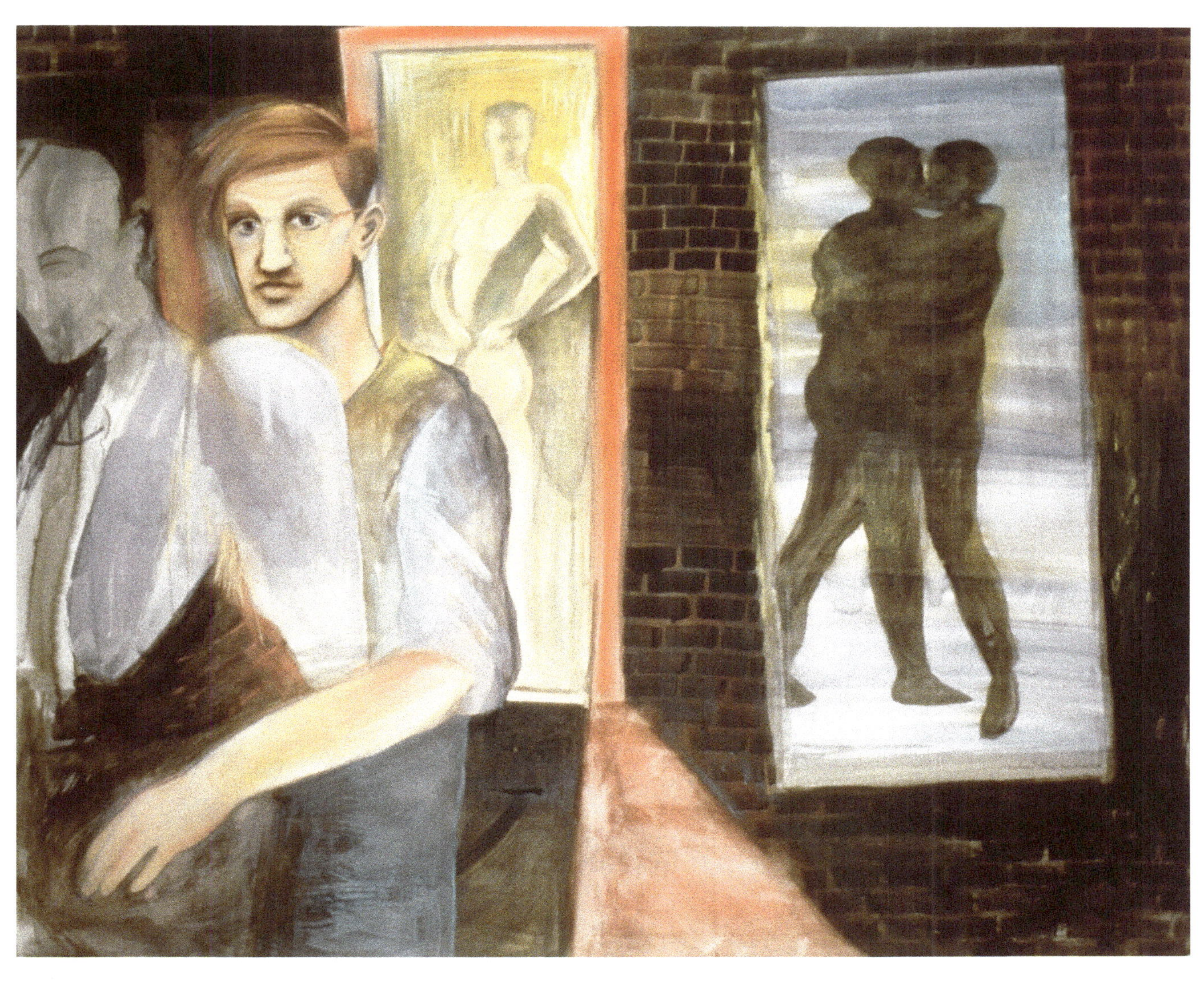

Untitled, 1989
Pastel, charcoal and watercolor on paper, 38" x 47"

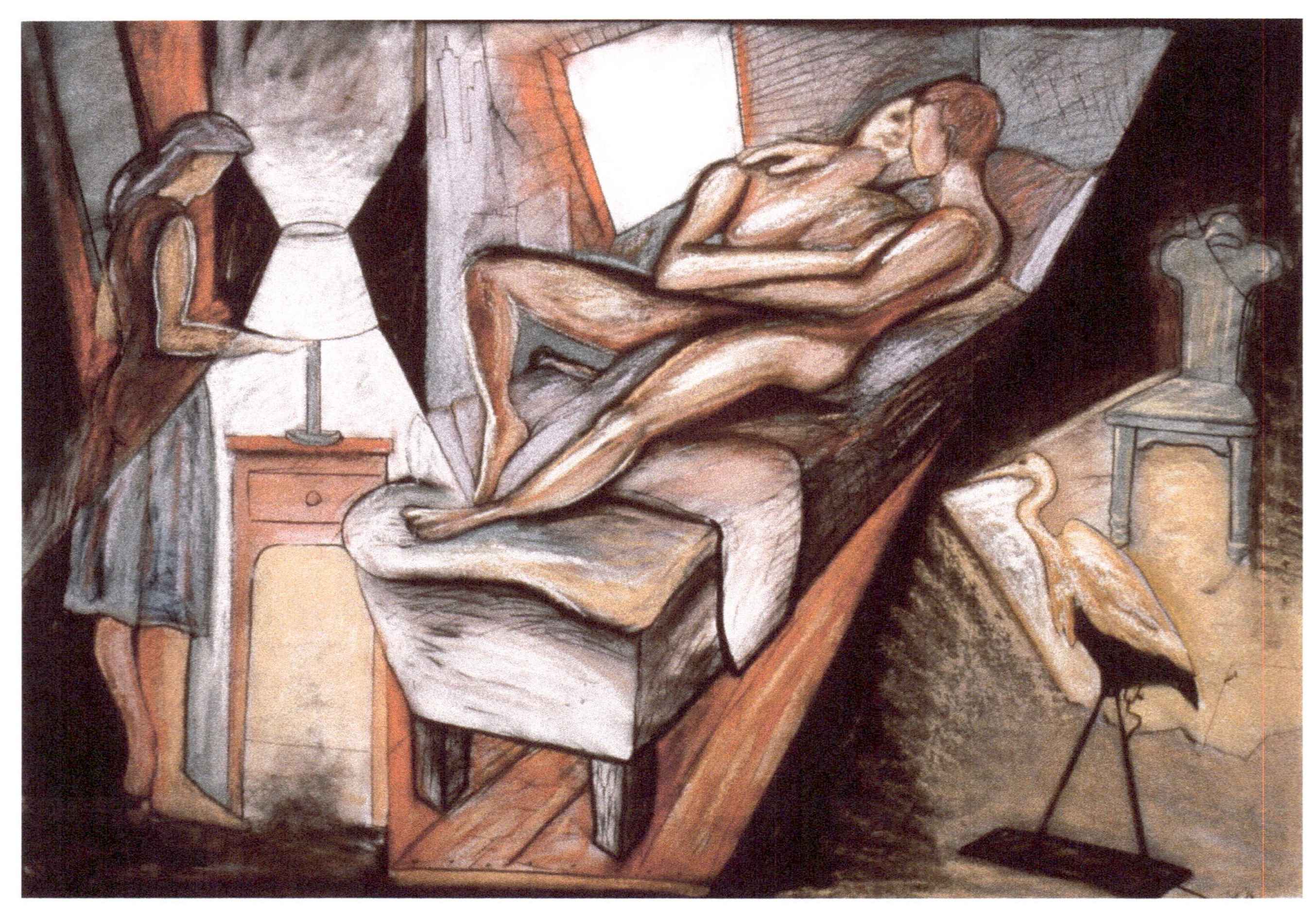

Interior, 1986
Pastel & charcoal on paper, 30" x 46"

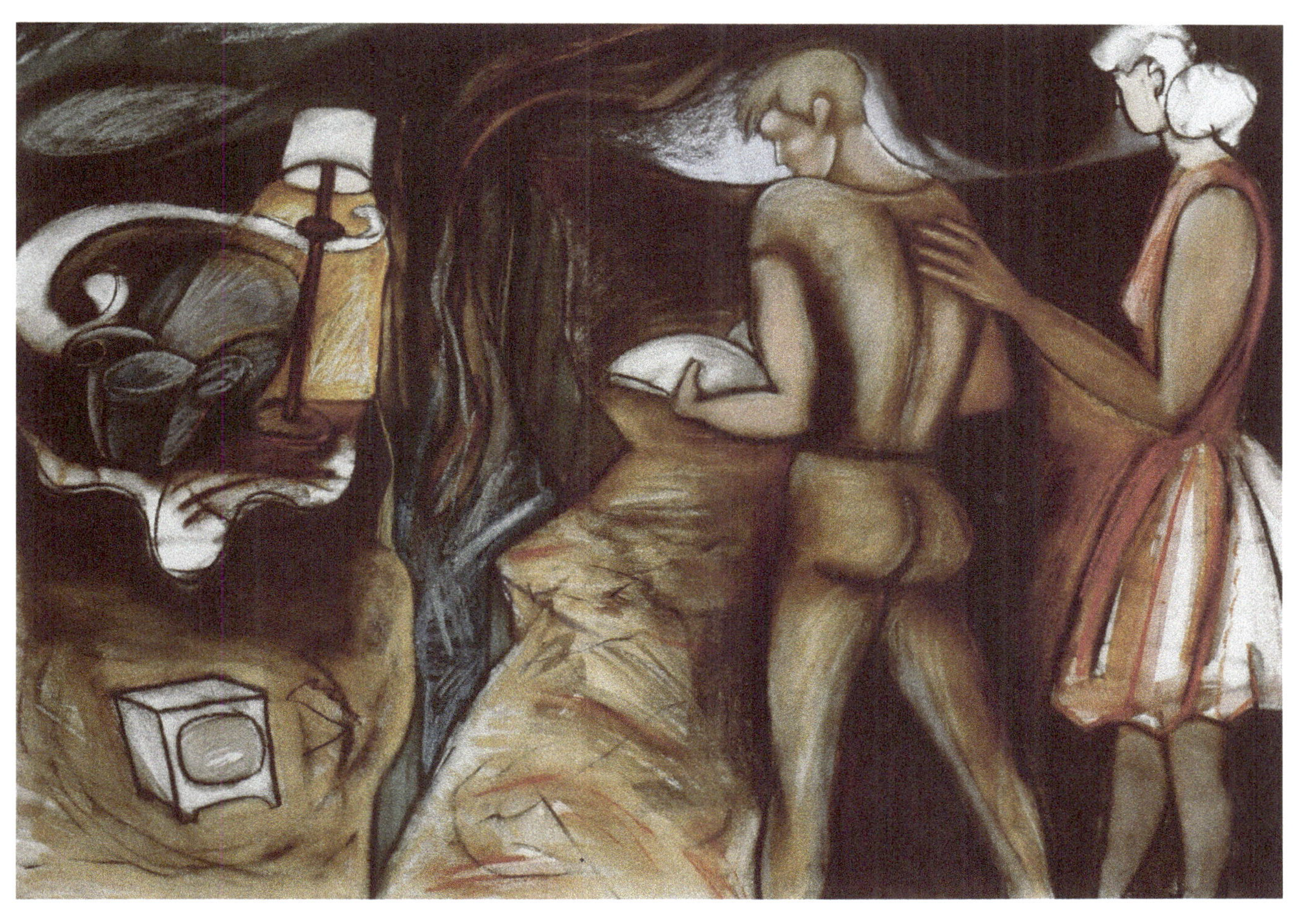

Trouble in Paradise, 1985
Pastel, charcoal and watercolor on paper, 27" x 39"
Private Collection, Los Angeles, CA

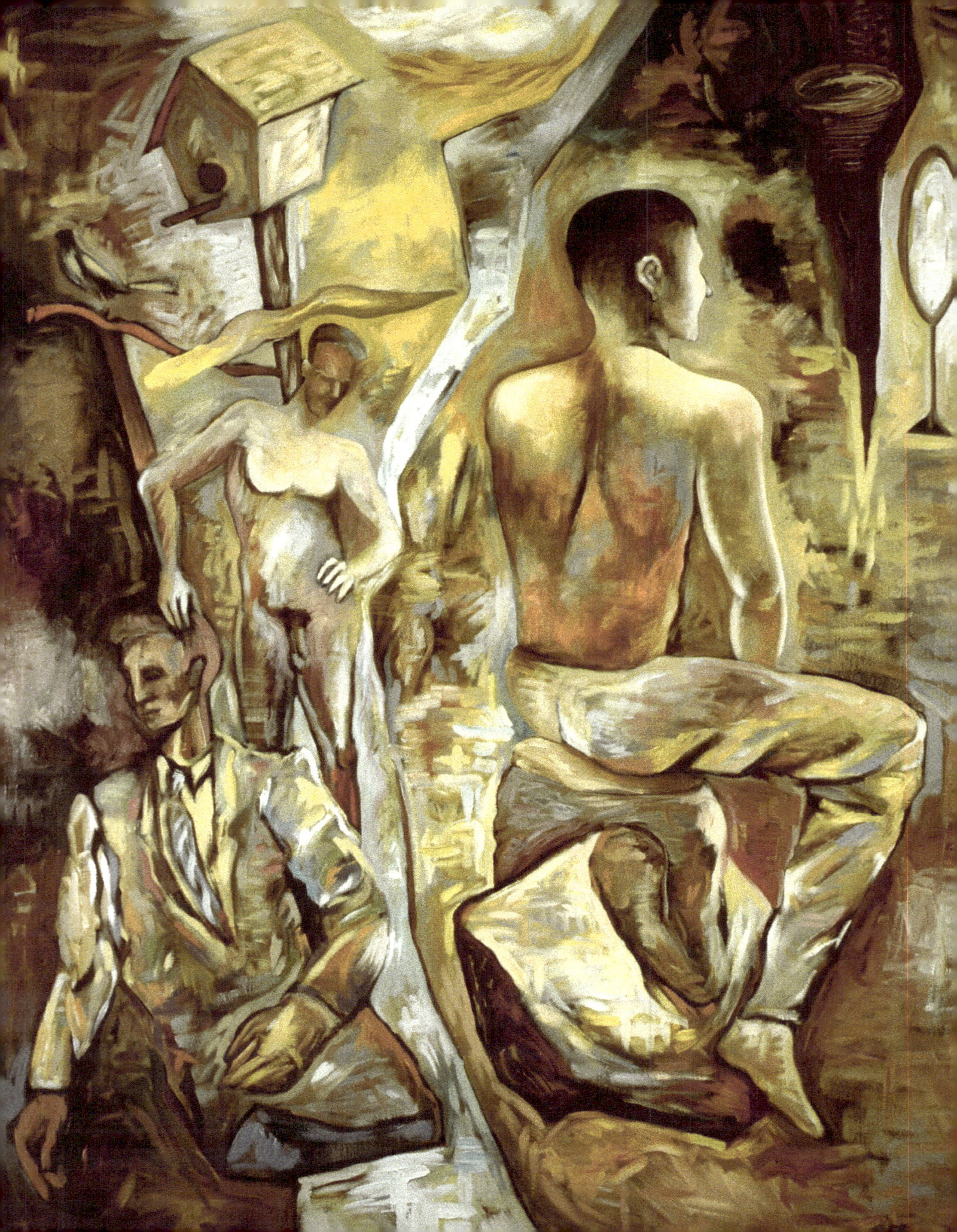

OPPOSITE

Spring, 1987
Oil on linen, 48" x 36"

BELOW

Holding On, Letting Go, 1987
Oil on masonite, 18" x 24"
Private Collection, Huntington Beach, CA

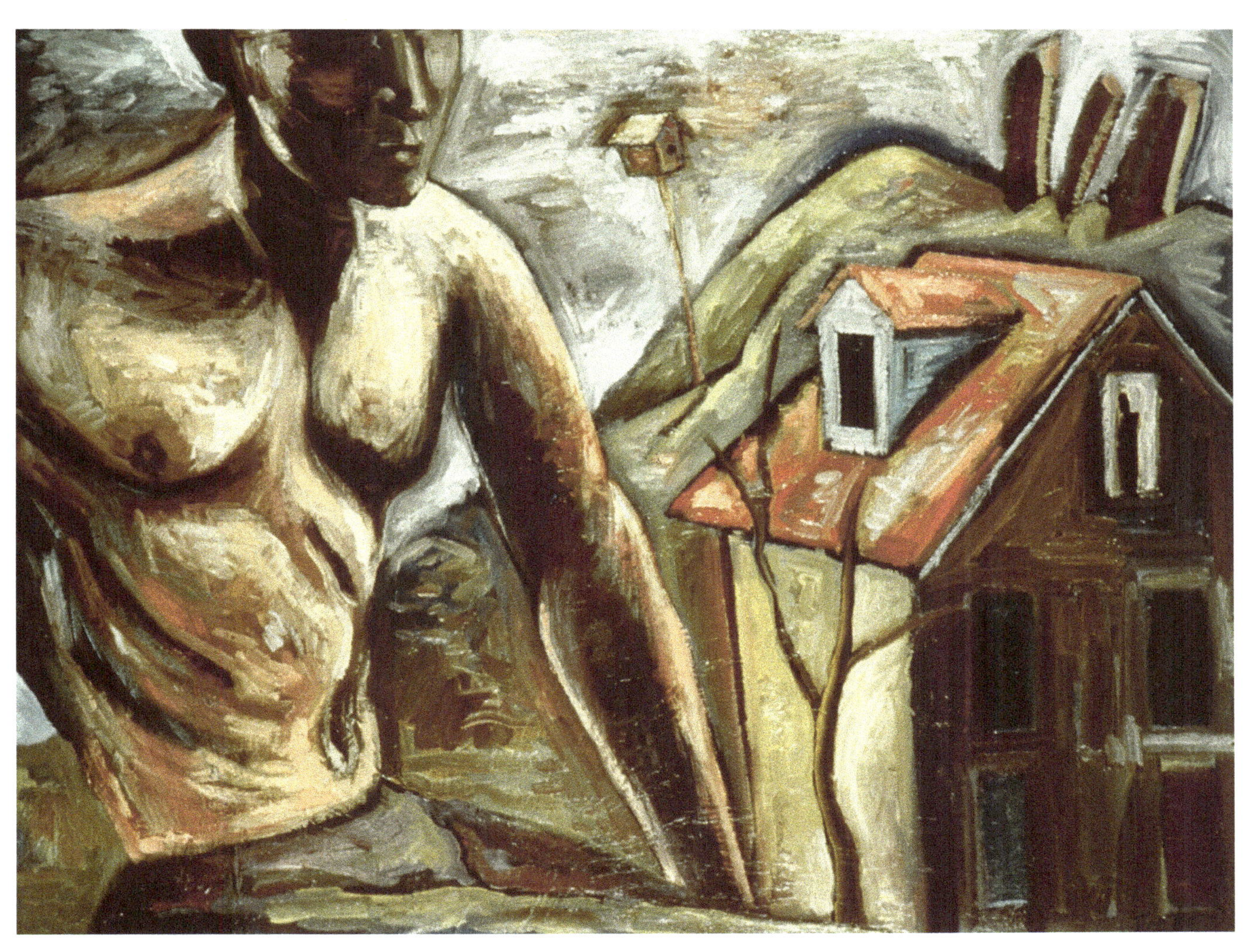

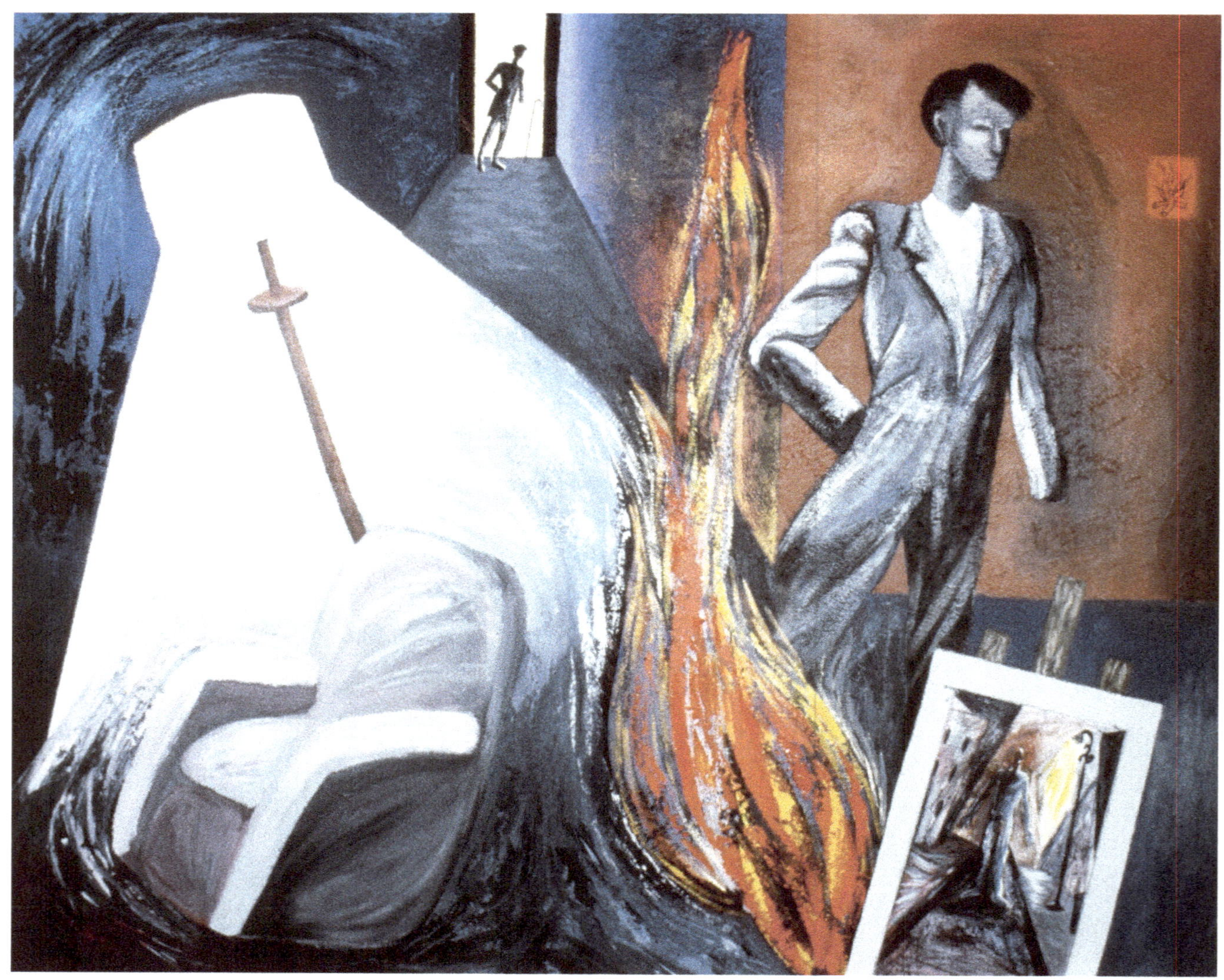

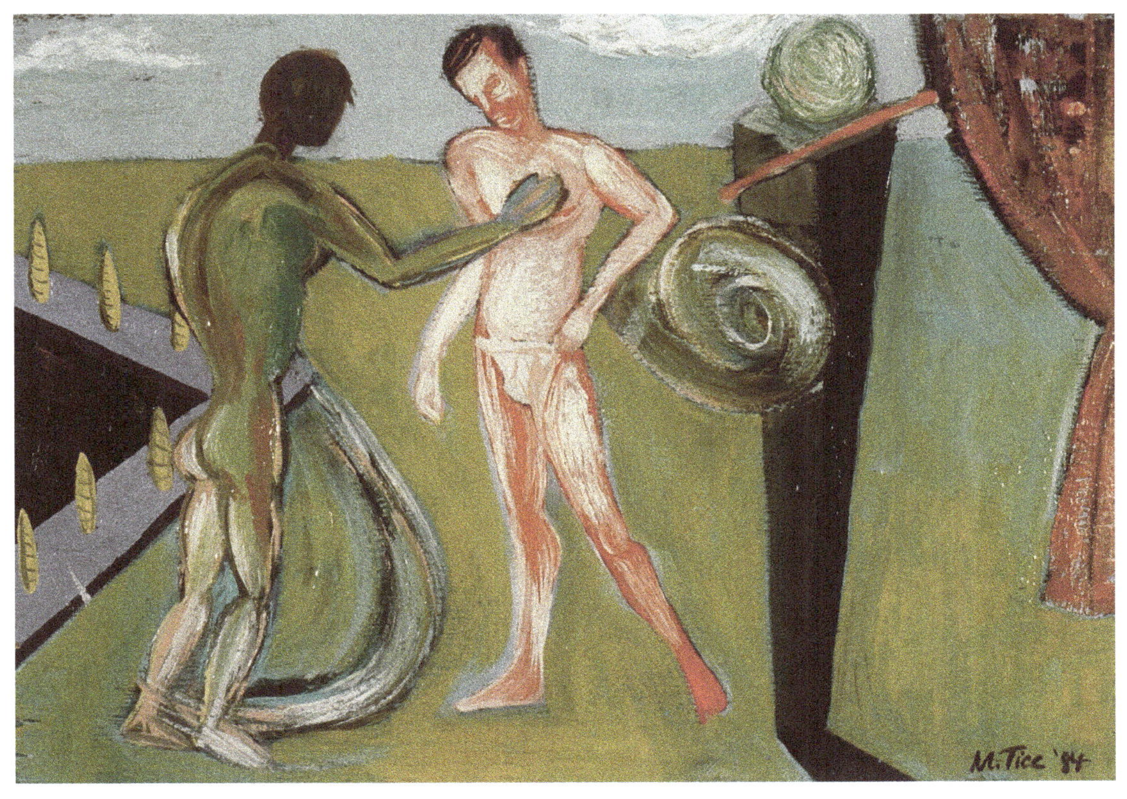

M.Tice '94

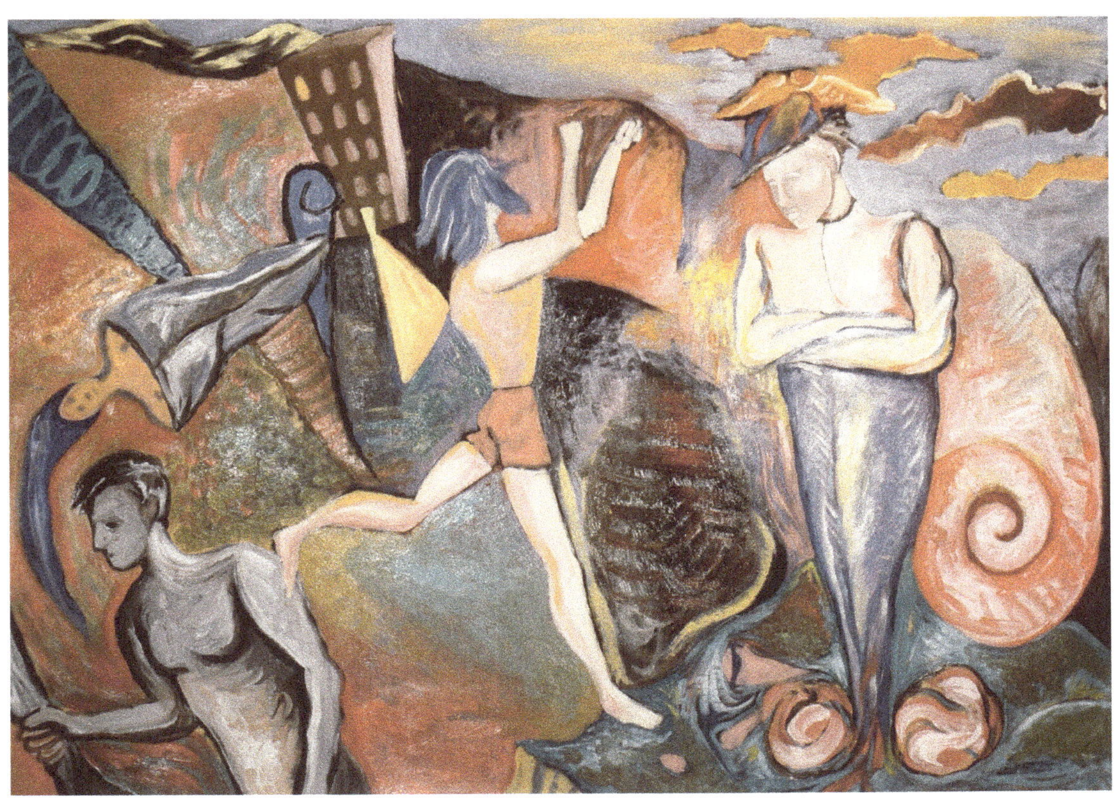

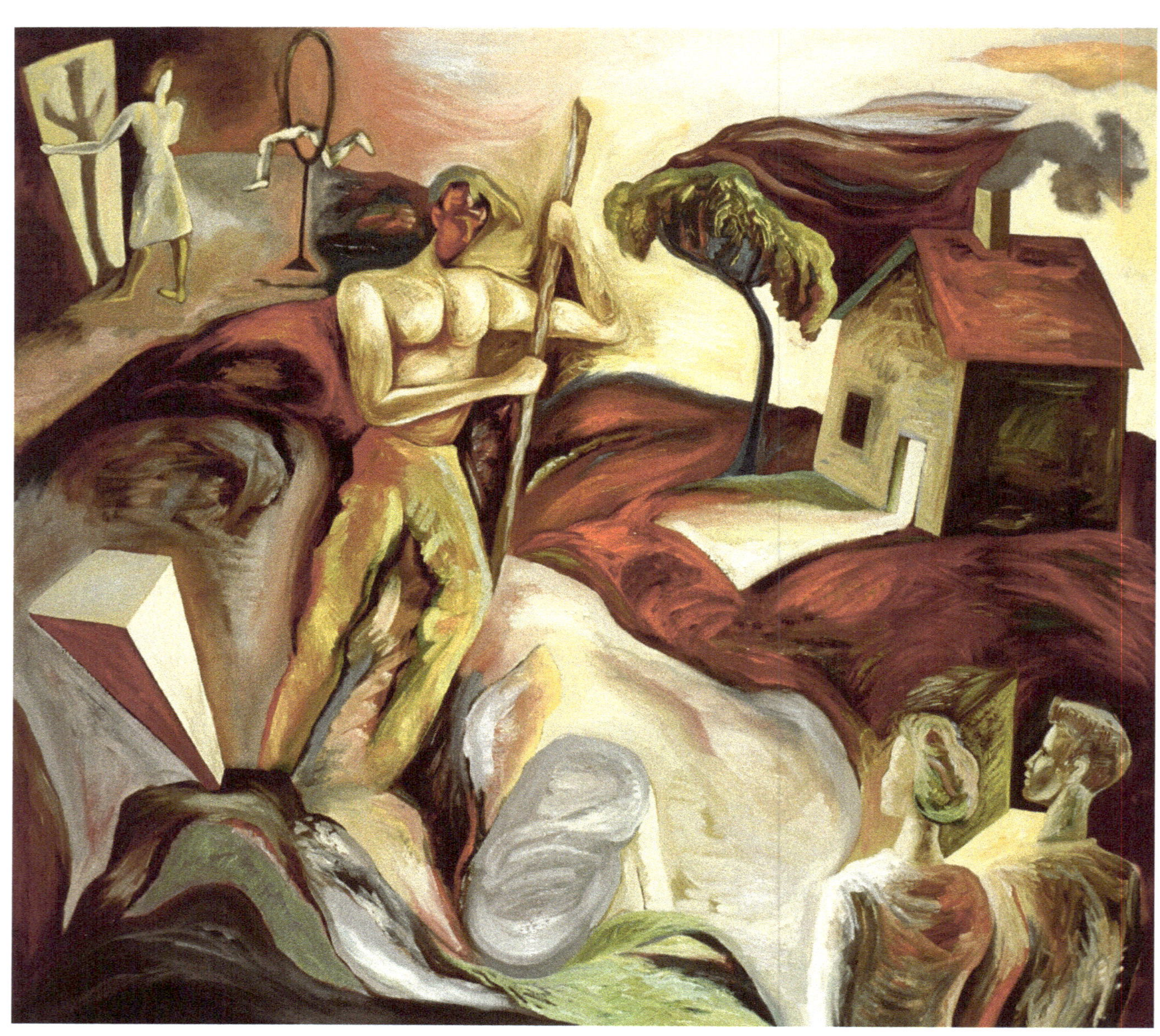

Alone on the Raft, 1986
Oil on canvas, 46" x 48"

1990's

UPS & DOWNS

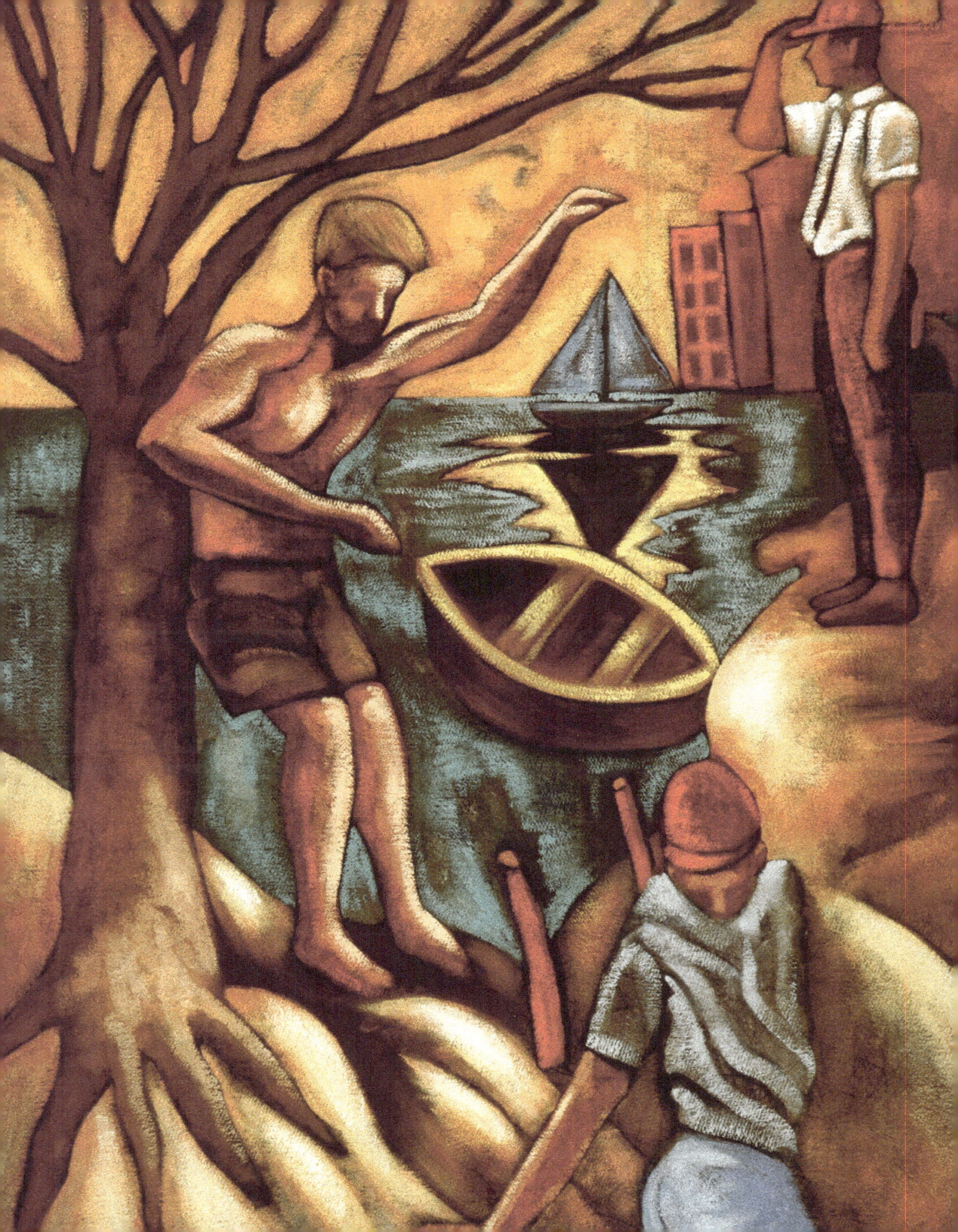

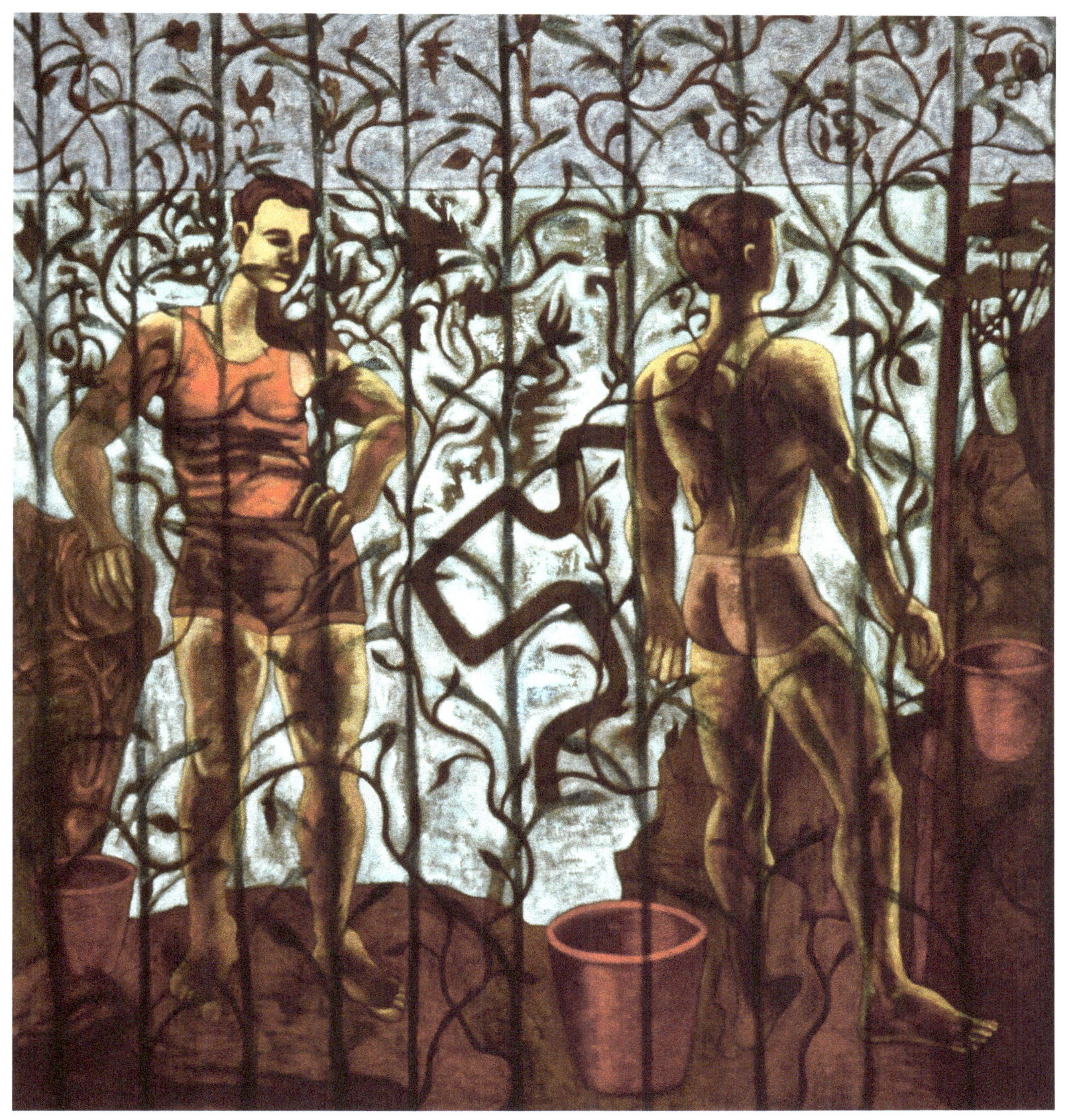

Spring Parting, 1992
Oil on canvas, 68" x 62"

43

ABOVE
Lingering Questions of a Child, 1997
Oil on paper, 28" x 40"

OPPOSITE
Comfort Zone, 1993
Oil & acrylic on paper, 30" x 22"
Private Collection, Columbia, SC

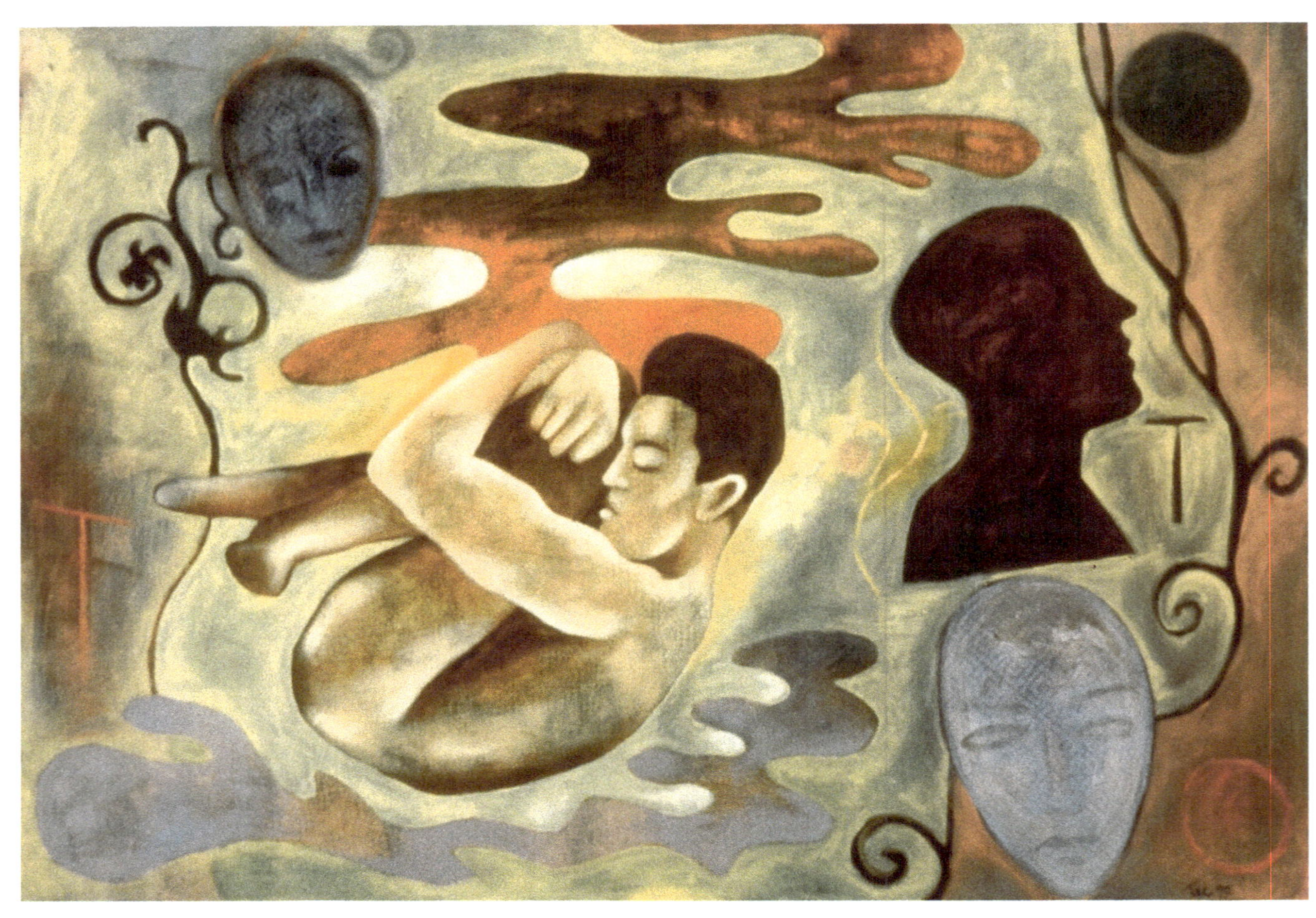

44

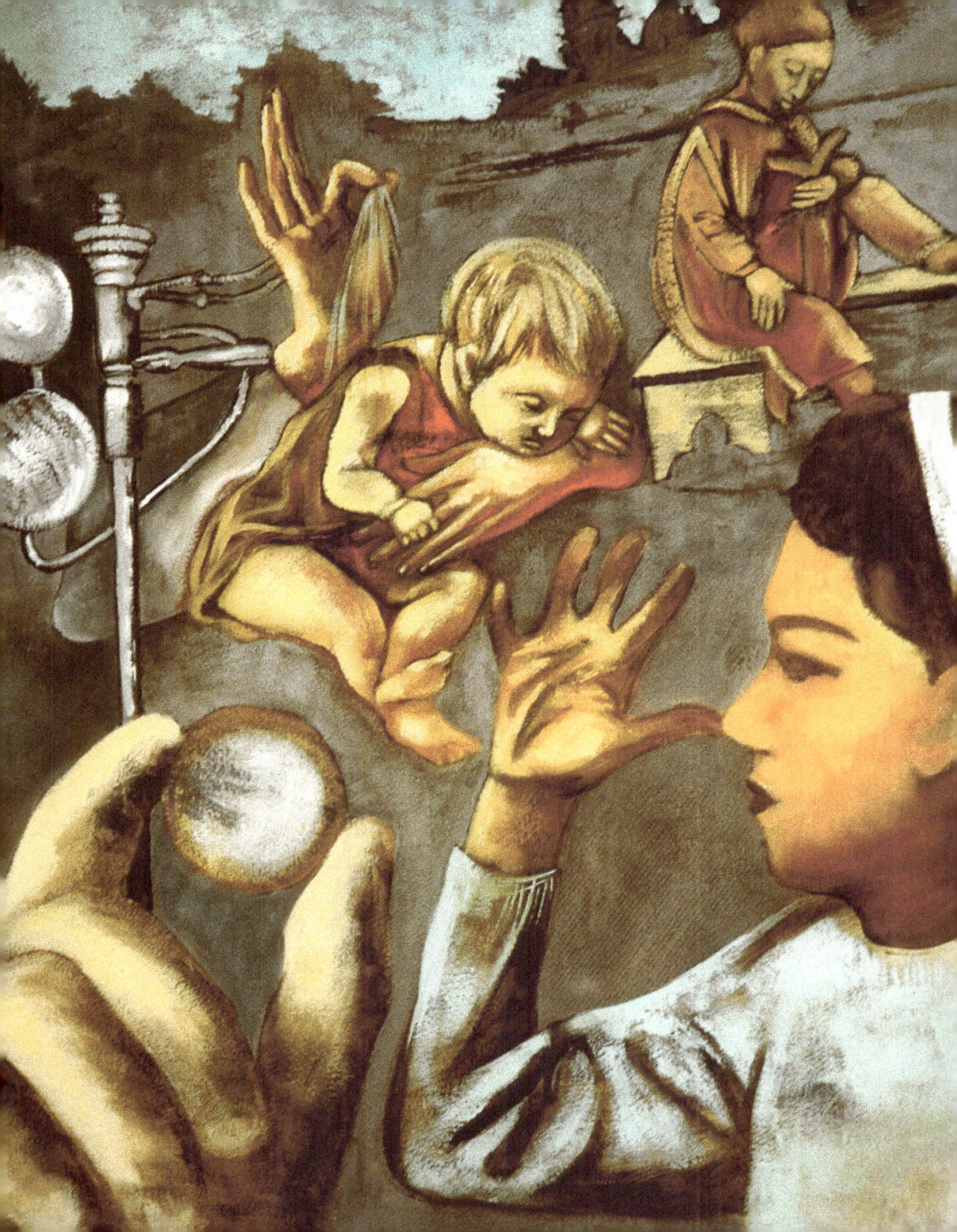

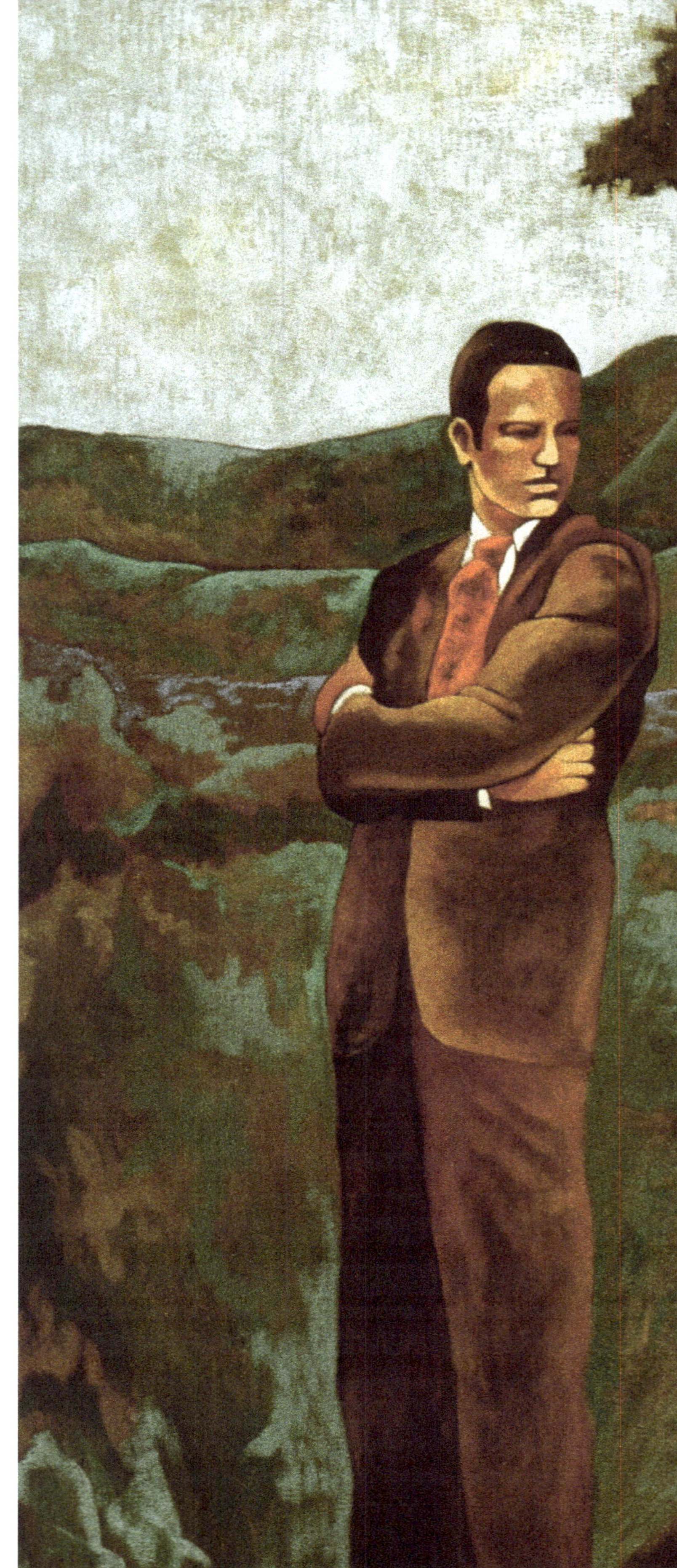

Two Men in a Landscape, 1996
Oil on canvas, 40" x 50"
Private Collection, Woodside, NY

FOLLOWING

Innocence & Delight, 1998
Oil on paper, 26" x 40"

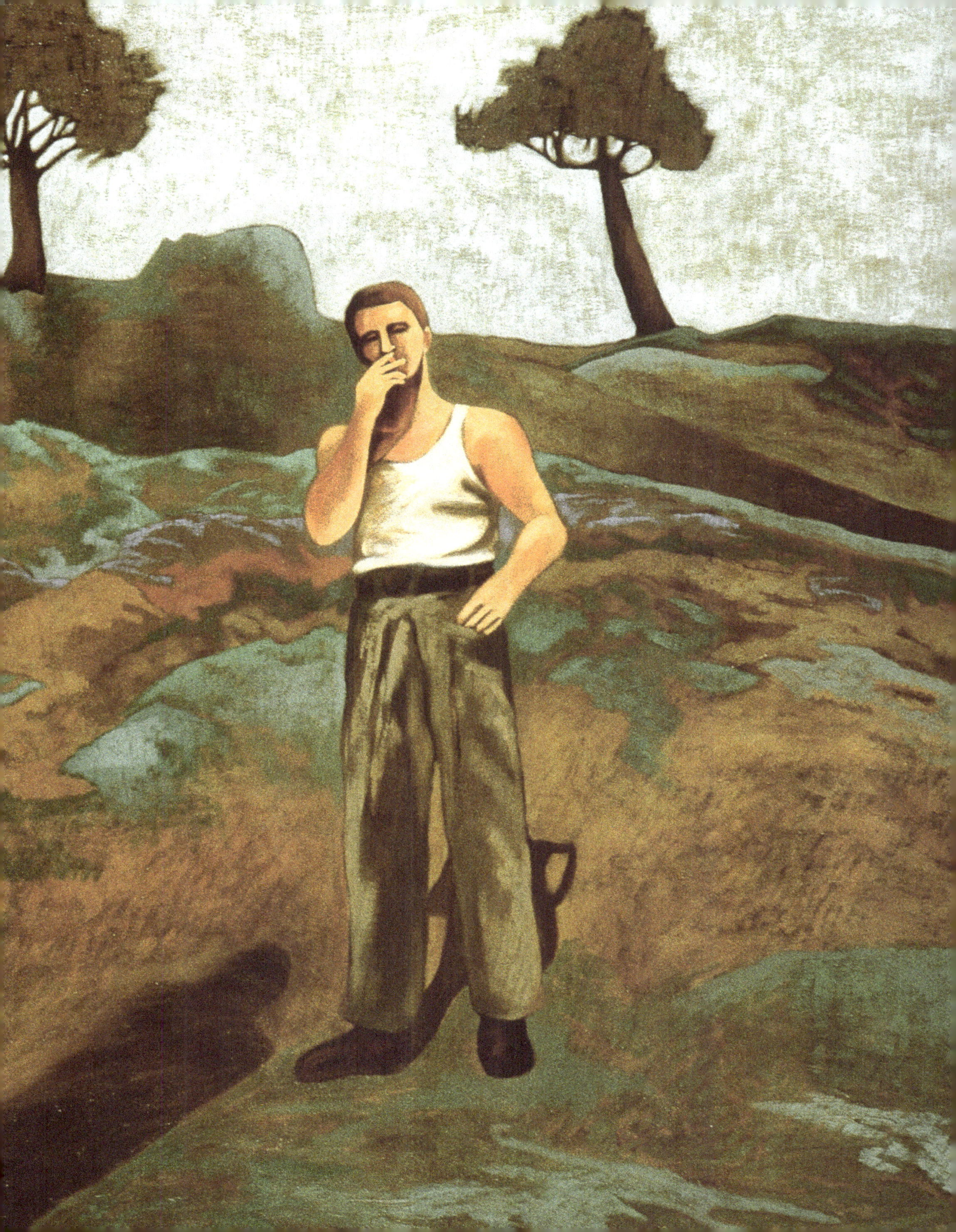

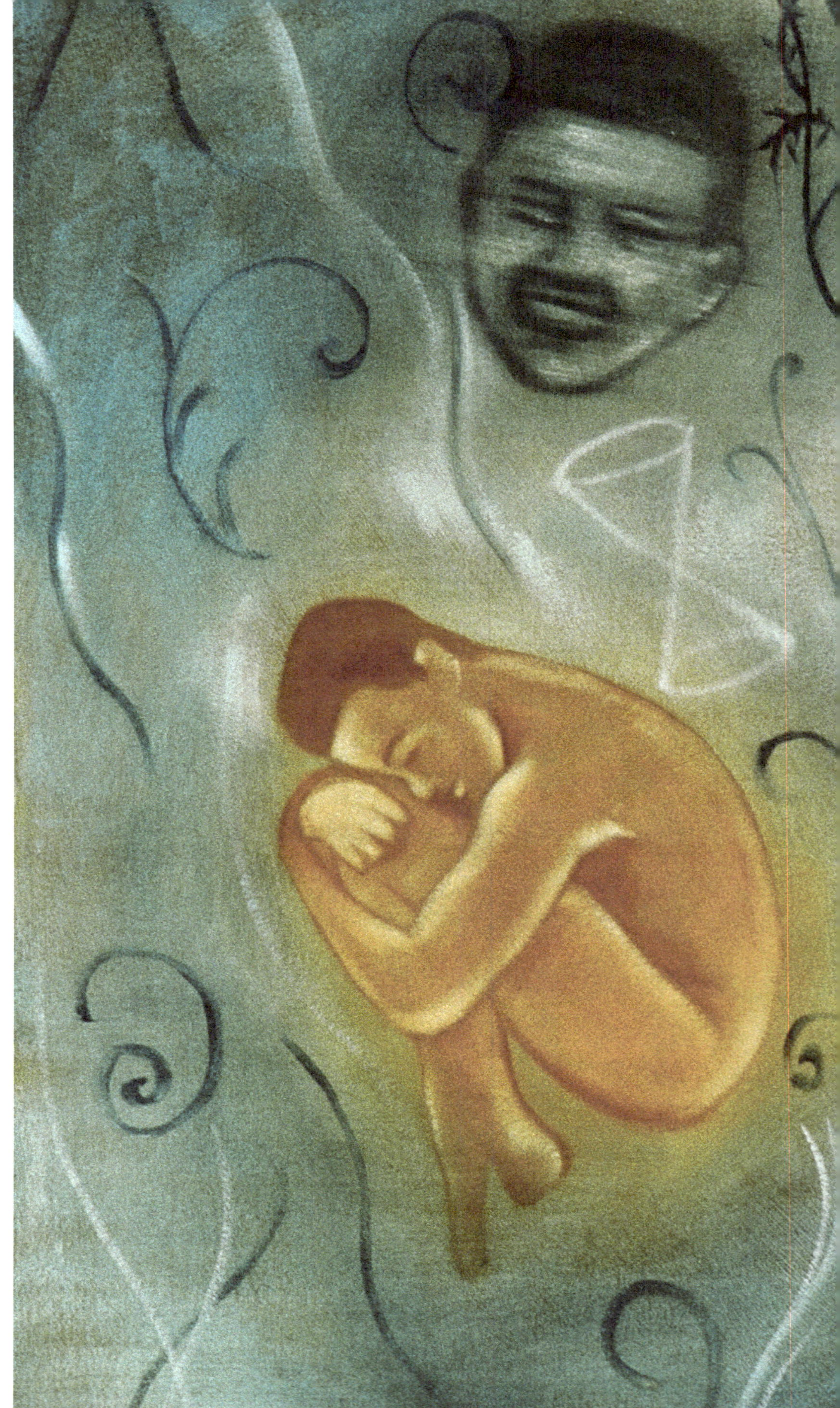

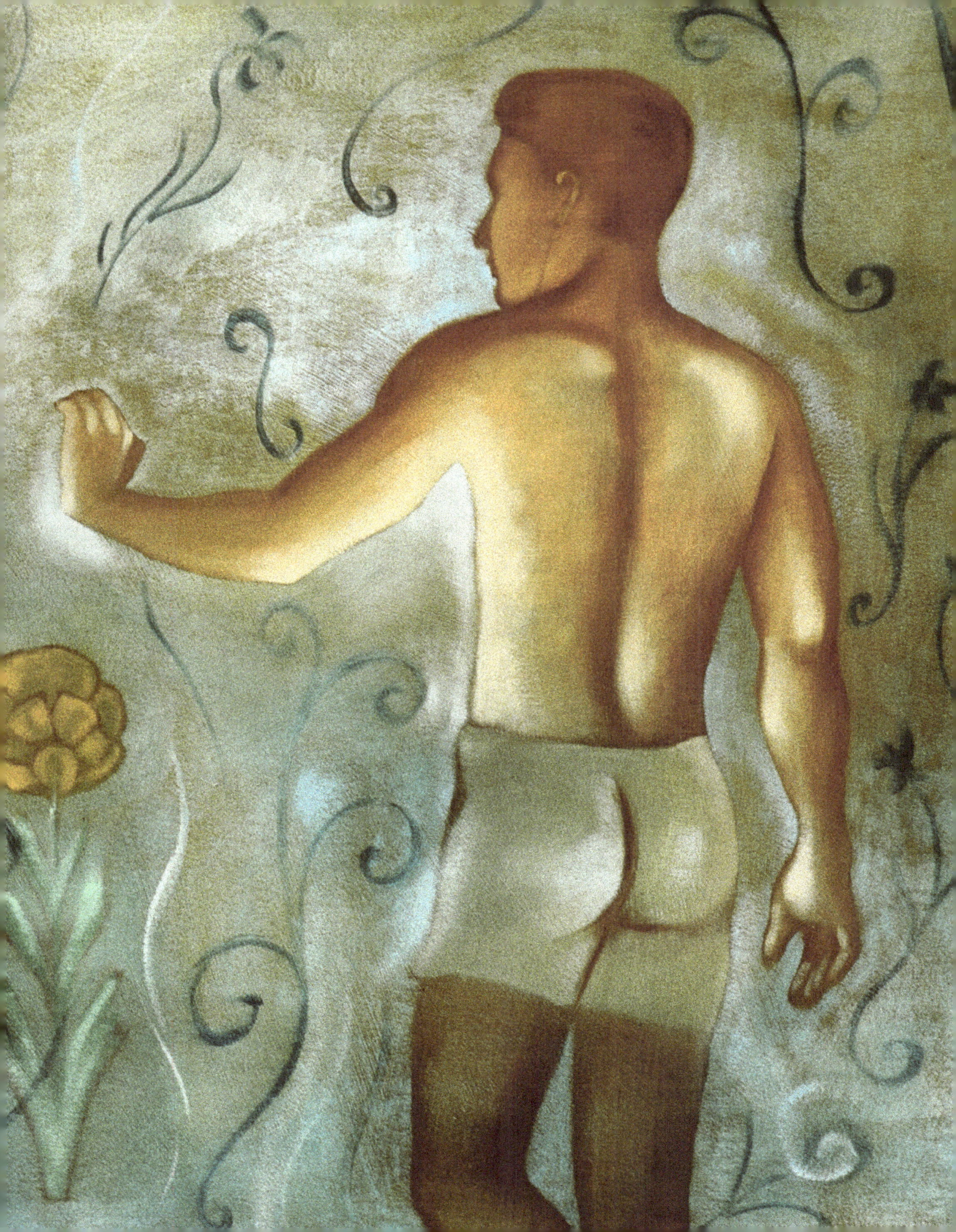

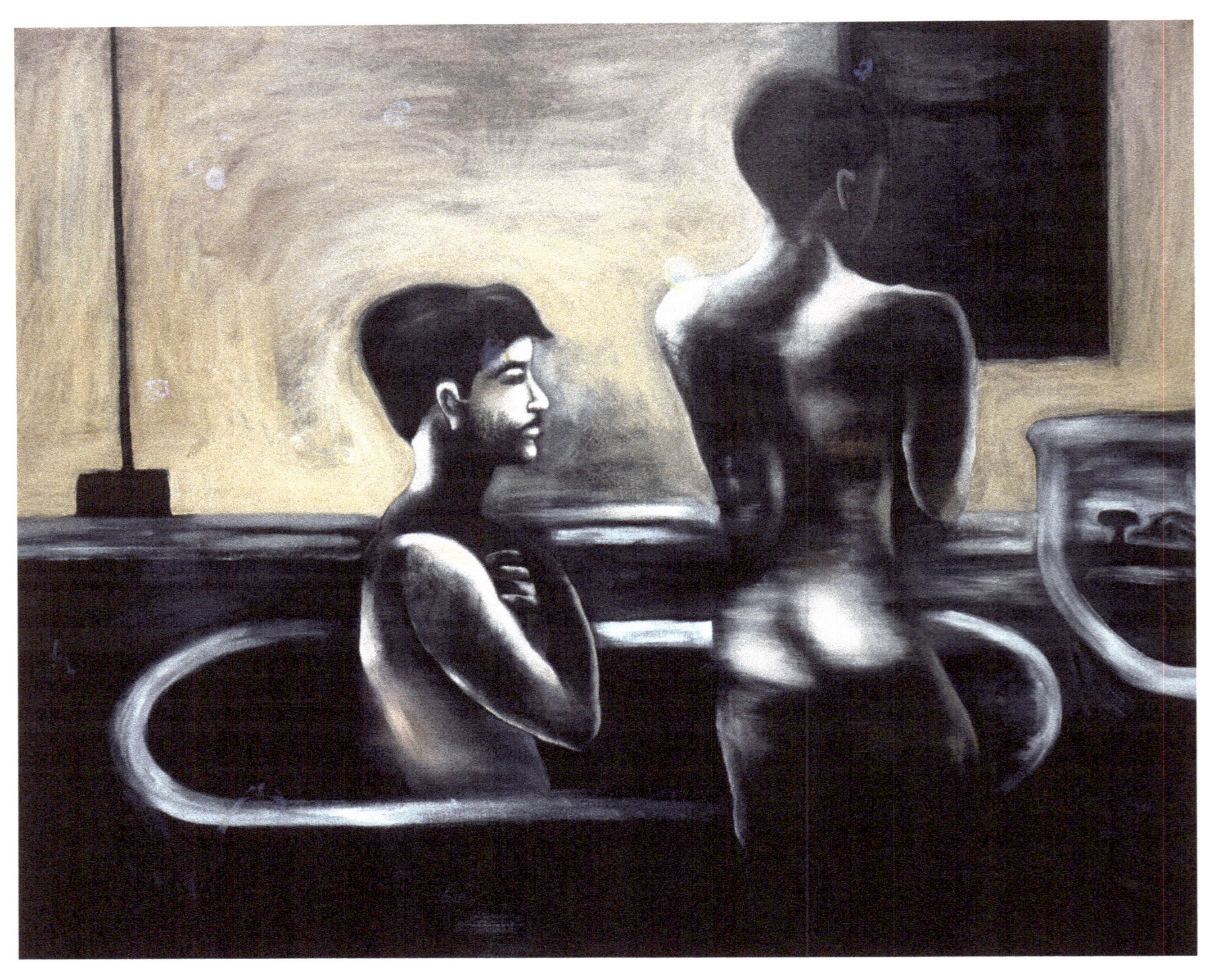

Bath, 1990
Oil on canvas, 48" x 60"
Private Collection, Huntington Beach, CA

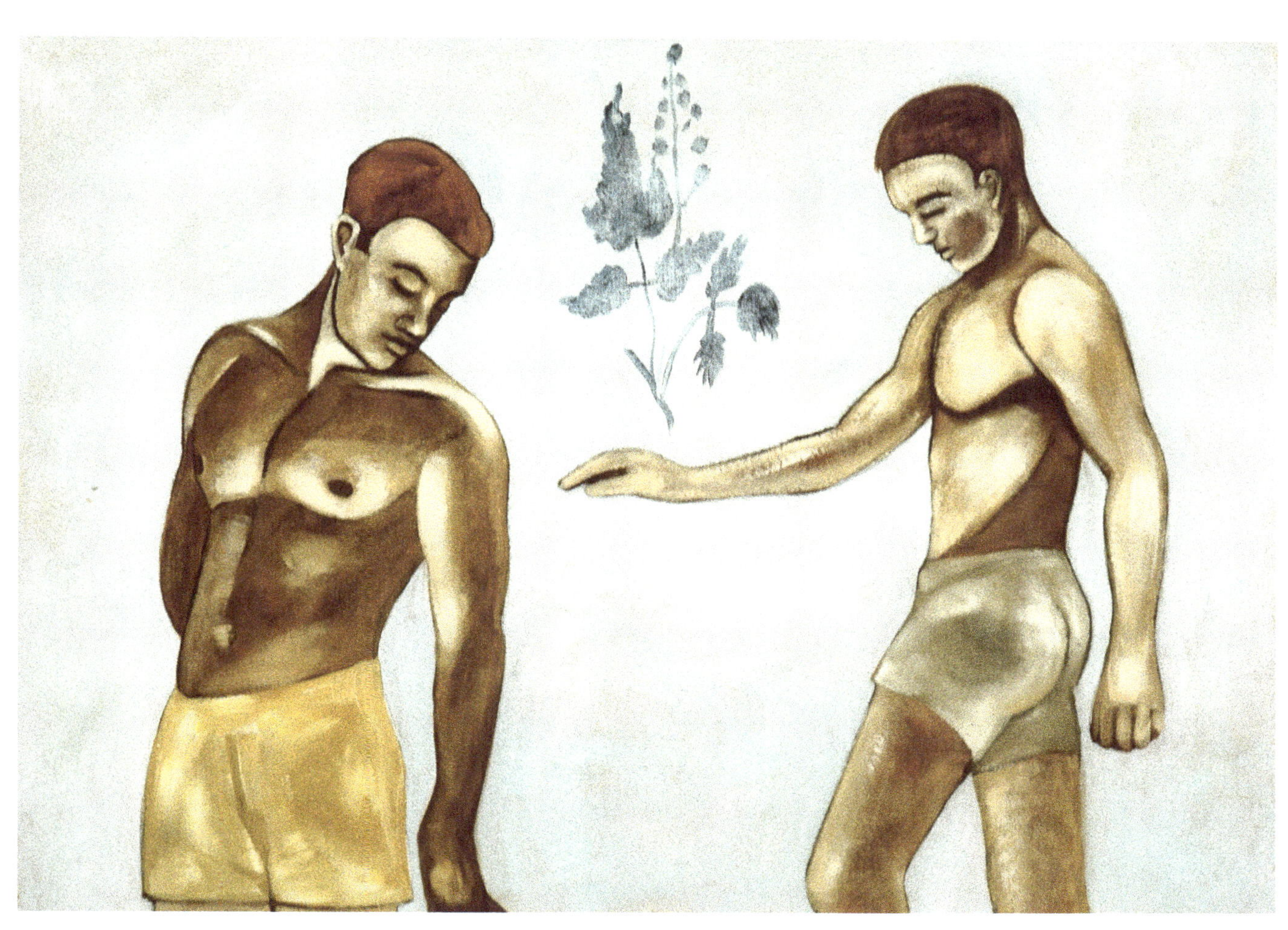

Untitled, 1997
Oil on paper, 28" x 40"

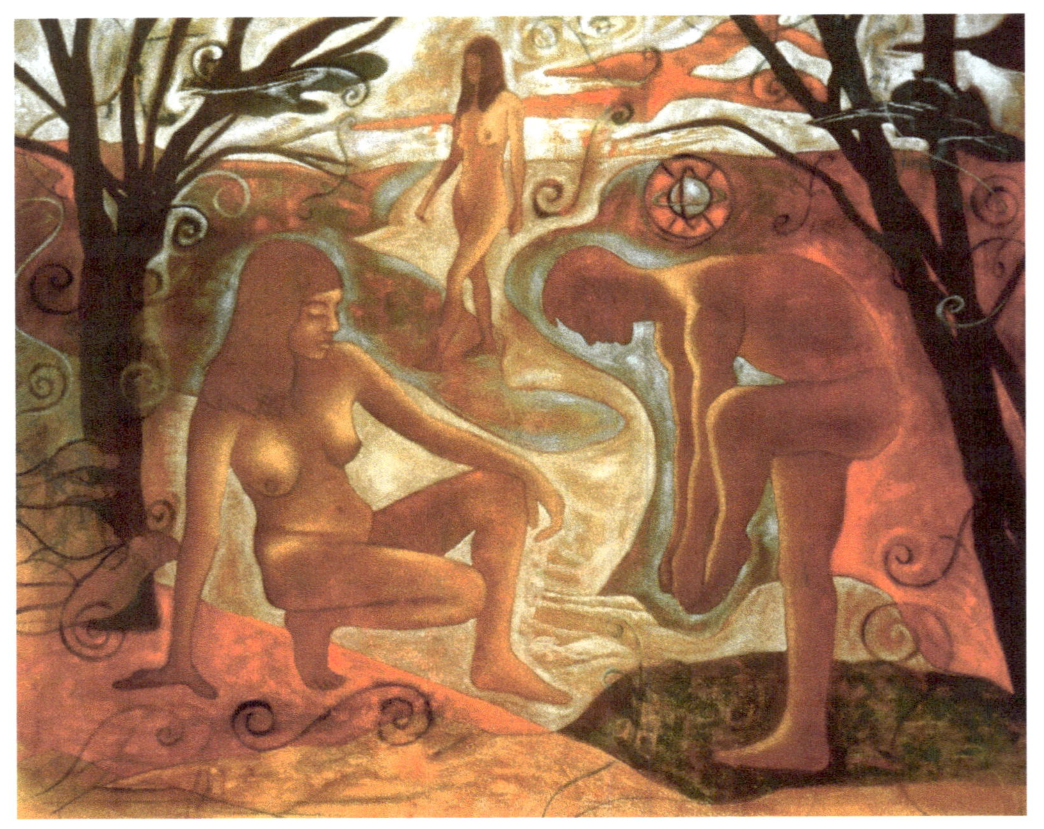

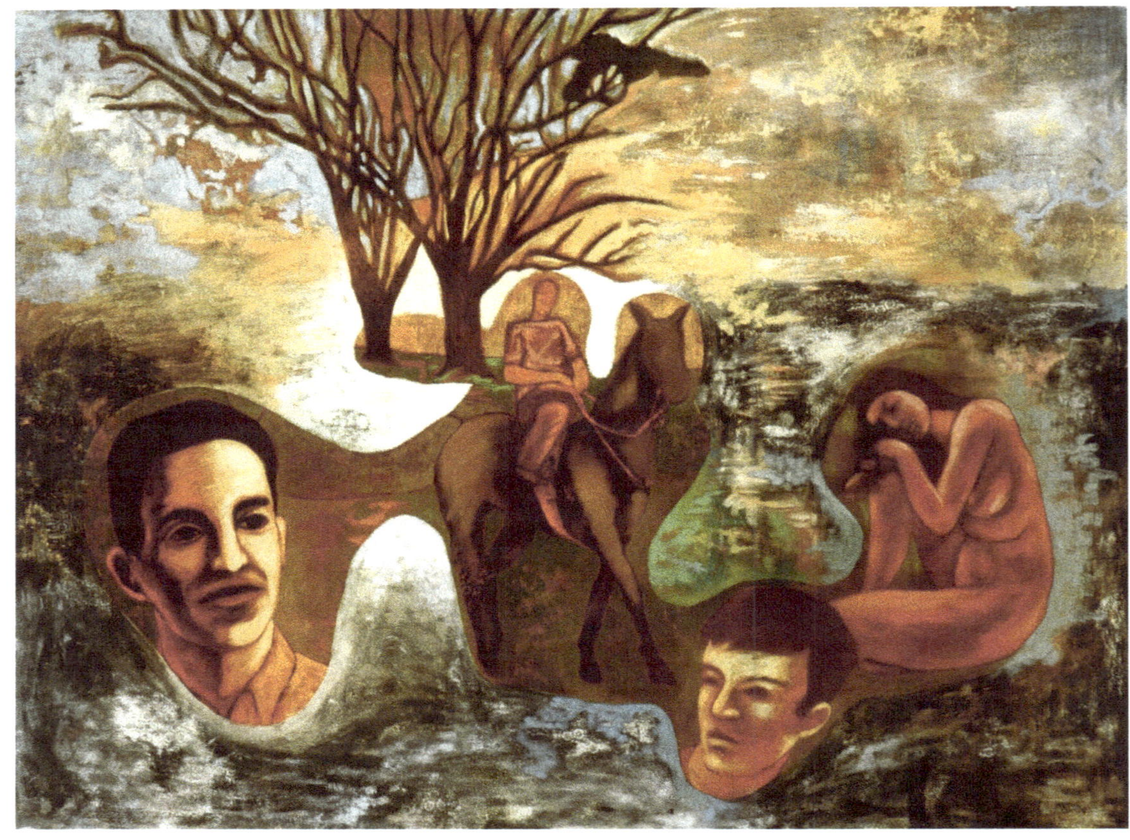

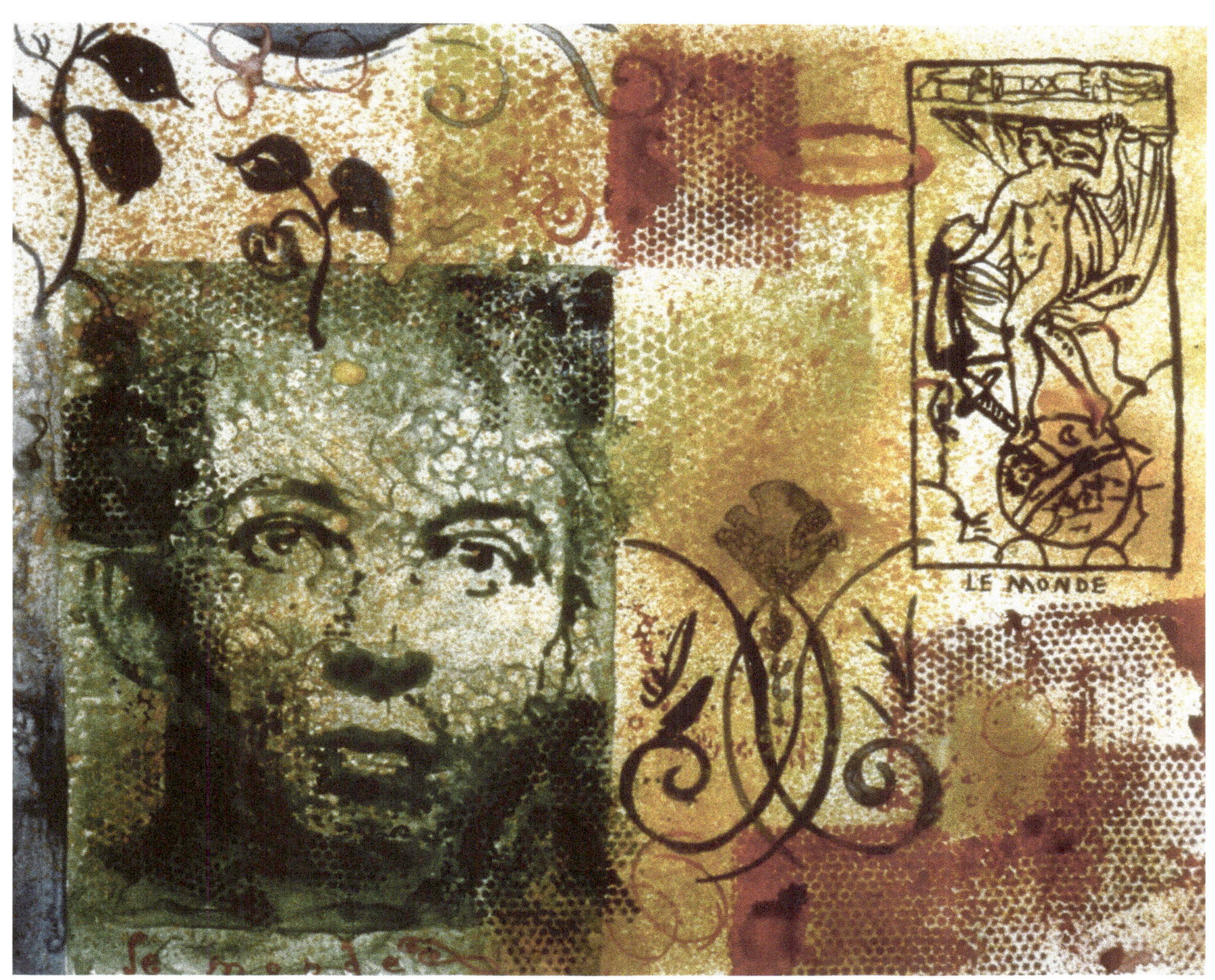

OPPOSITE TOP

Entrance to the Forest, 1997
Oil on linen, 48"x 60"
Private Collection, Belle Harbor, NY

OPPOSITE BOTTOM

La Poza del Angel, 1994
Oil & acrylic on paper, 38" x 47"

ABOVE

Le Monde, 1998
Monotype on paper, 16" x 19 1/2"

BELOW
An Odd Request, 1999
Oil on wood, 14" x 18"
Private Collection, Chapel Hill, NC

OPPOSITE
Friendly Neighbors, 1999
Oil & acrylic on canvas, 60" x 54"

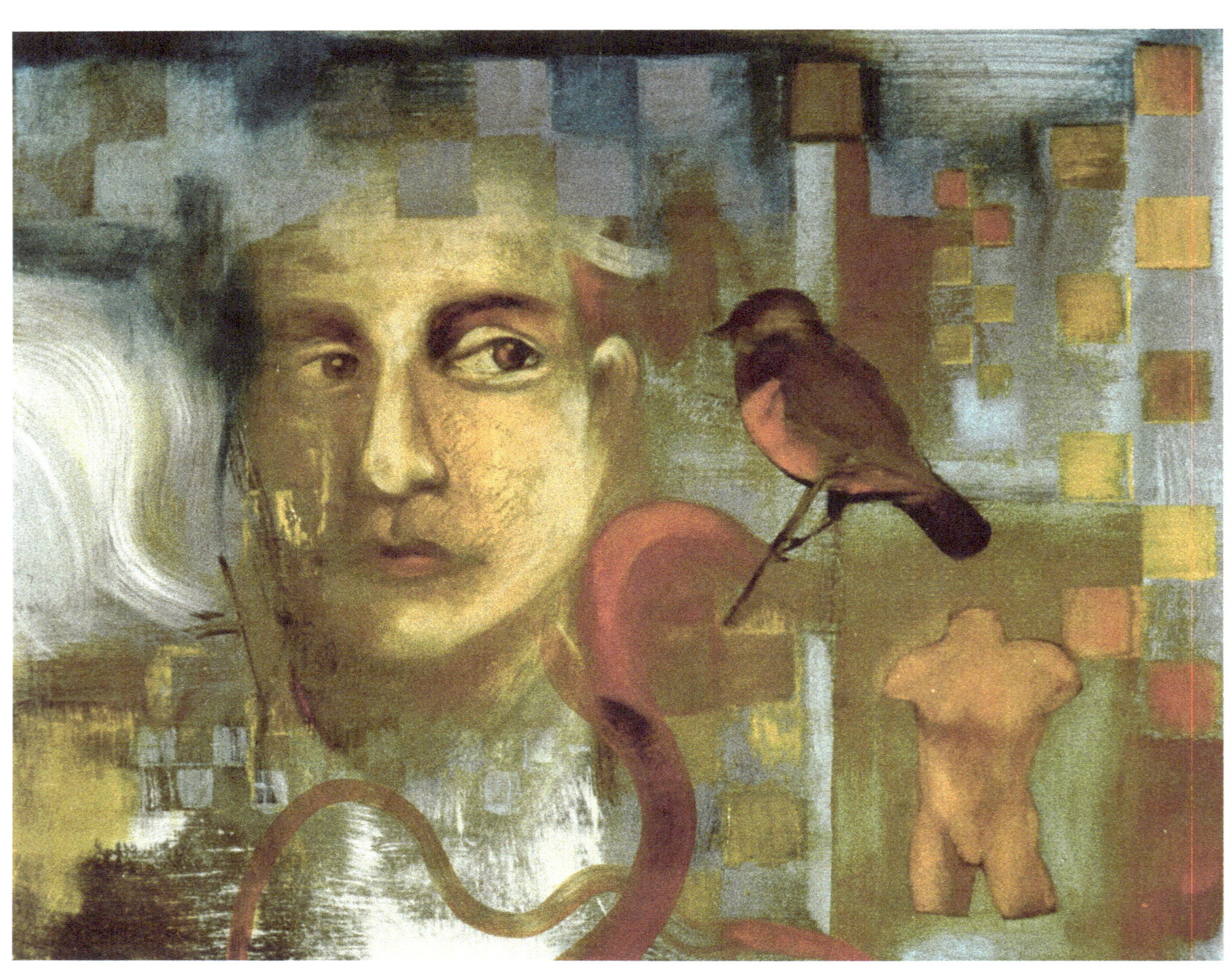

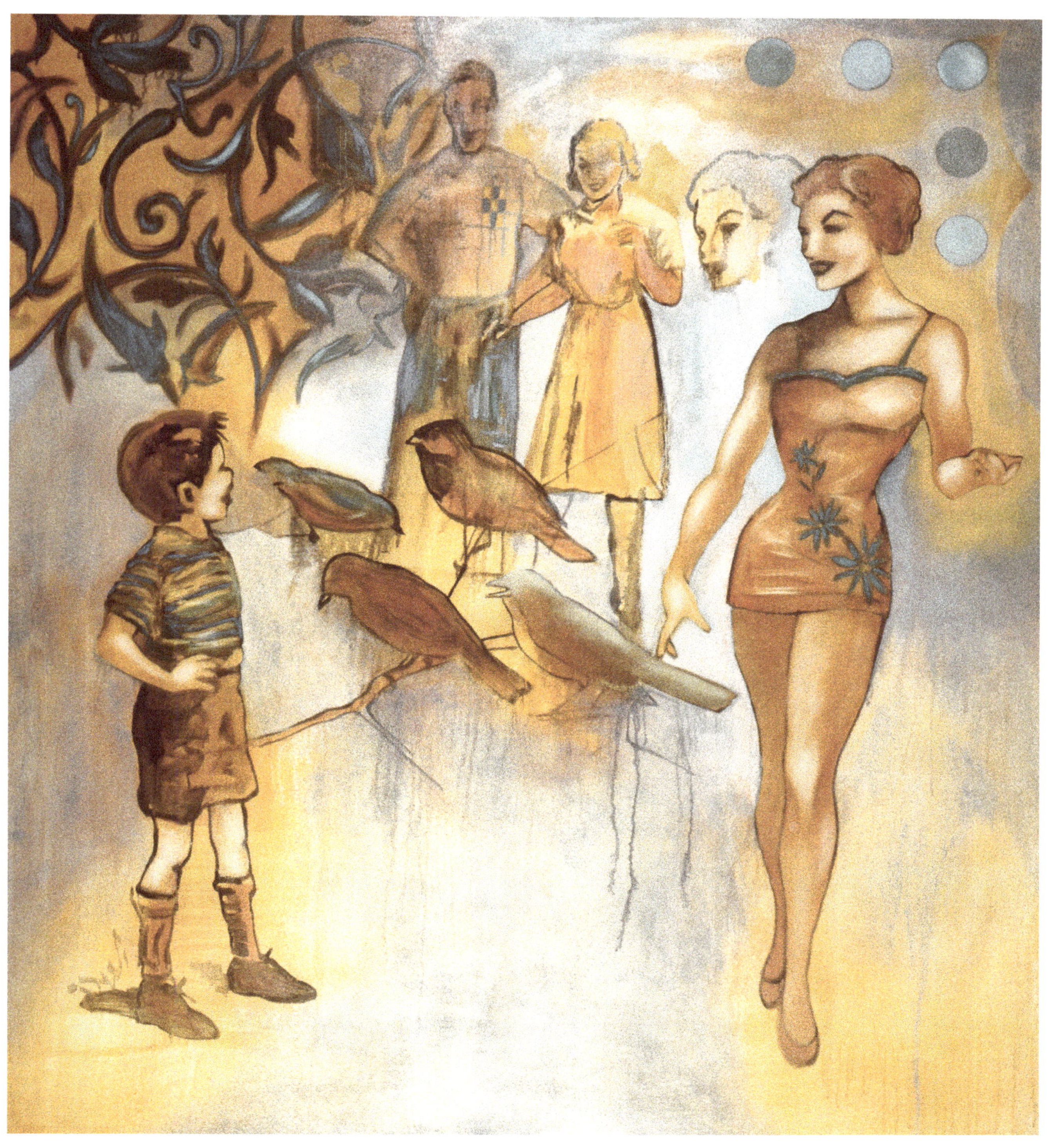

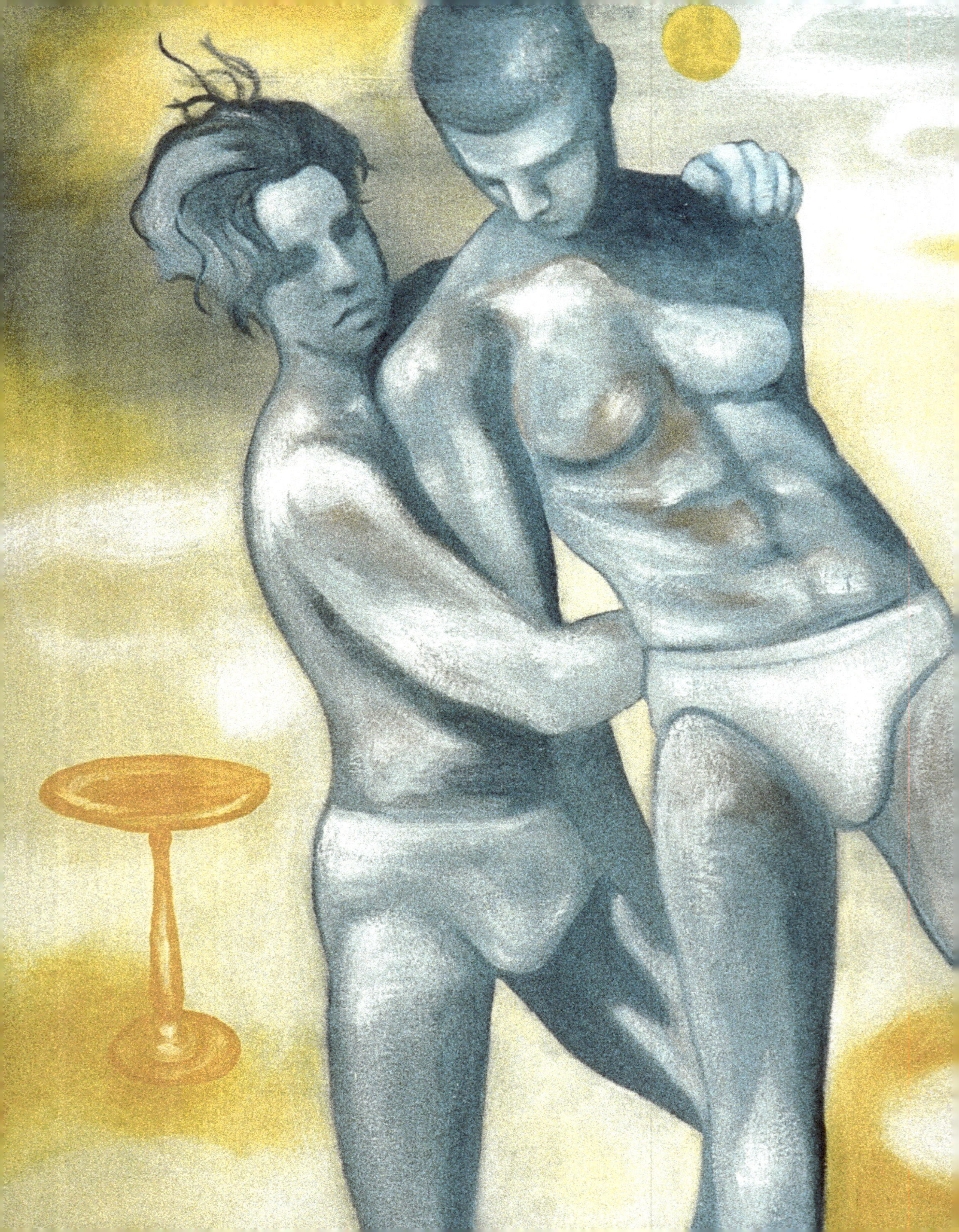

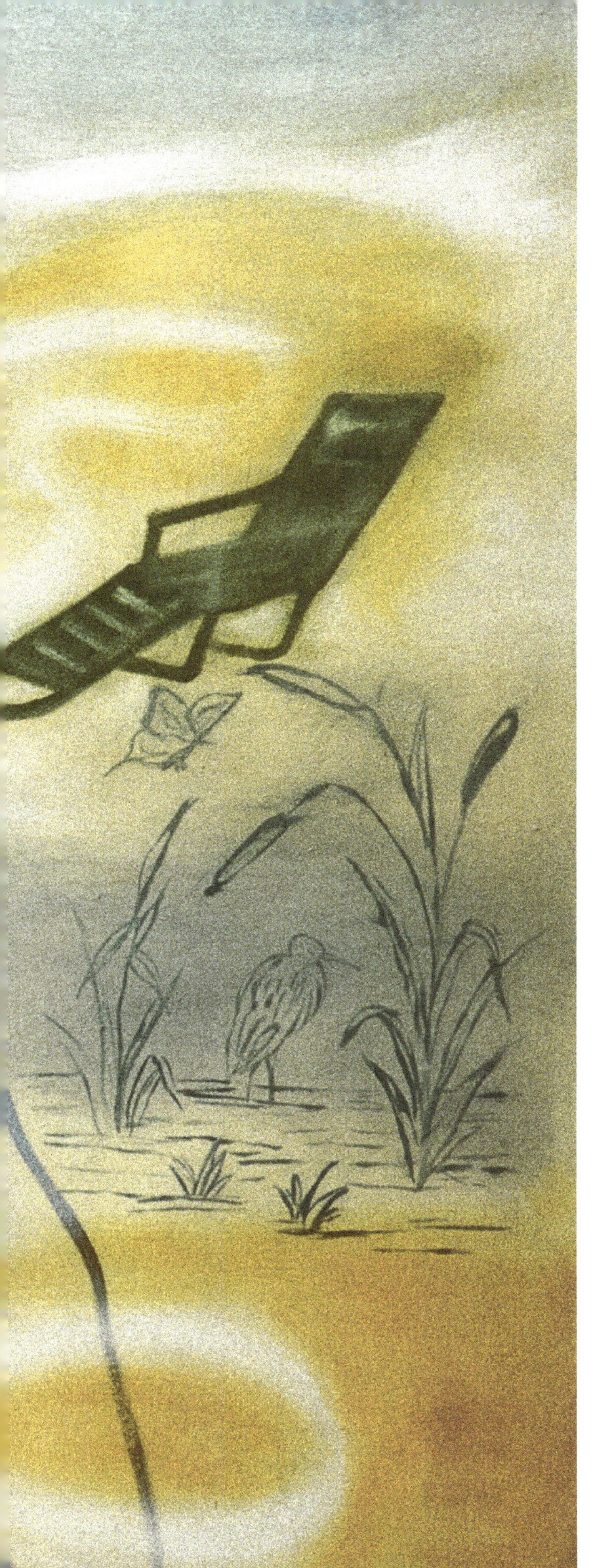

Tryst, 1998
Oil on canvas, 42" x 50"

BELOW

Dear World, 1997
Watercolor on paper, 29 1/2" x 41"

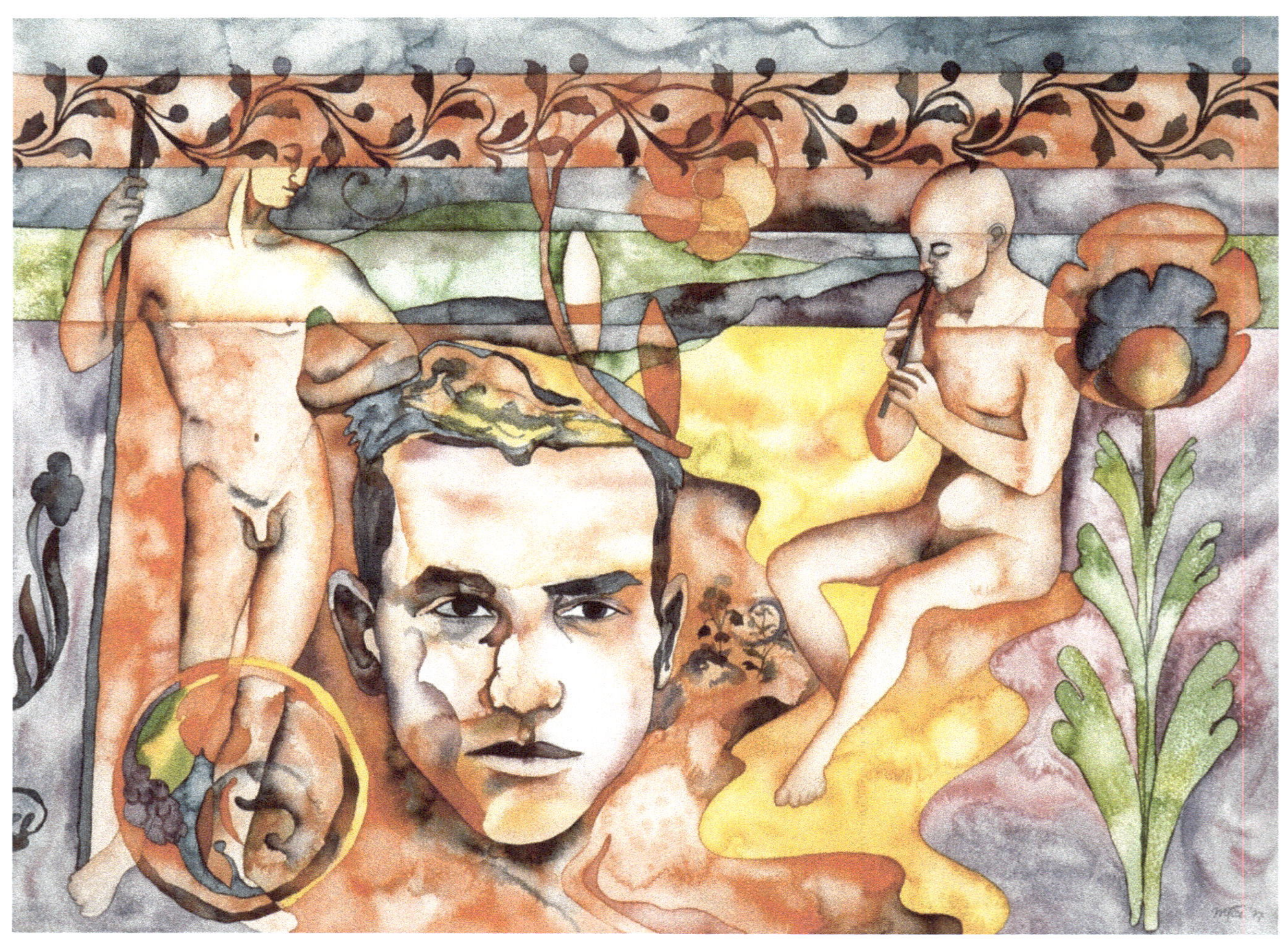

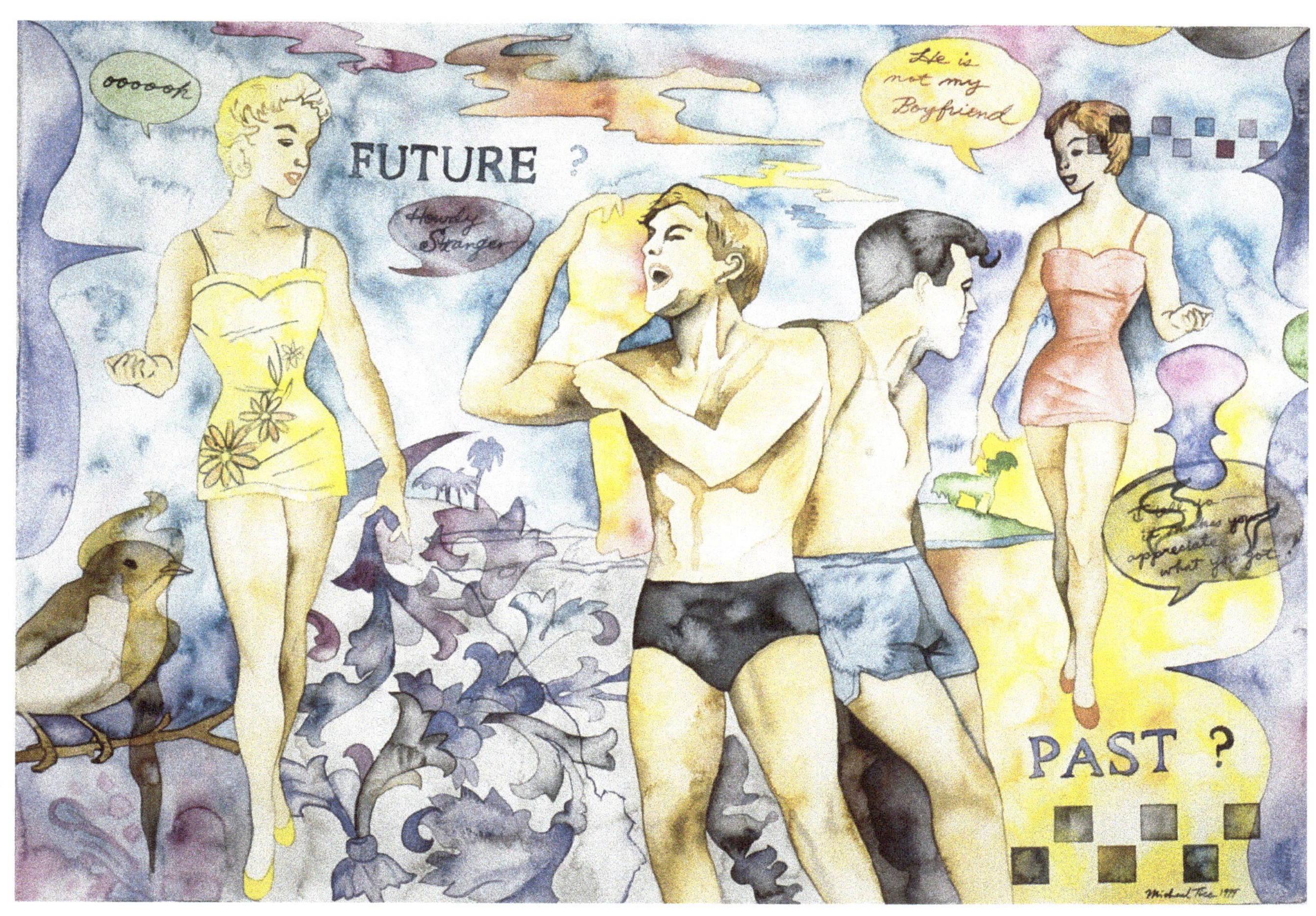

Future? Past?, 1999
Watercolor on paper, 25" x 36"

First Time, 1998
Monotype on paper, 11"x 17"

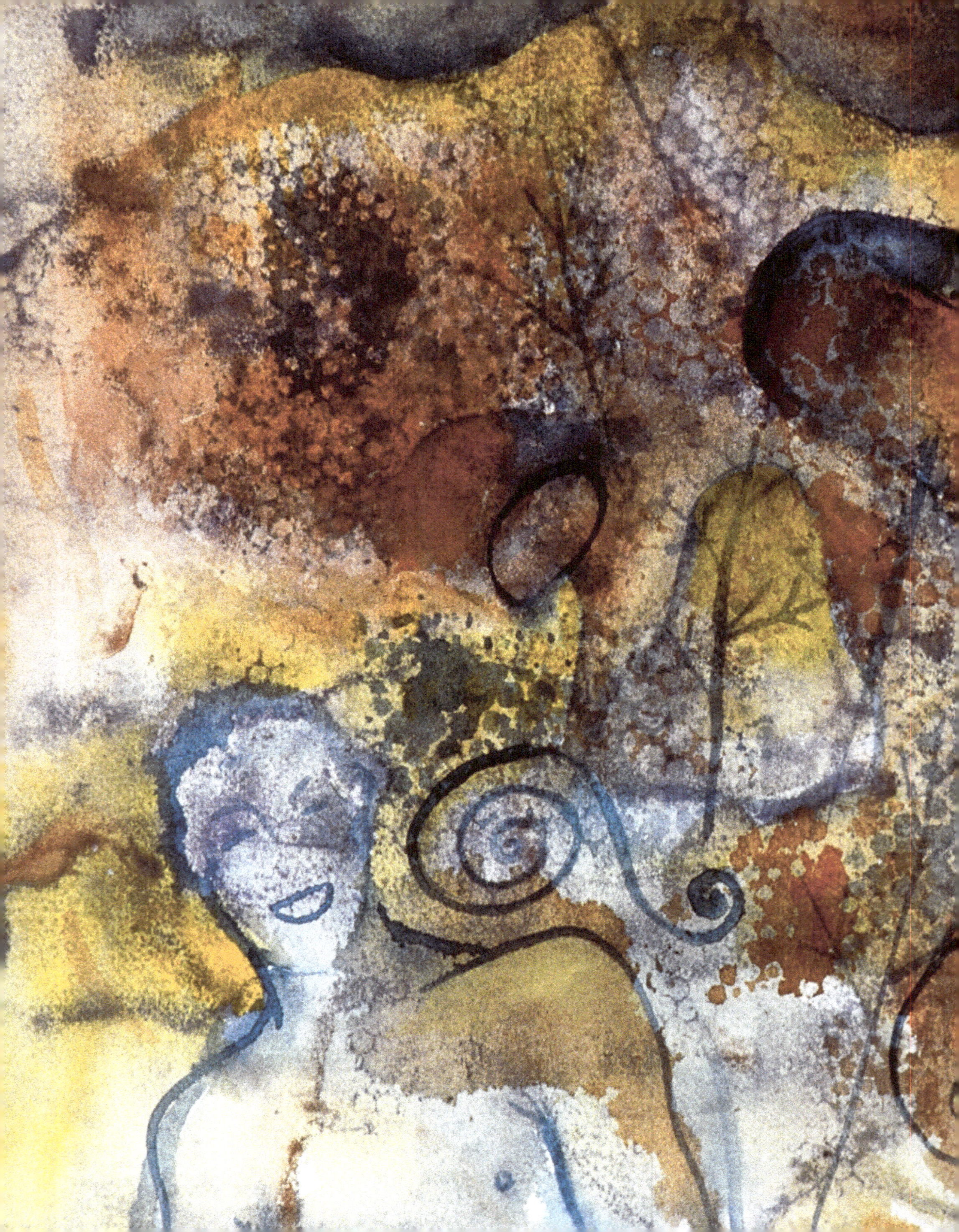

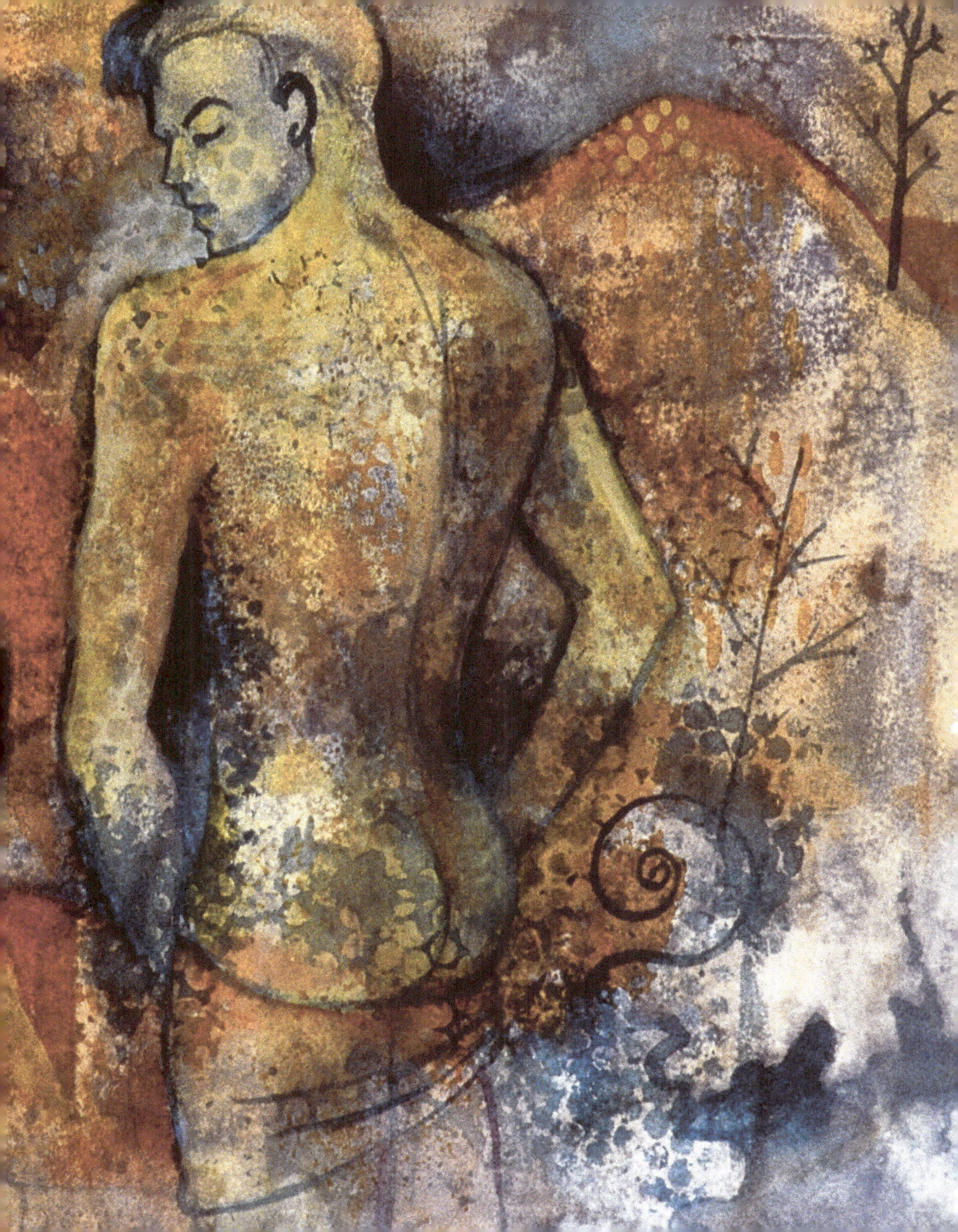

A Dream Deferred, 1996
Oil on paper, 28" x 40"
Private Collection

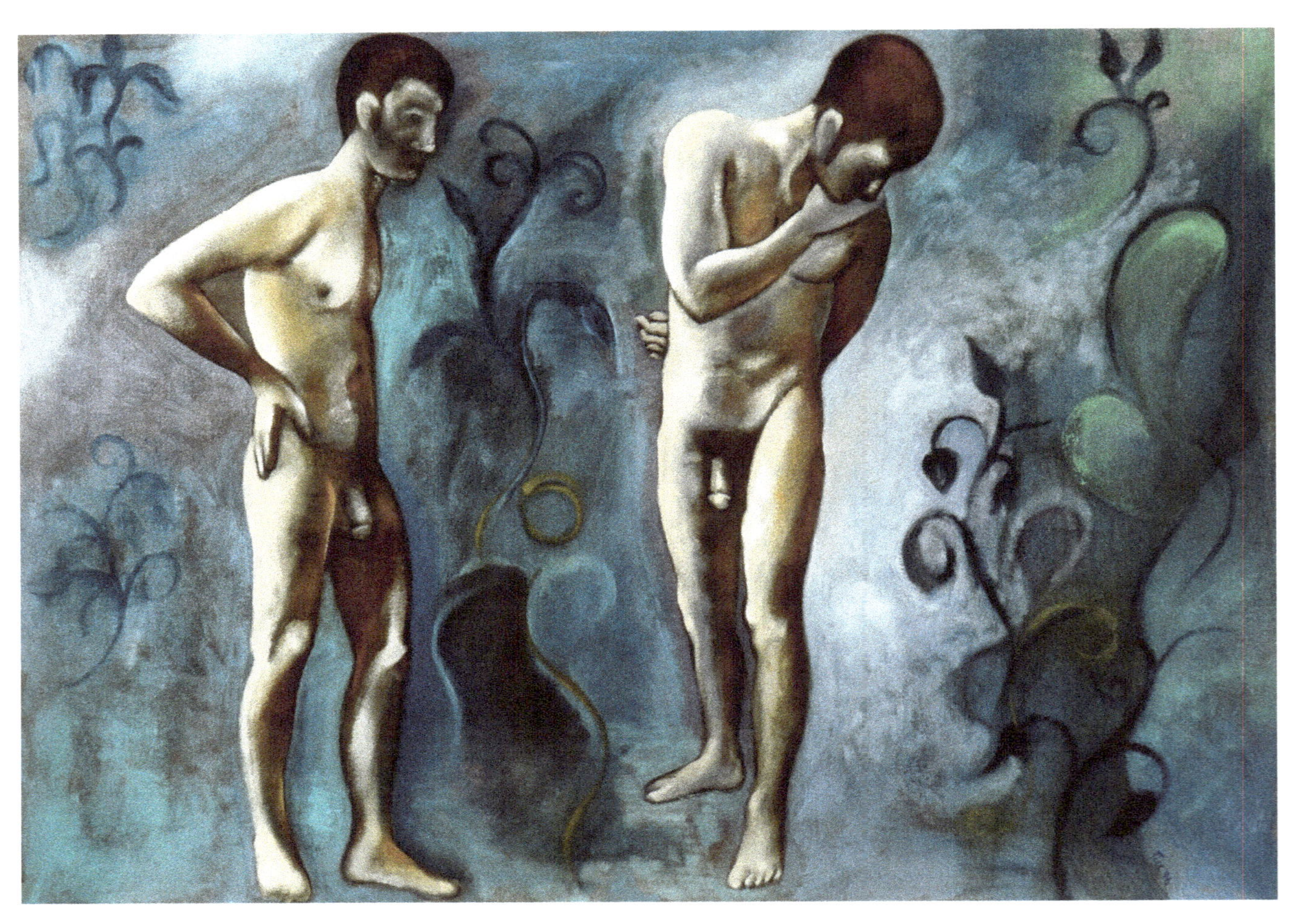

62

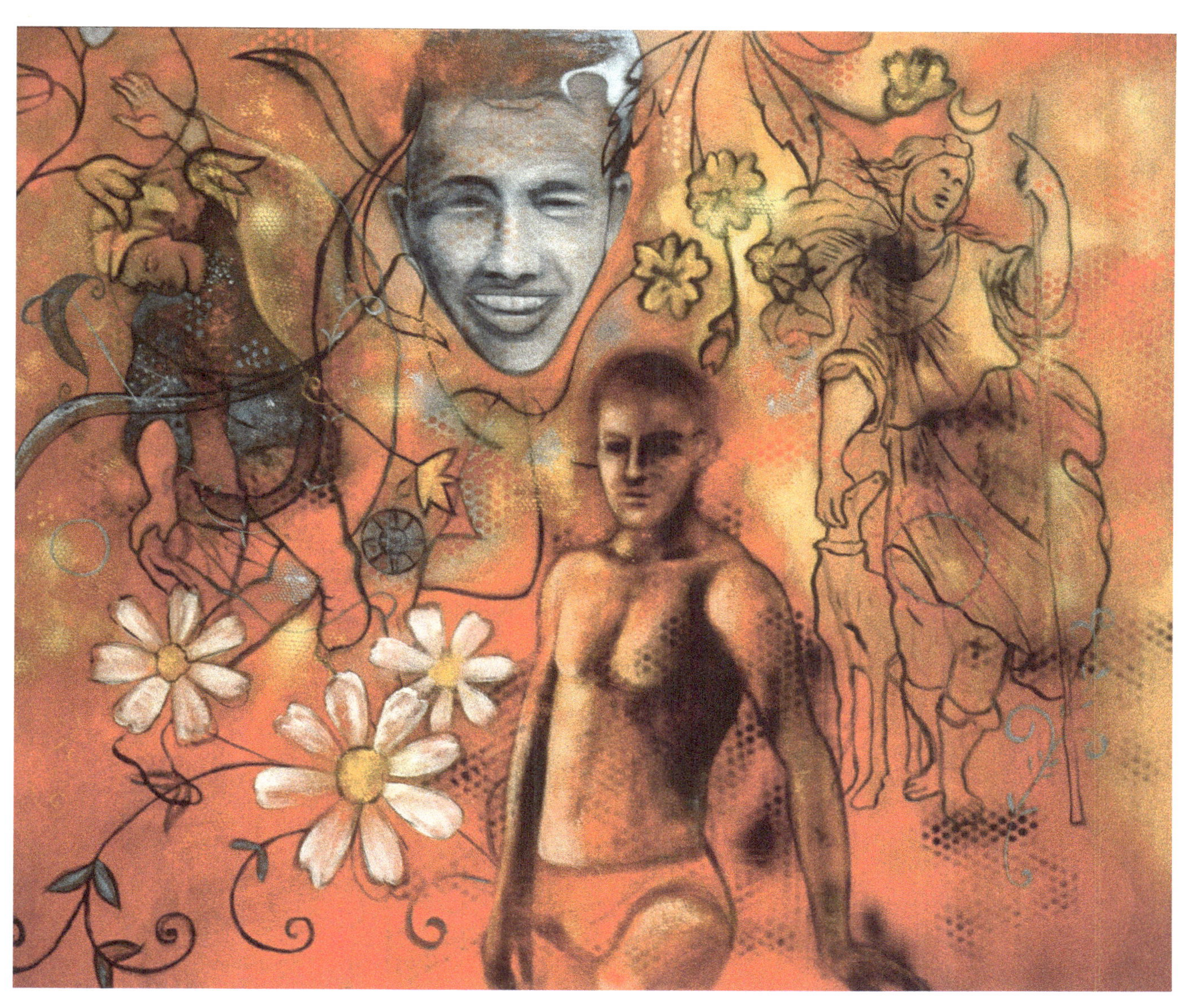

MoonBoy, 1998
Oil on linen, 50" x 60"

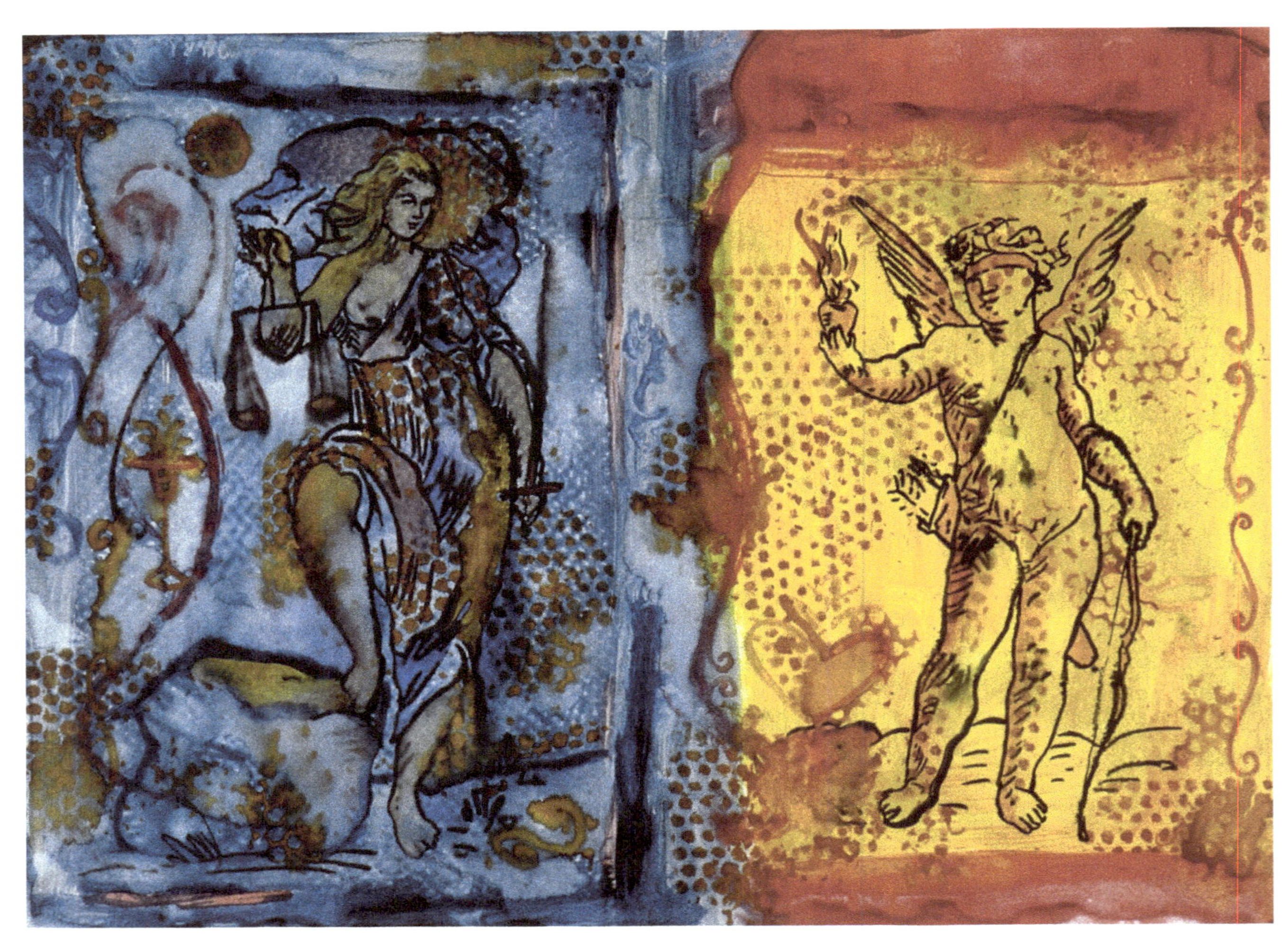

Sun in Libra, 1998
Monotype on paper, 12" x 16"

64

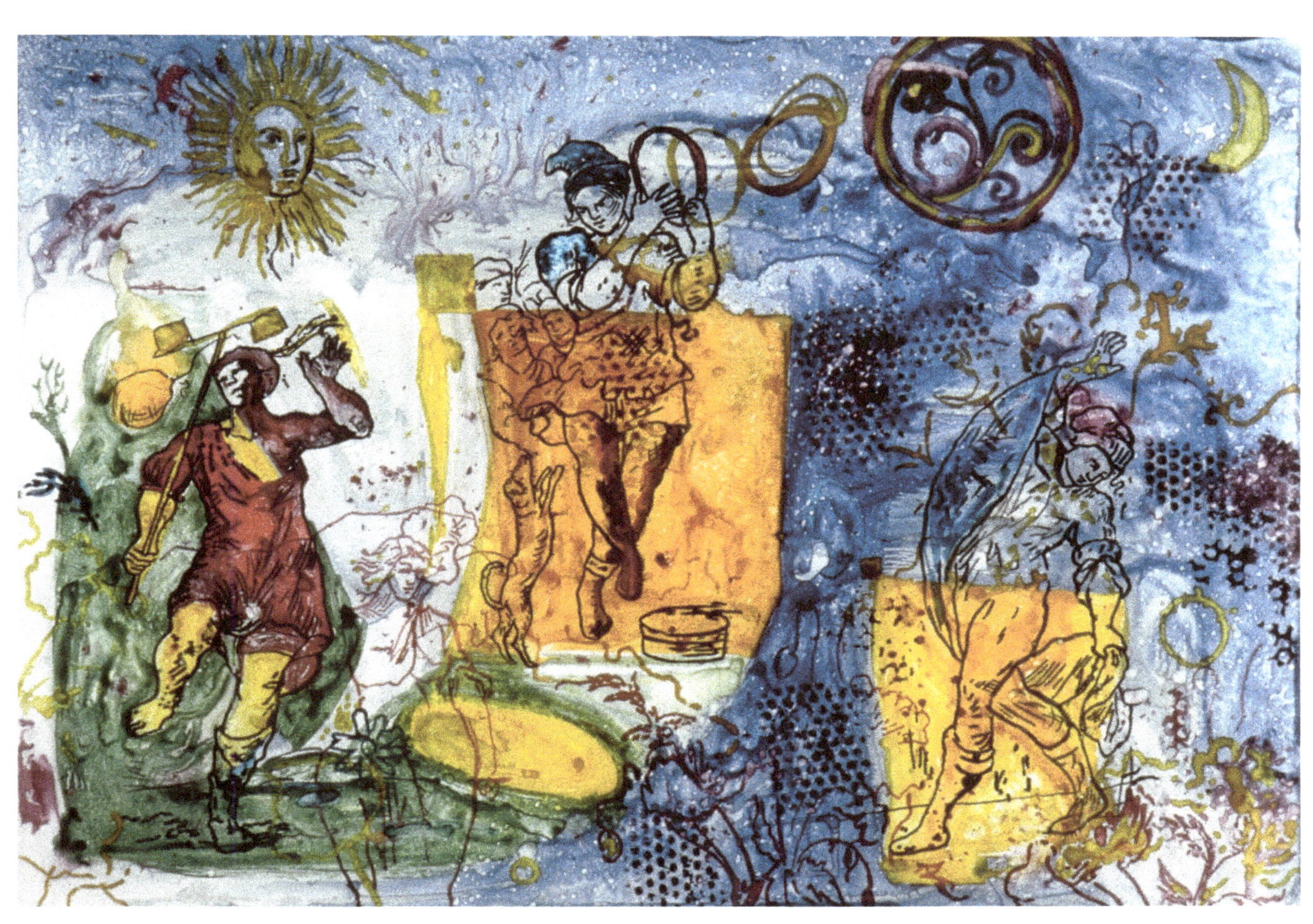

Change Fools the Magician, 1998
Monotype on paper, 16 3/4" x 24"
Private Collection, Durham, NC

FOLLOWING

Magician's Son, 1992
Oil on paper, 14" x 10"
Private Collection, Brooklyn, NY

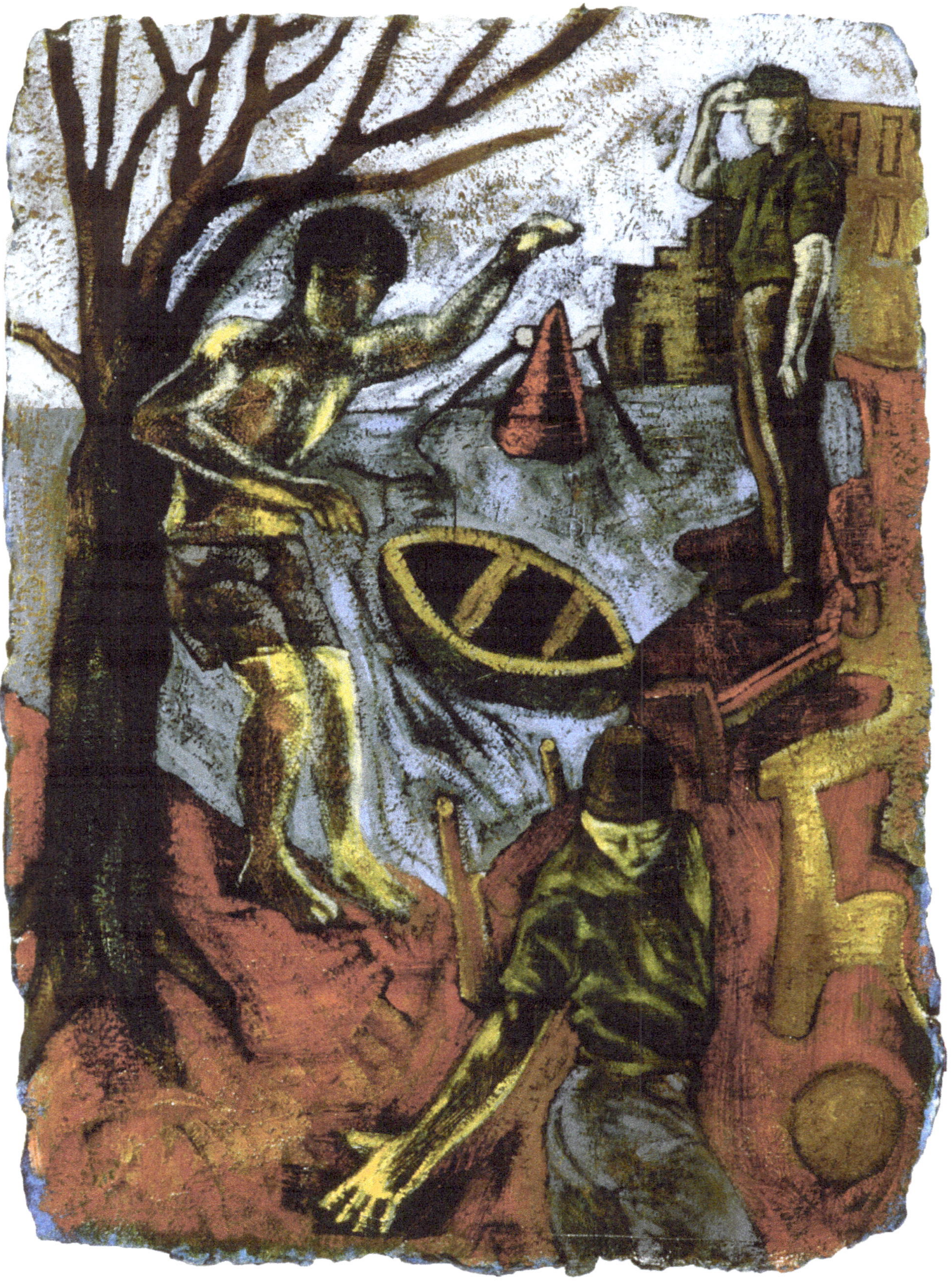

2000's / Current

INNOCENCE & EXPERIENCE

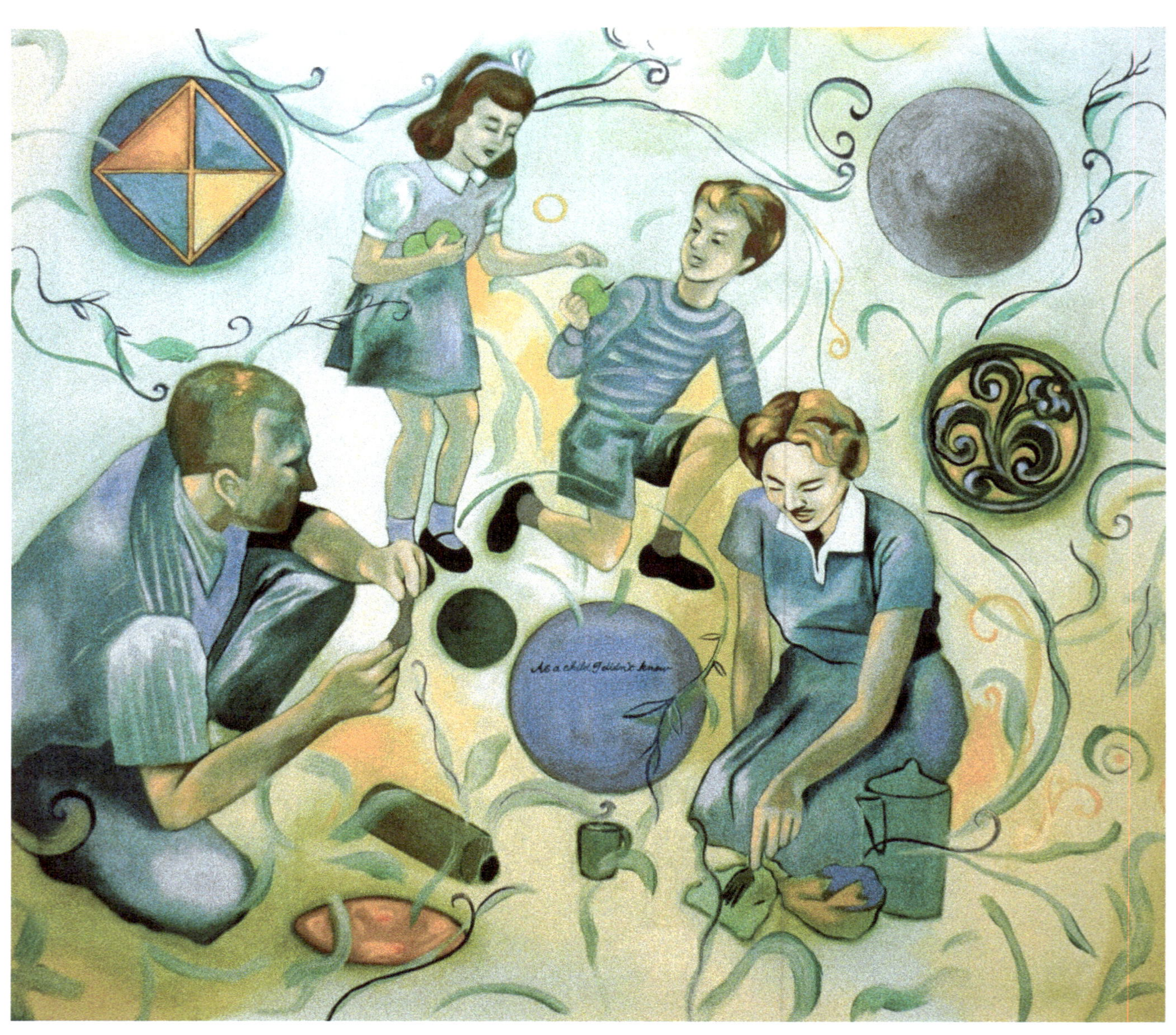

ABOVE

As A Child I Didn't Know, 2001
Oil on canvas, 42" x 48"
Private Collection, Hong Kong

OPPOSITE

Easter Sunday, 2001
Oil & acrylic on paper, 35" x 23 1/2"
Private Collection, Cincinatti, OH

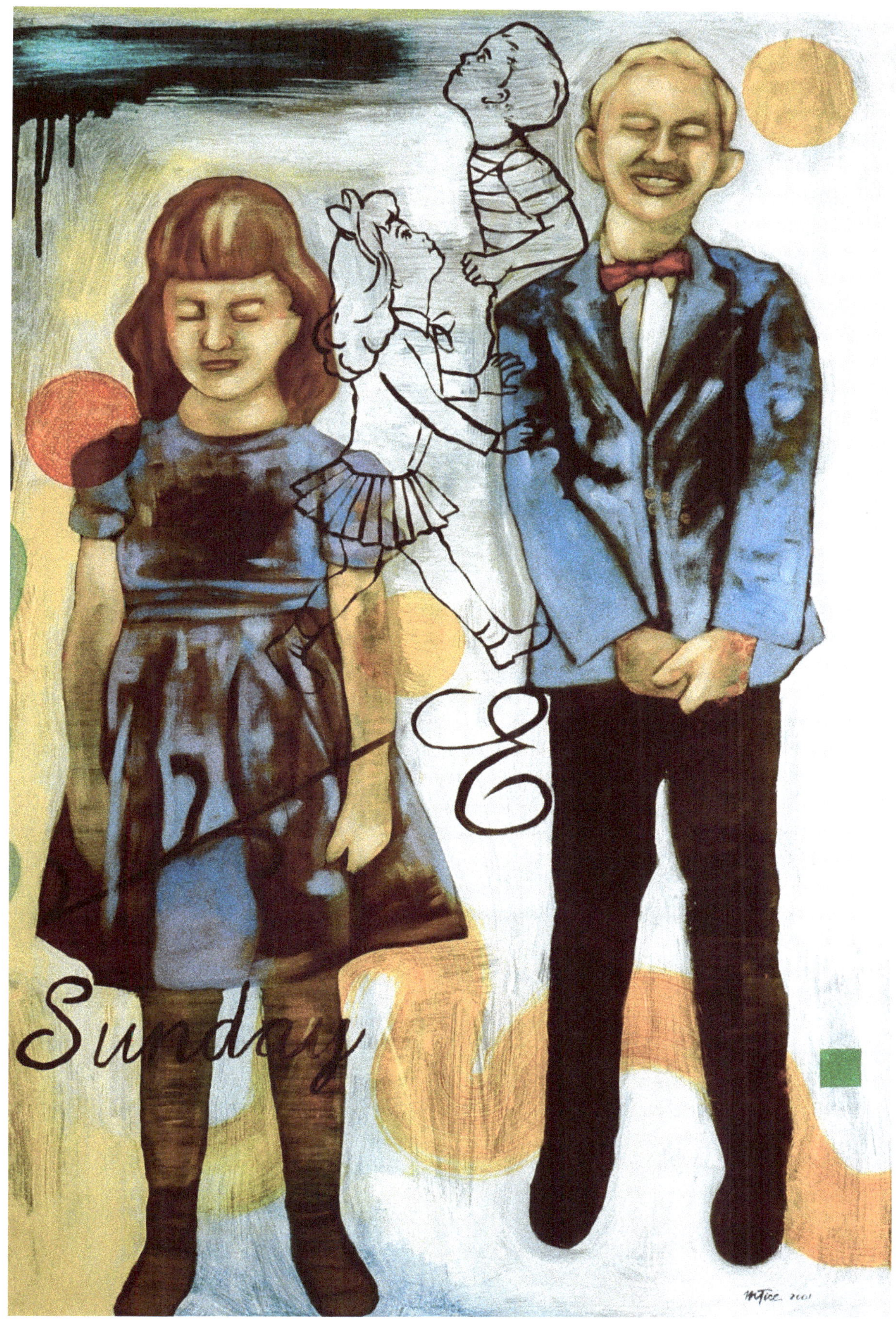

Sunday

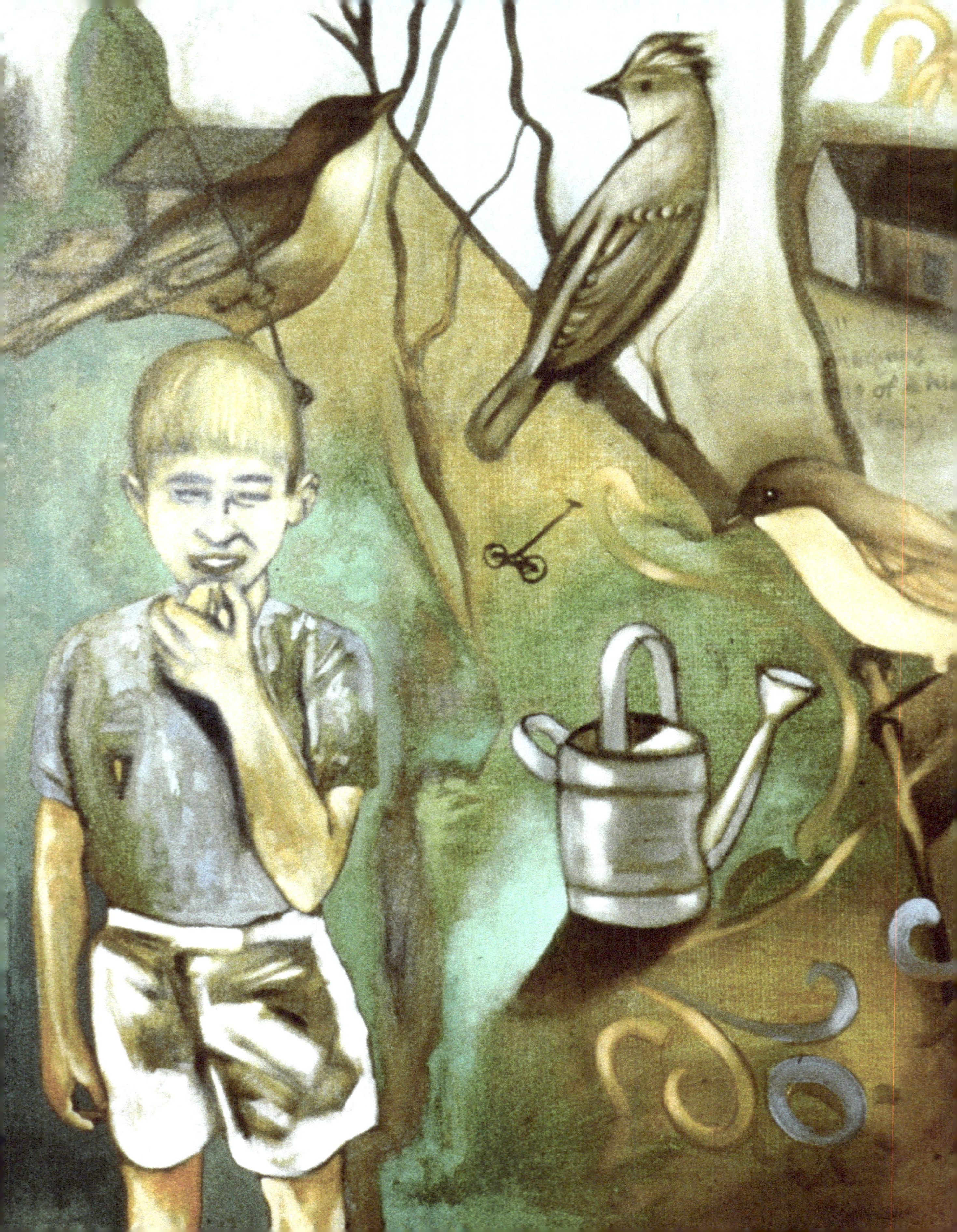

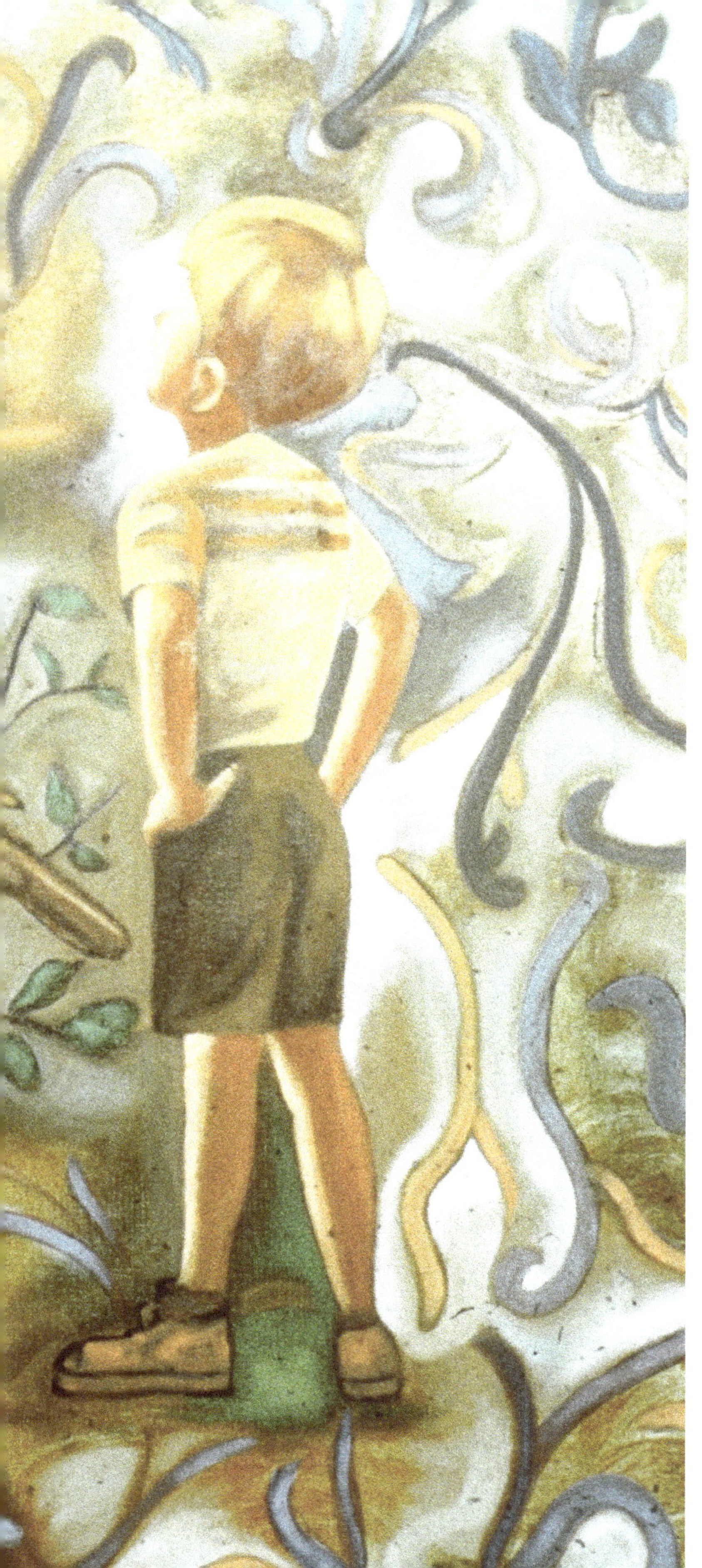

Bonner Street, 2000
Oil on canvas, 35" x 44"

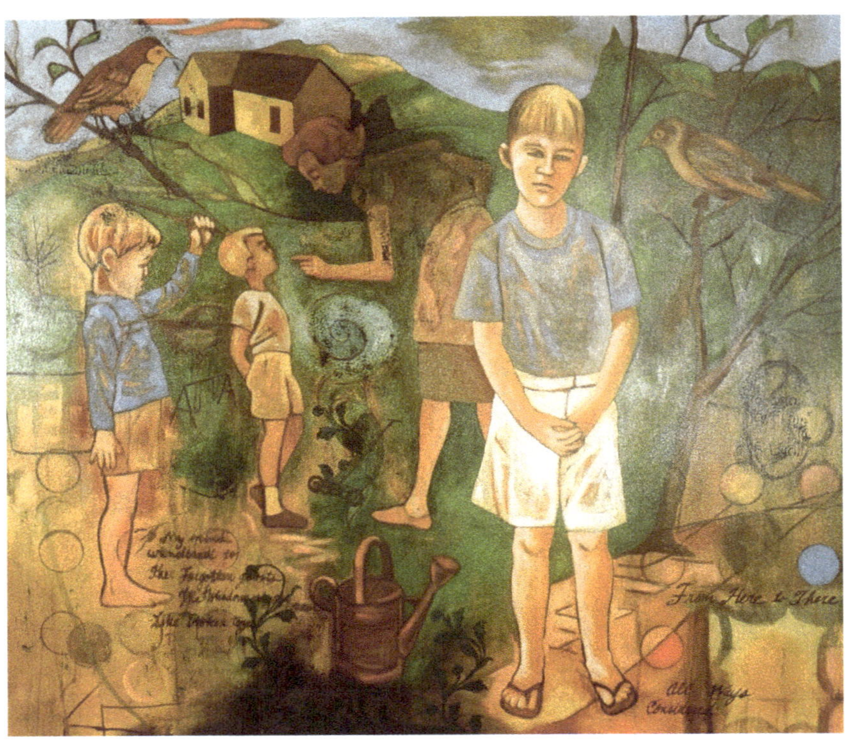

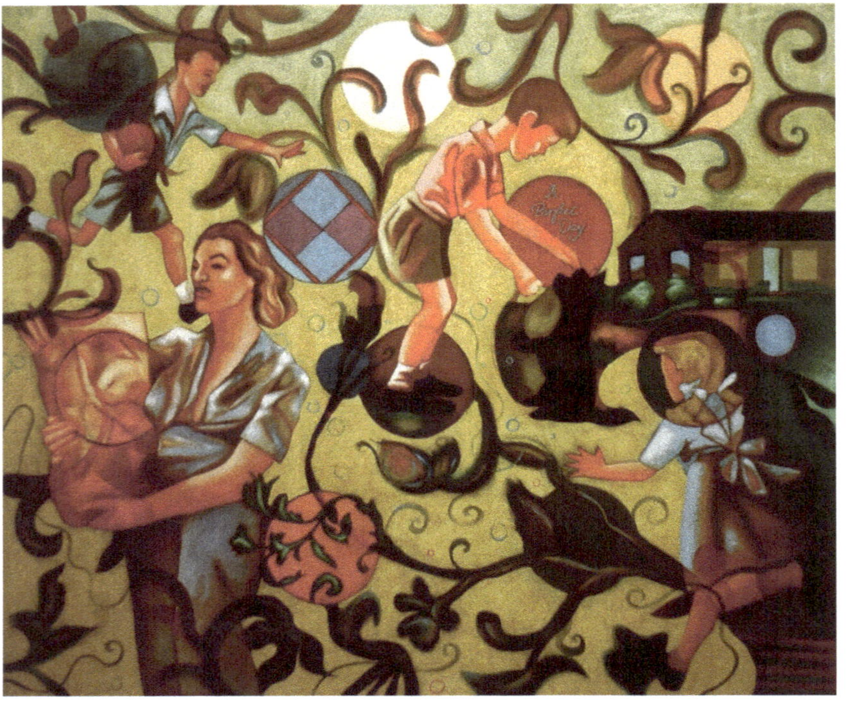

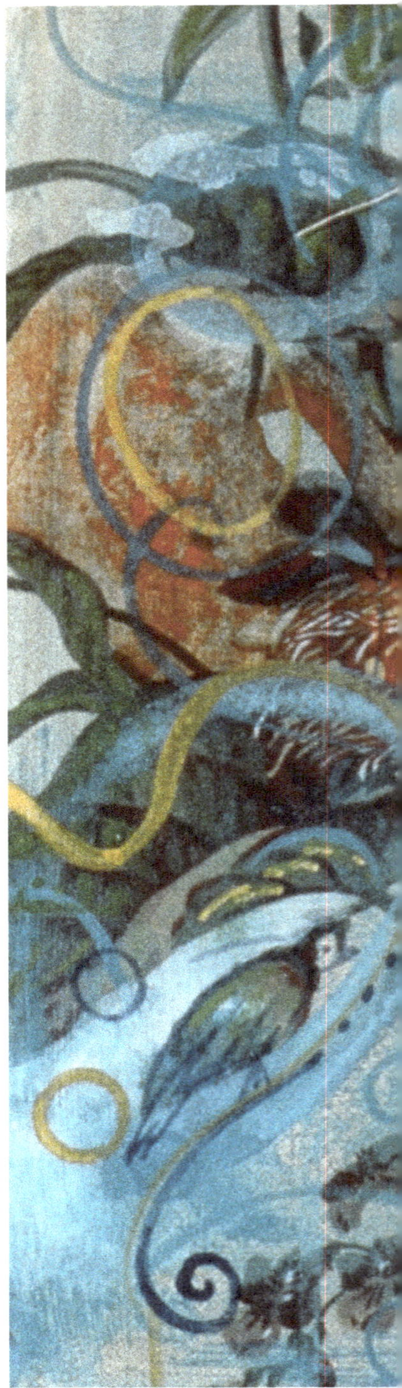

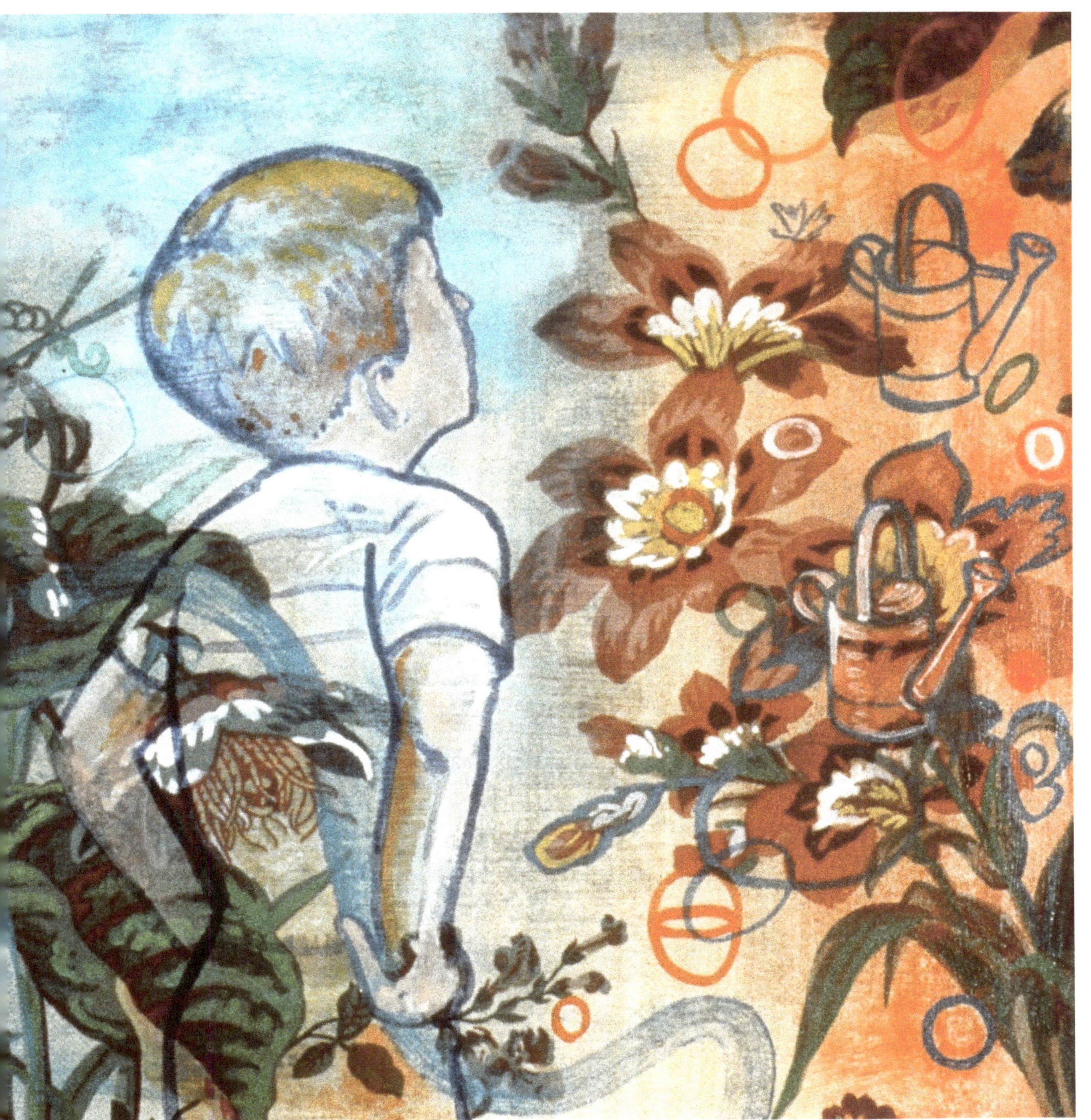

OPPOSITE TOP
From Here to There, 2000
Oil on canvas, 44" x 50"

OPPOSITE BOTTOM
A Perfect Day, 2000
Oil on canvas, 50" x 60"

ABOVE
Little Alien, III, 2000
Acrylic on fabric, 12" x 16"

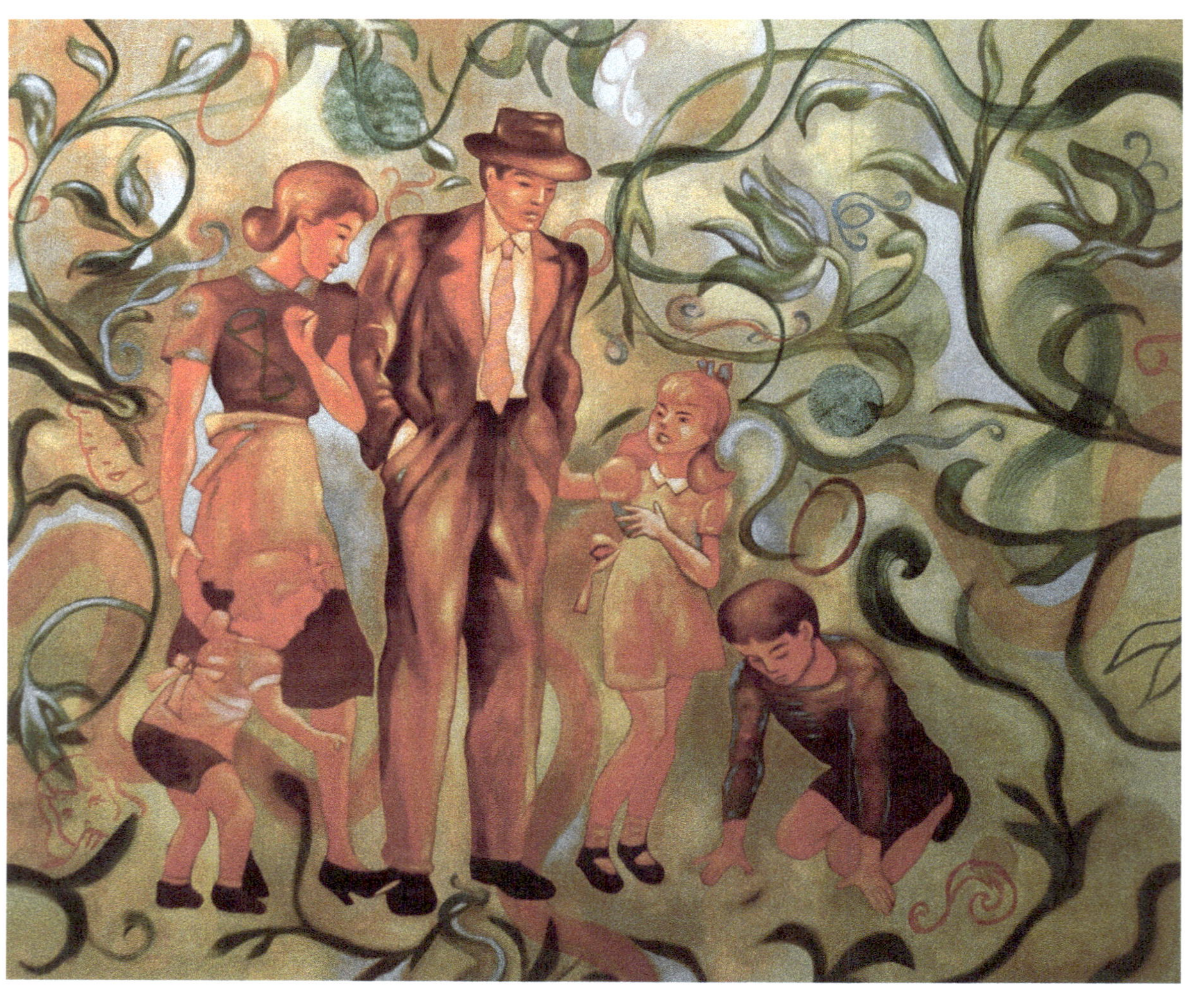

Nothing Out of the Ordinary to the Casual Observer, 2001
Oil on canvas, 60" x 72"

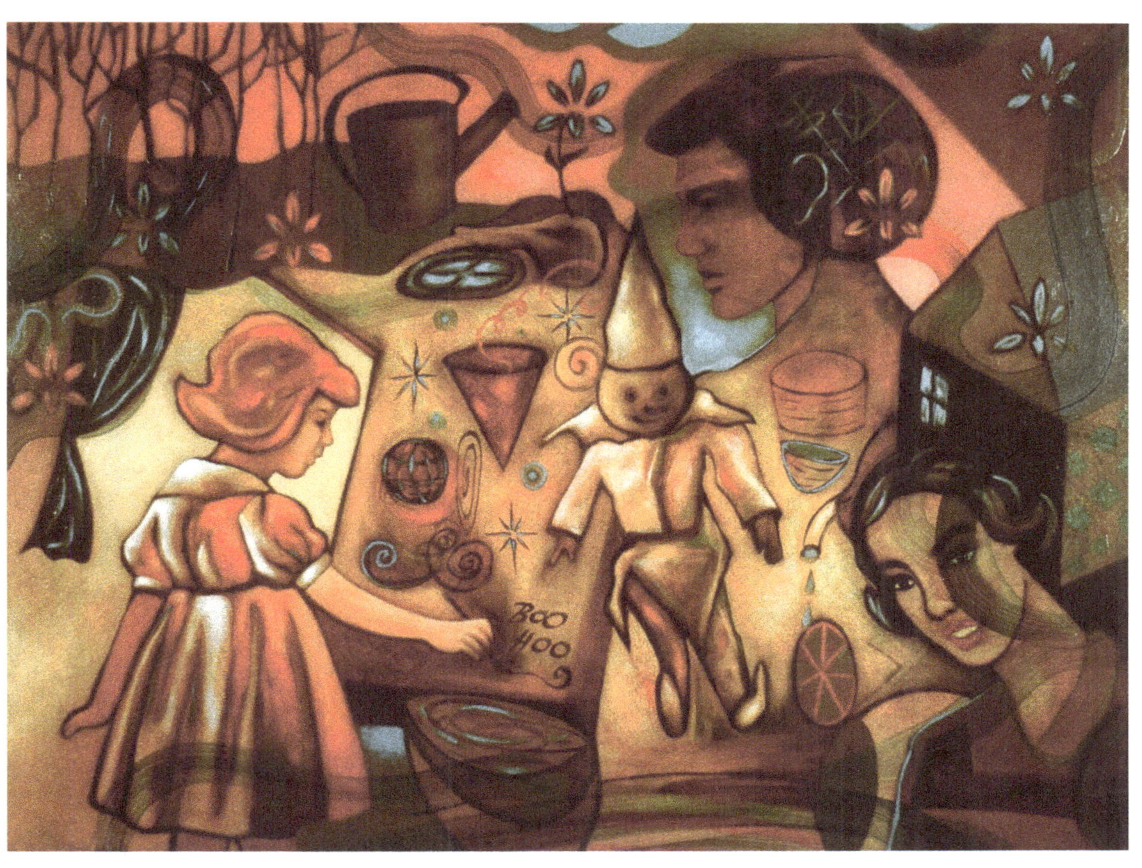

ABOVE

Quiet Calm and Little-Known, 2004
Oil on canvas, 30" x 40"

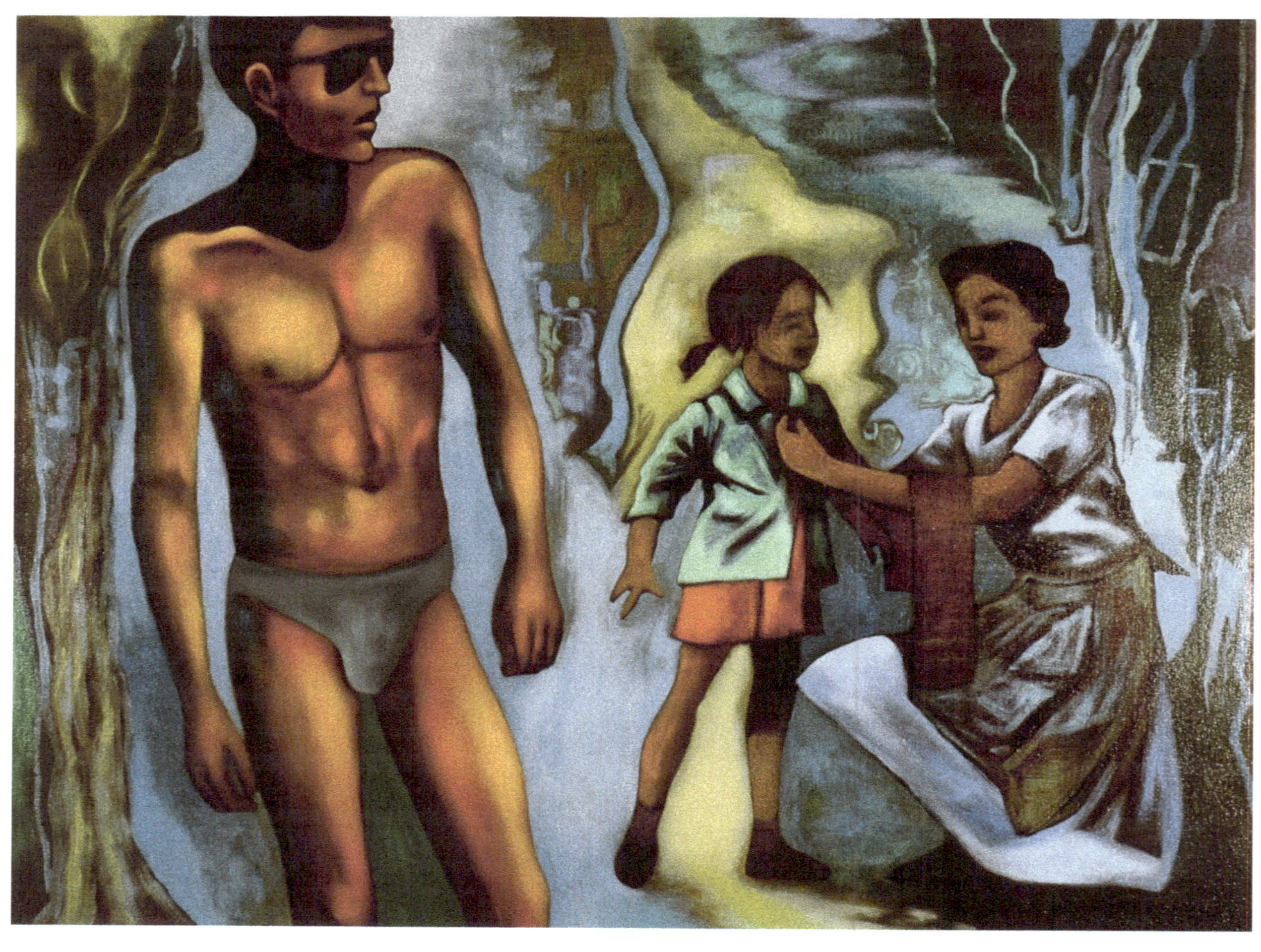

Homeland Security, 2003
Oil on canvas, 30" x 40"

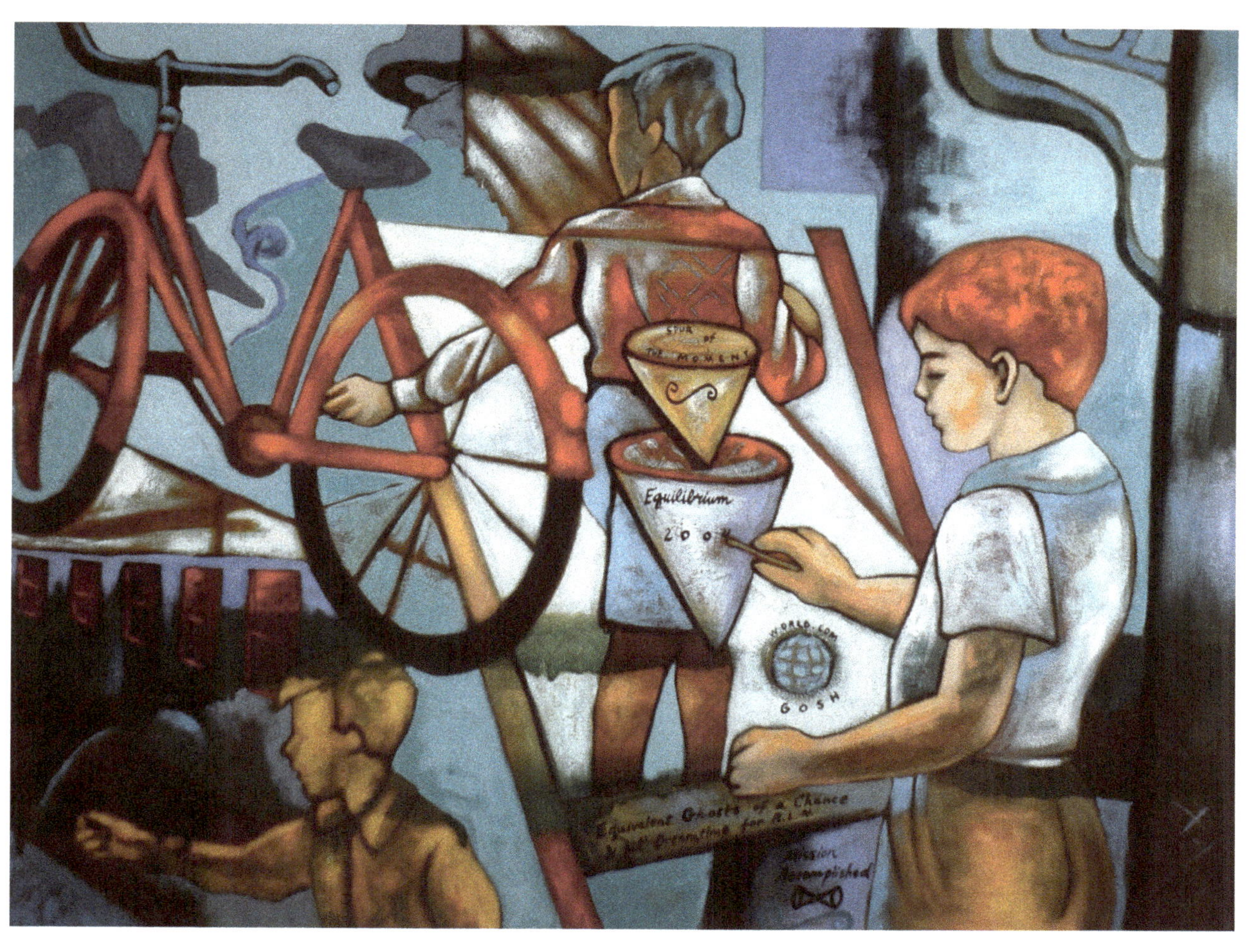

Equilibrium, 2004
Oil on canvas, 30" x 40"

Portrait, 2005
Oil on wood, 16" x 20"

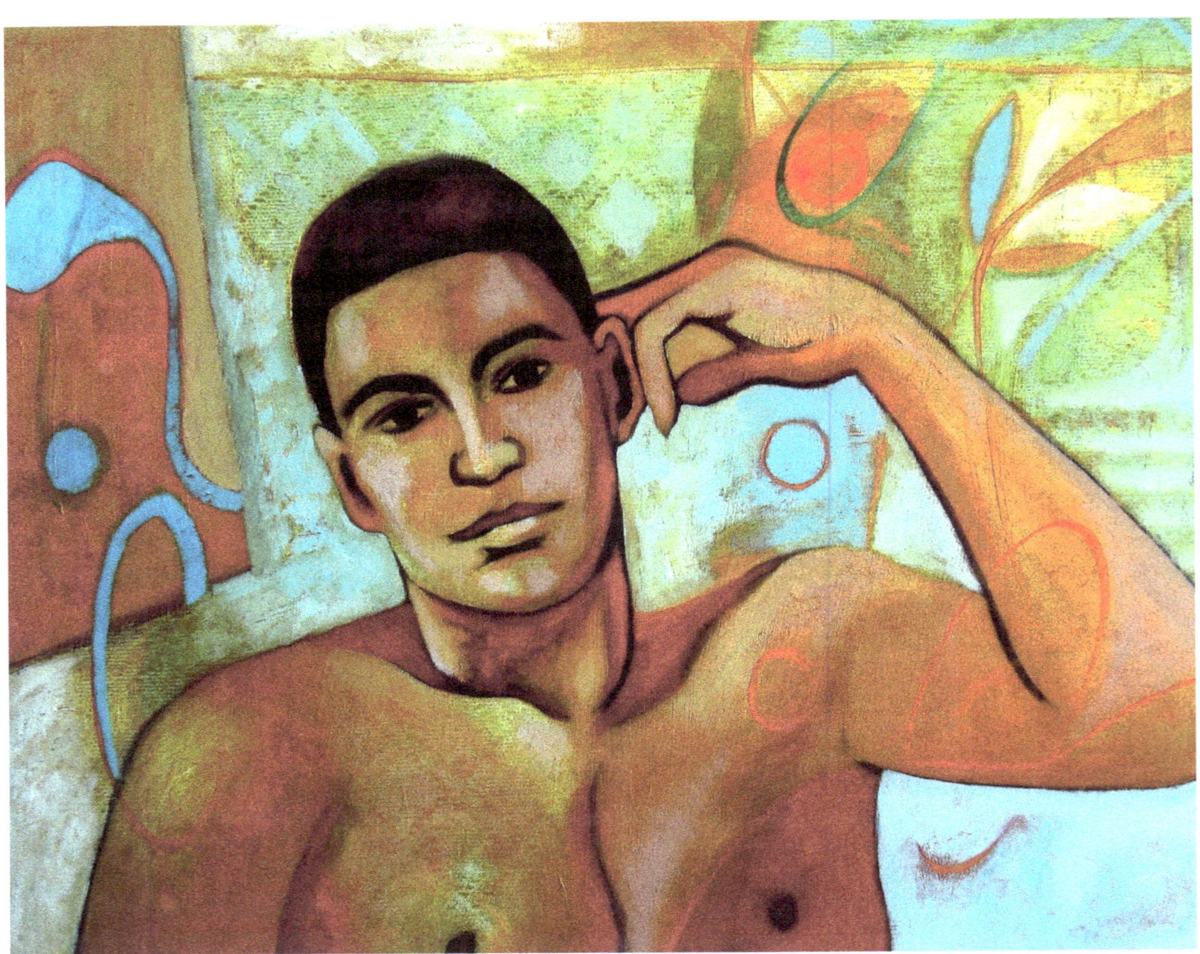

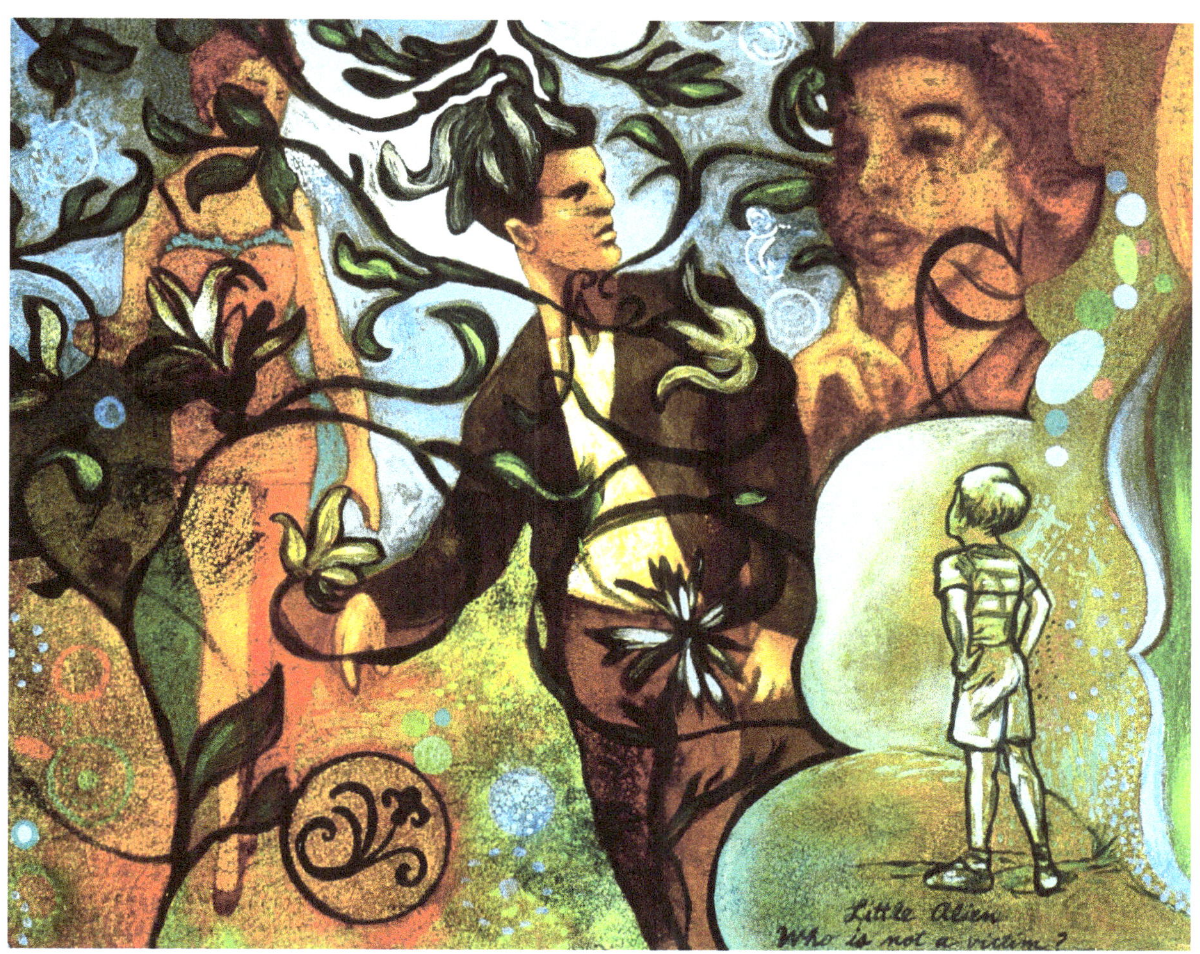

Little Alien, 2000
Oil on masonite, 16" x 20"

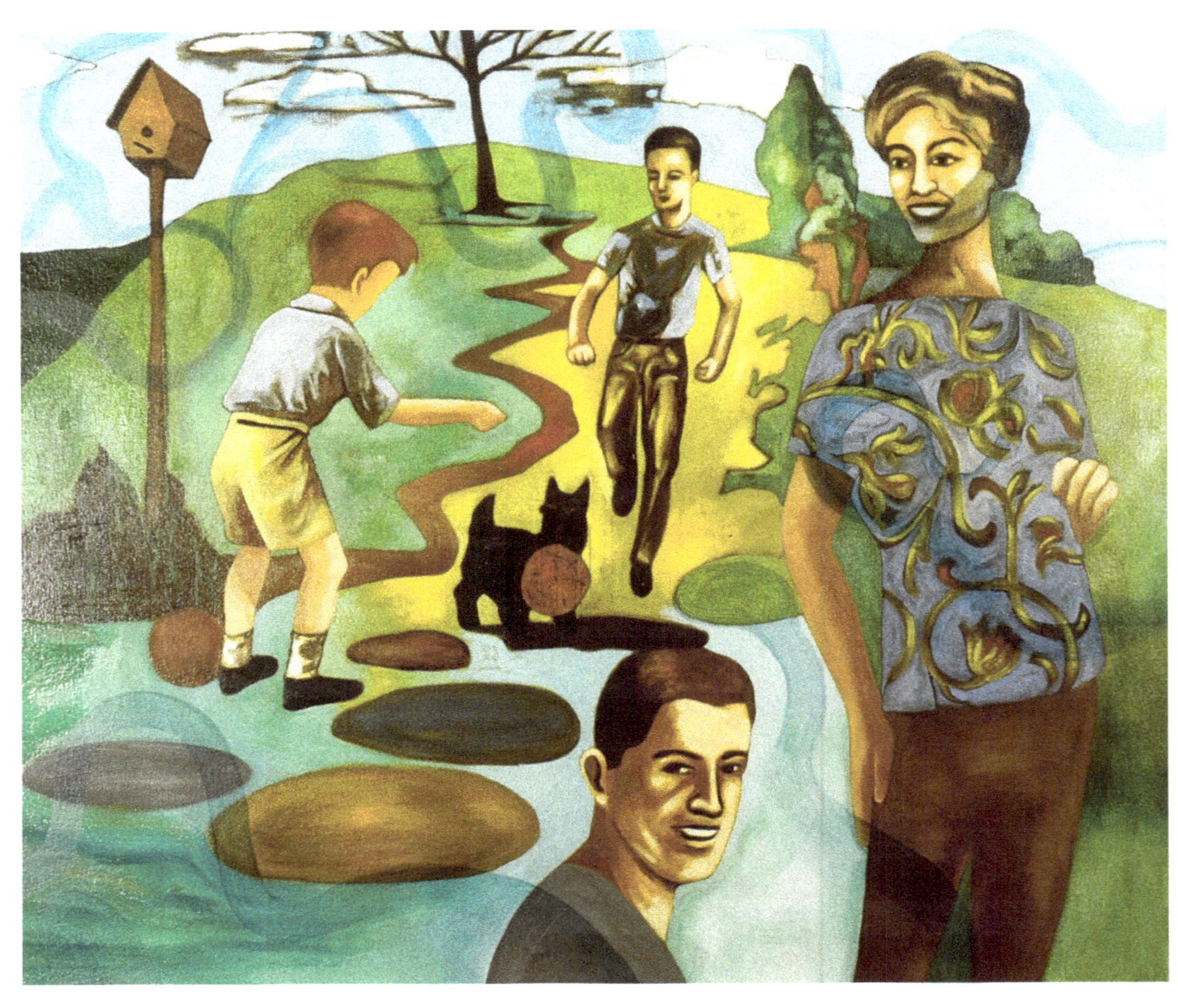

80

Good Fortune, 2003
Oil on wood, 12" x 16"

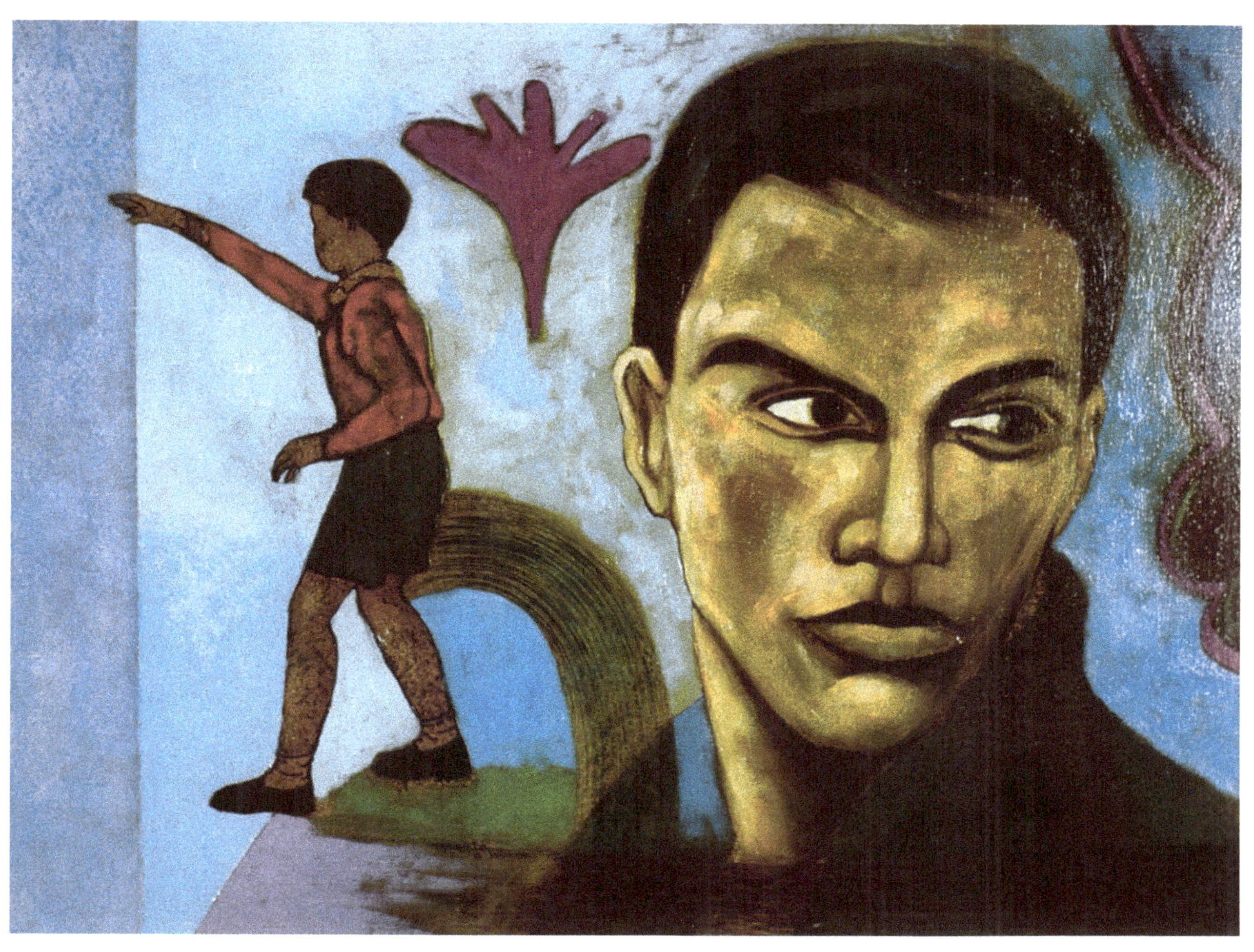

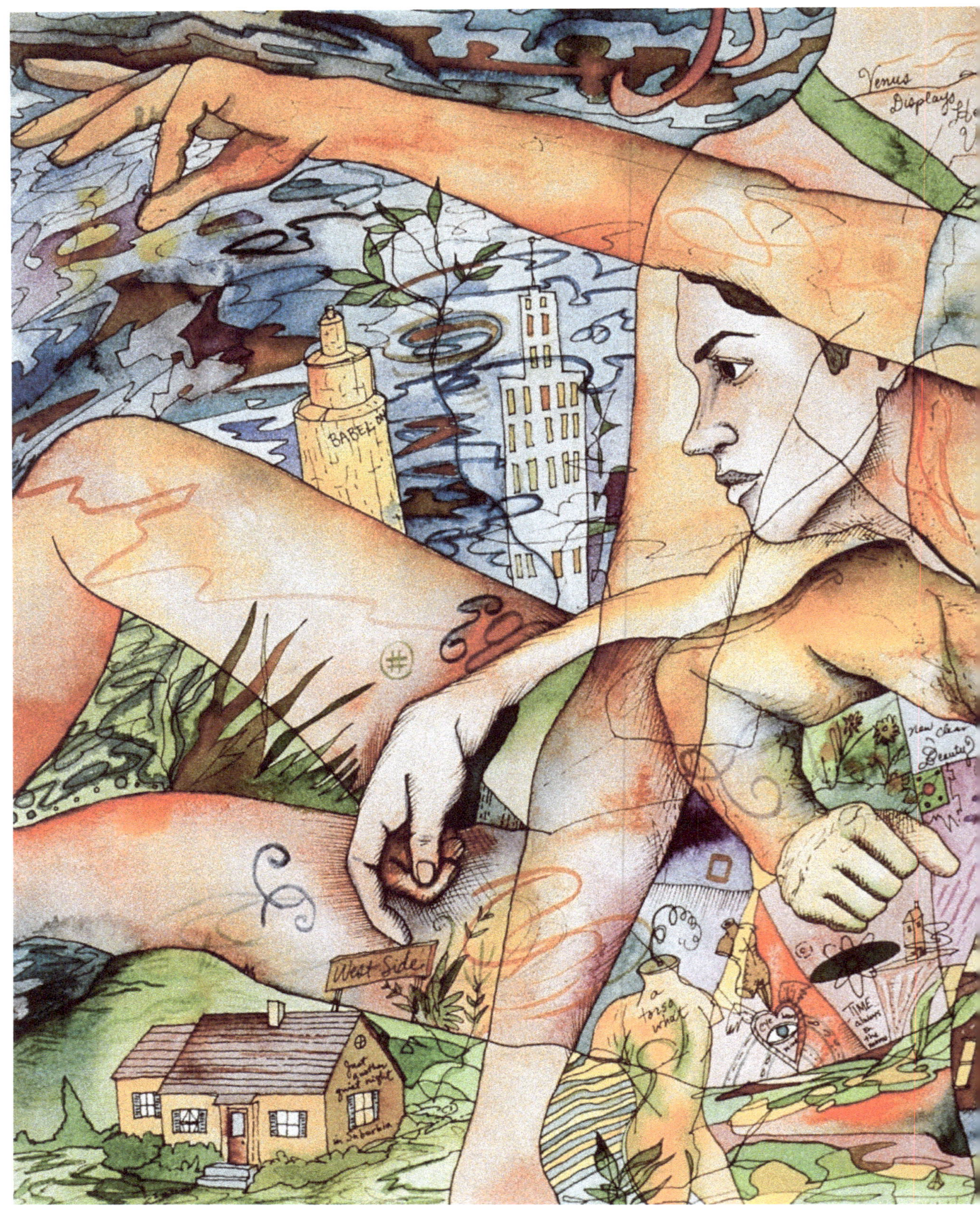

Venus Displays Her
BABEL on
West Side
Just another quiet night in Suburbia
New Clear Beauty
TIME always ...
a torso what

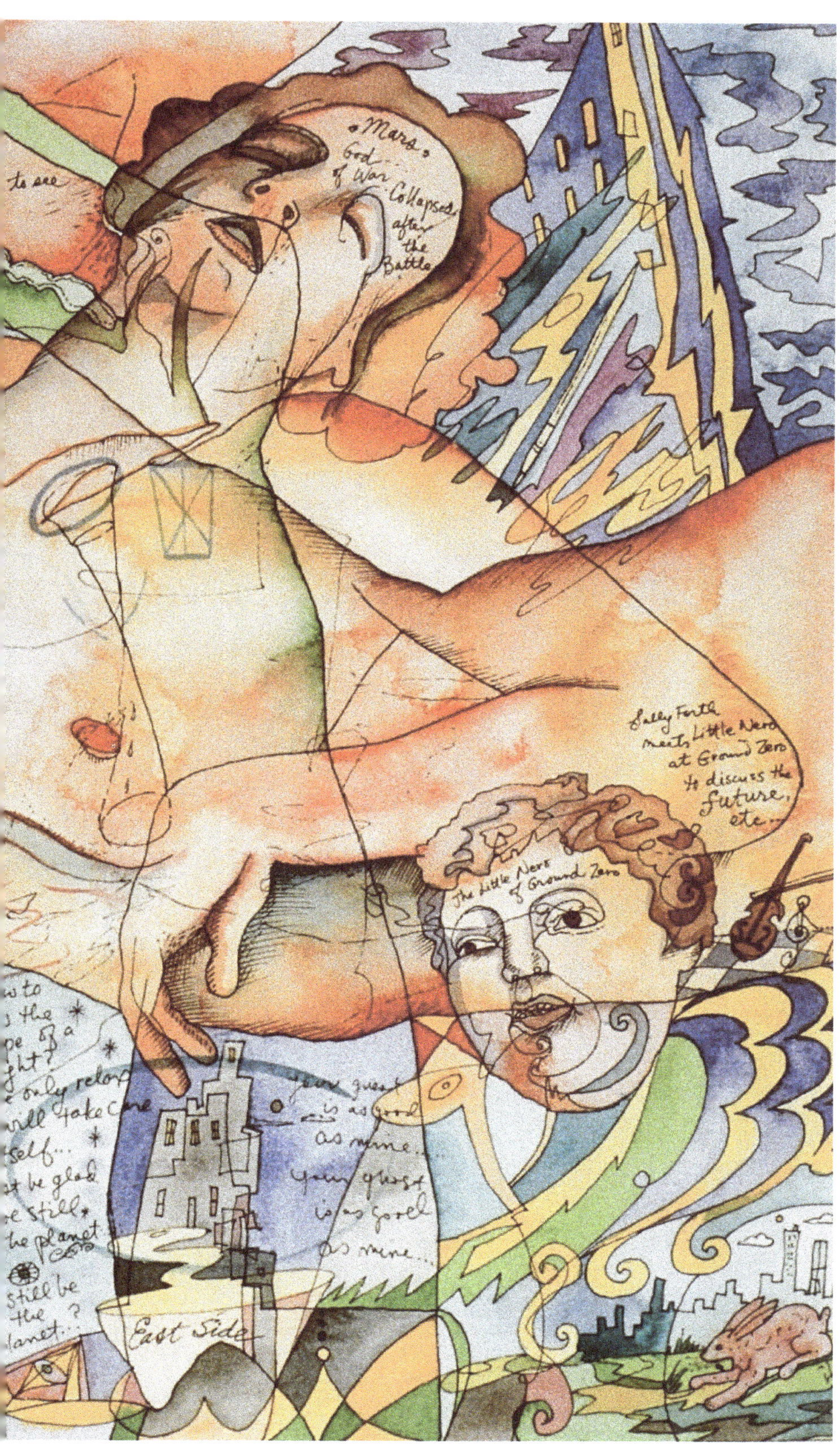

Venus & Mars, 2002
Ink & watercolor on paper,
20" x 26"

FOLLOWING

*Calling Muses, Angels
and Judge Mentals,* 2003
Watercolor on paper, 26" x 40"

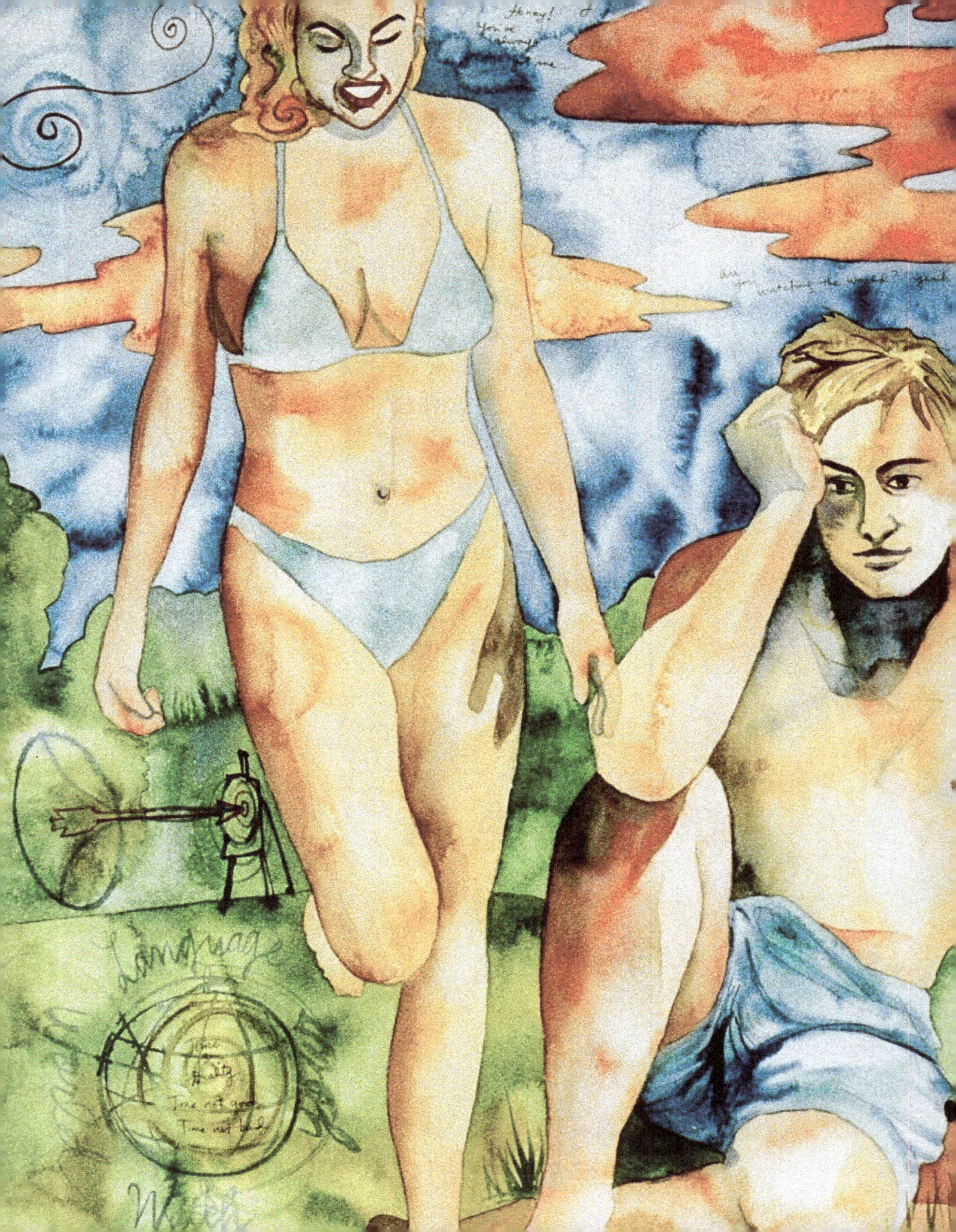

Honey!
You've always
...me
Are you watching the world? yeah
Language
Time not good.
Time not bad.

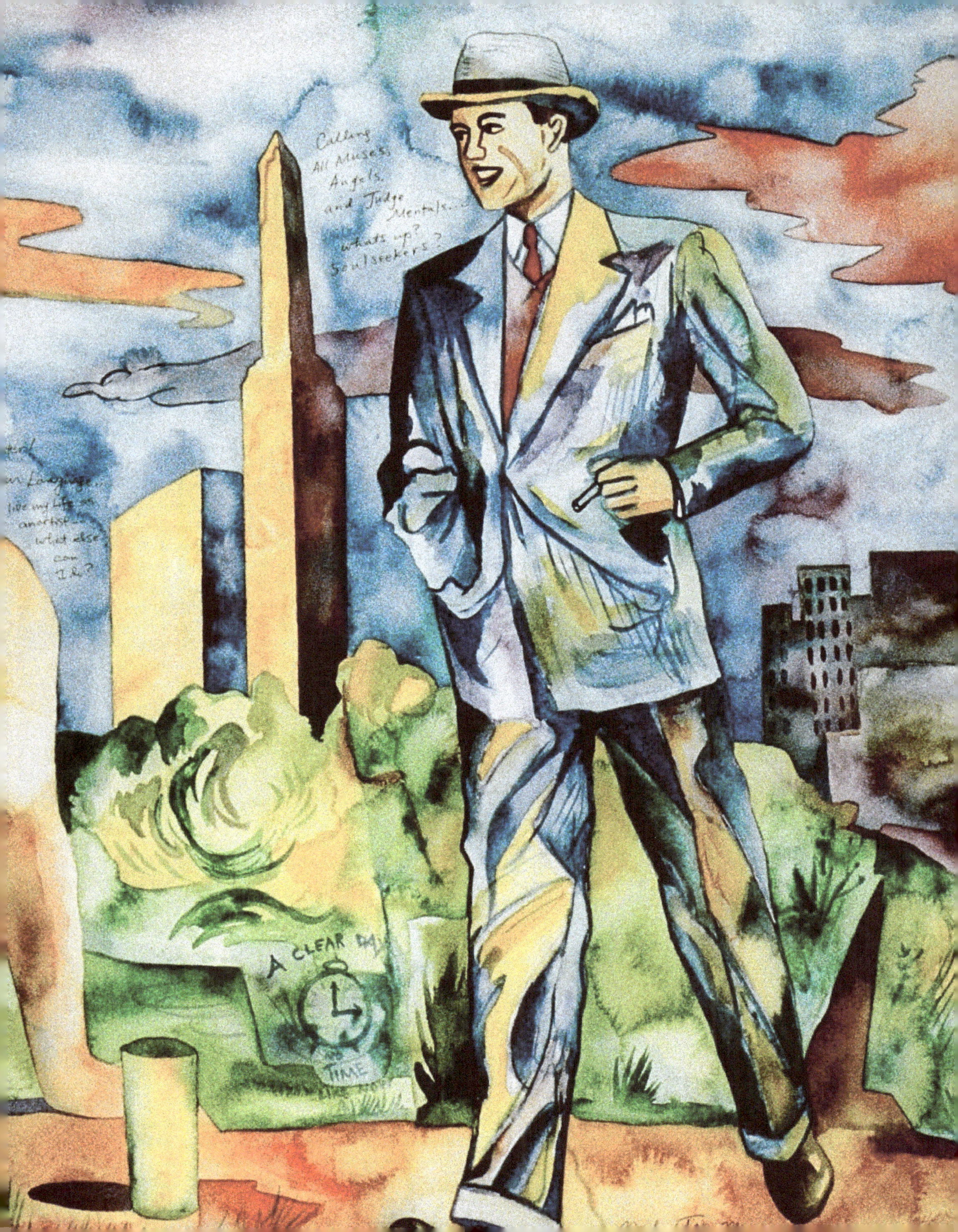

Calling
All Muses,
Angels,
and Judge
Mental...
whats up?
Soulseekers?
an Language...
live my Life as
anarchist...
what else
can
I do?
A CLEAR DAY
TIME

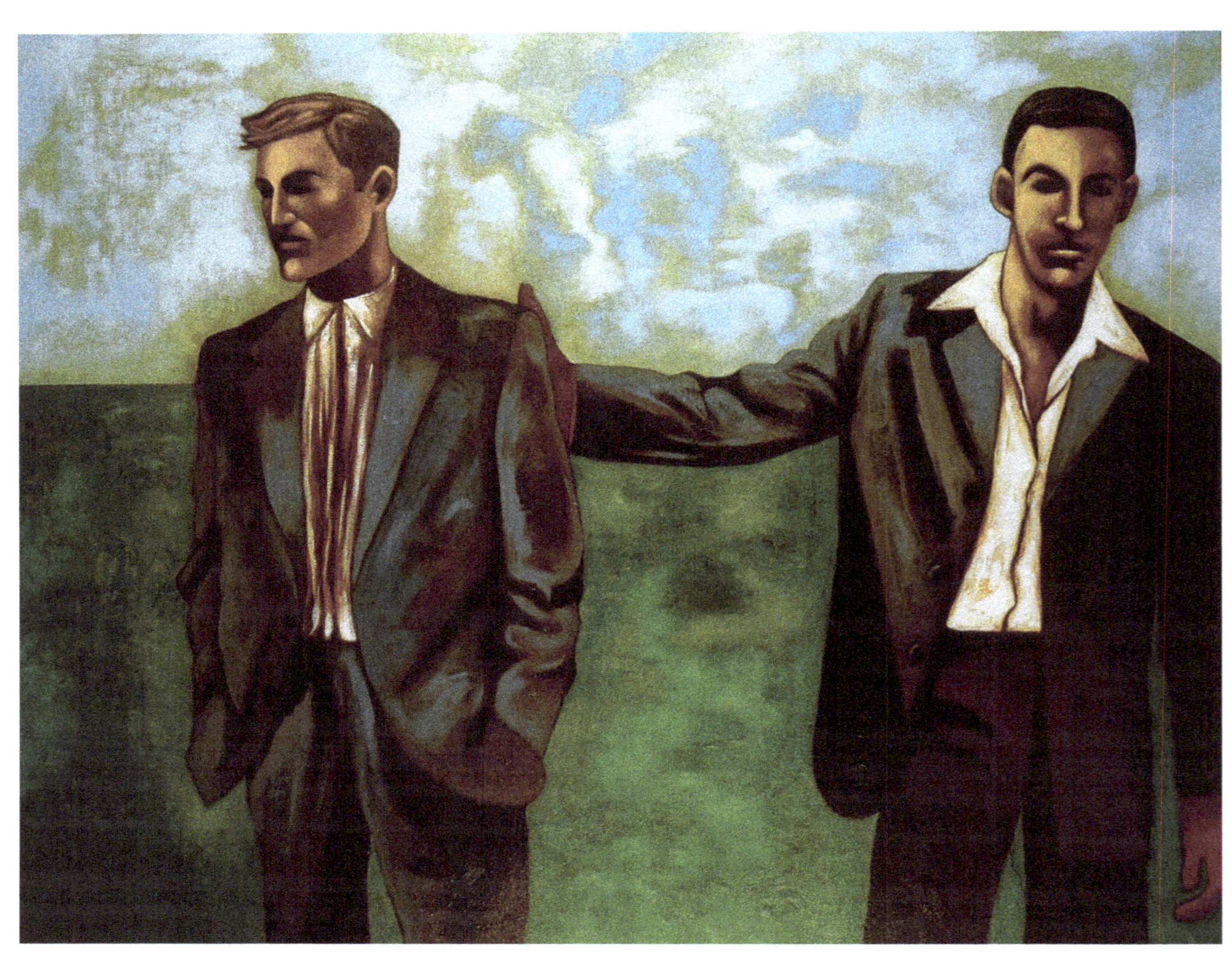

ABOVE

Couple, 2003
Oil on canvas, 42" x 52"

OPPOSITE

Thank You, 2003
Oil on wood, 16" x 12"

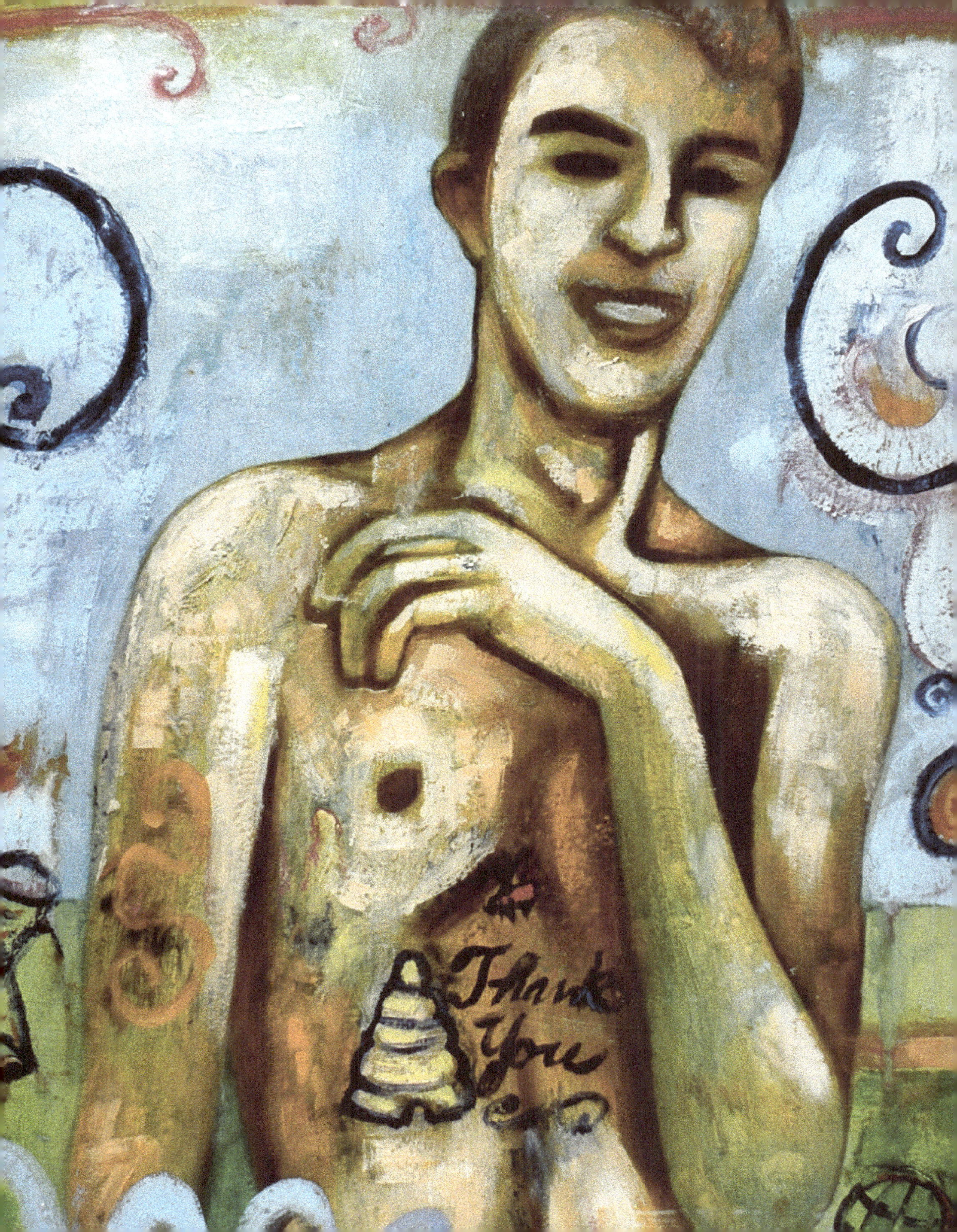
Thank
You

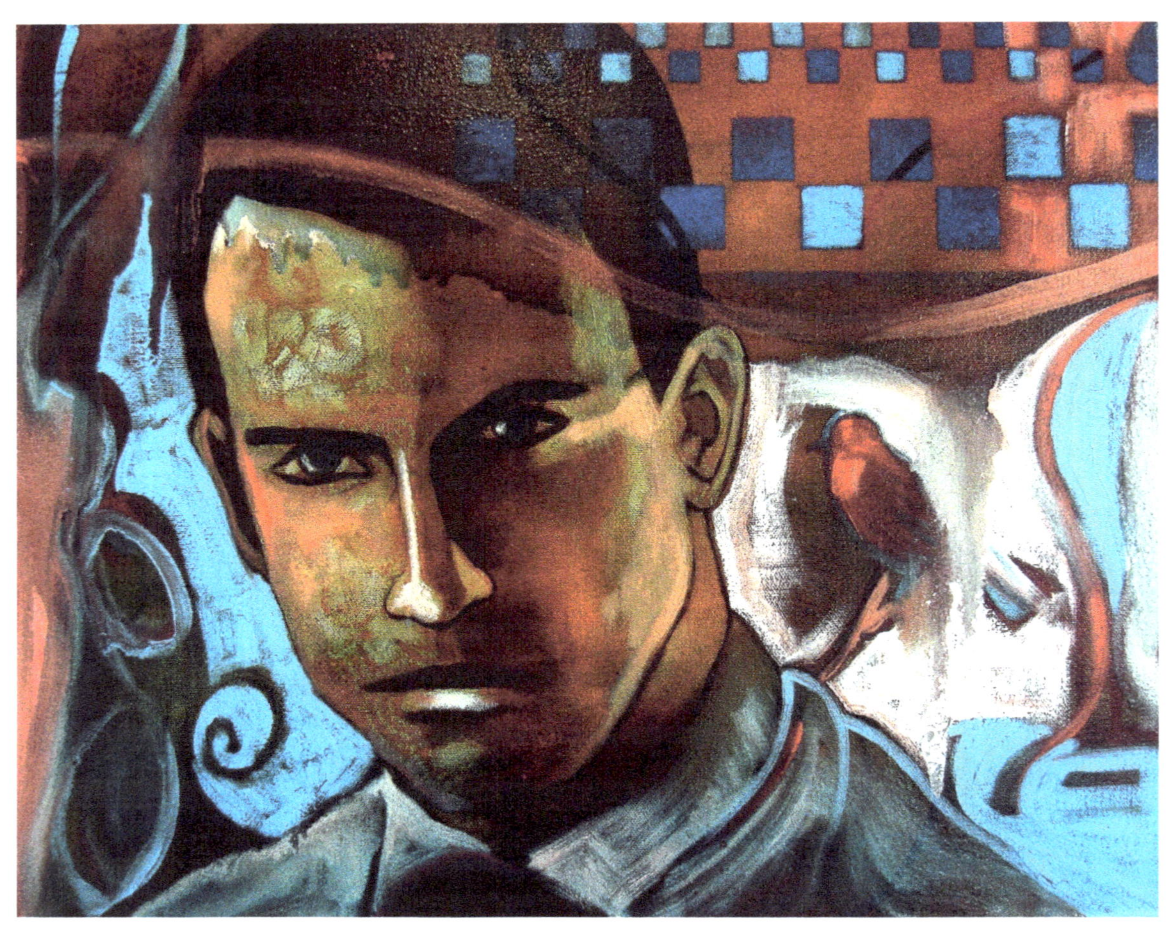

Portrait Study, 2011
Oil on canvas, 16" x 20"
Private Collection, Jersey City, NJ

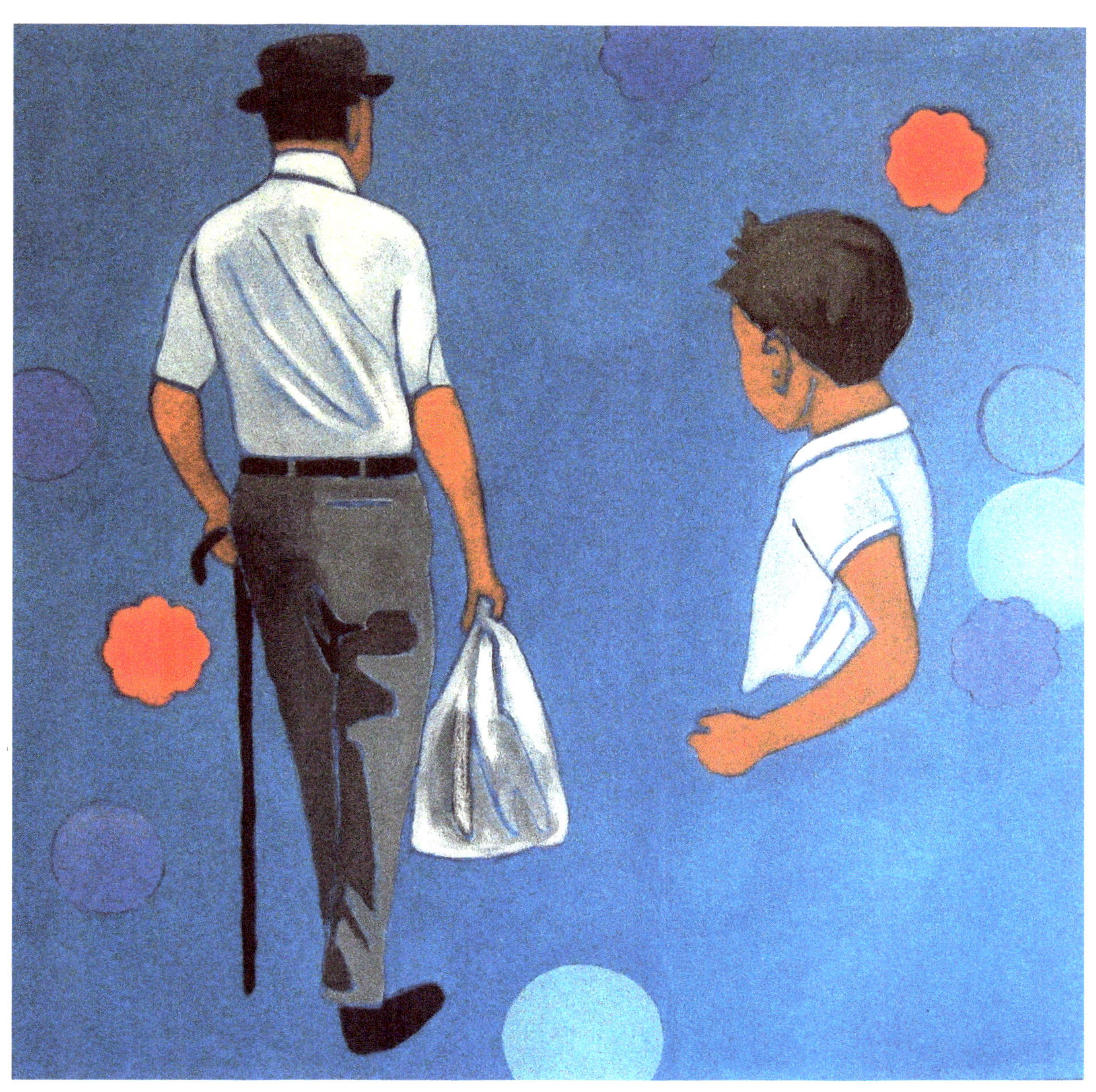

On We Go, 2011
30" x 30", Oil on canvas

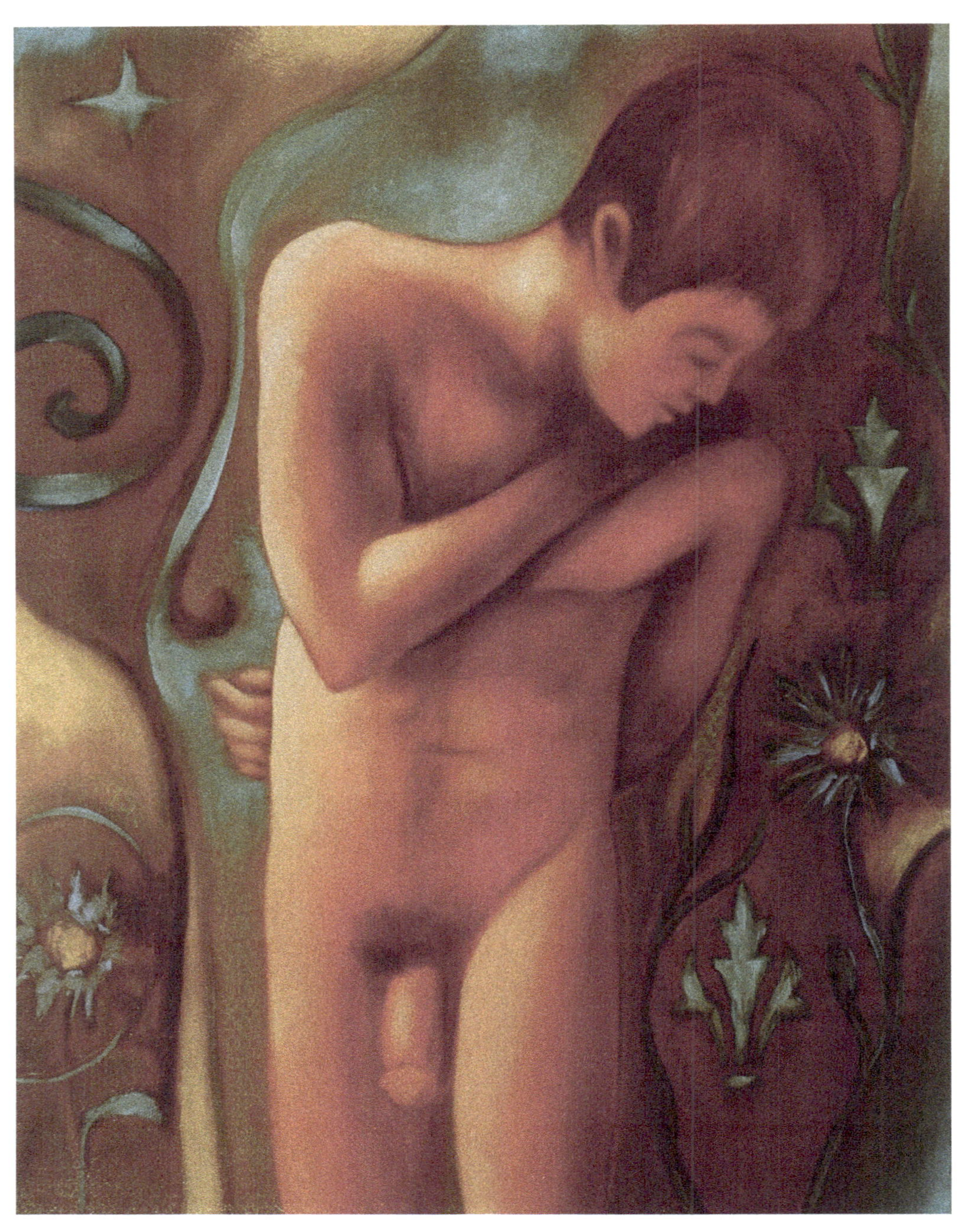

Lune D'Or, 2003
Oil on canvas, 18" x 14"

90

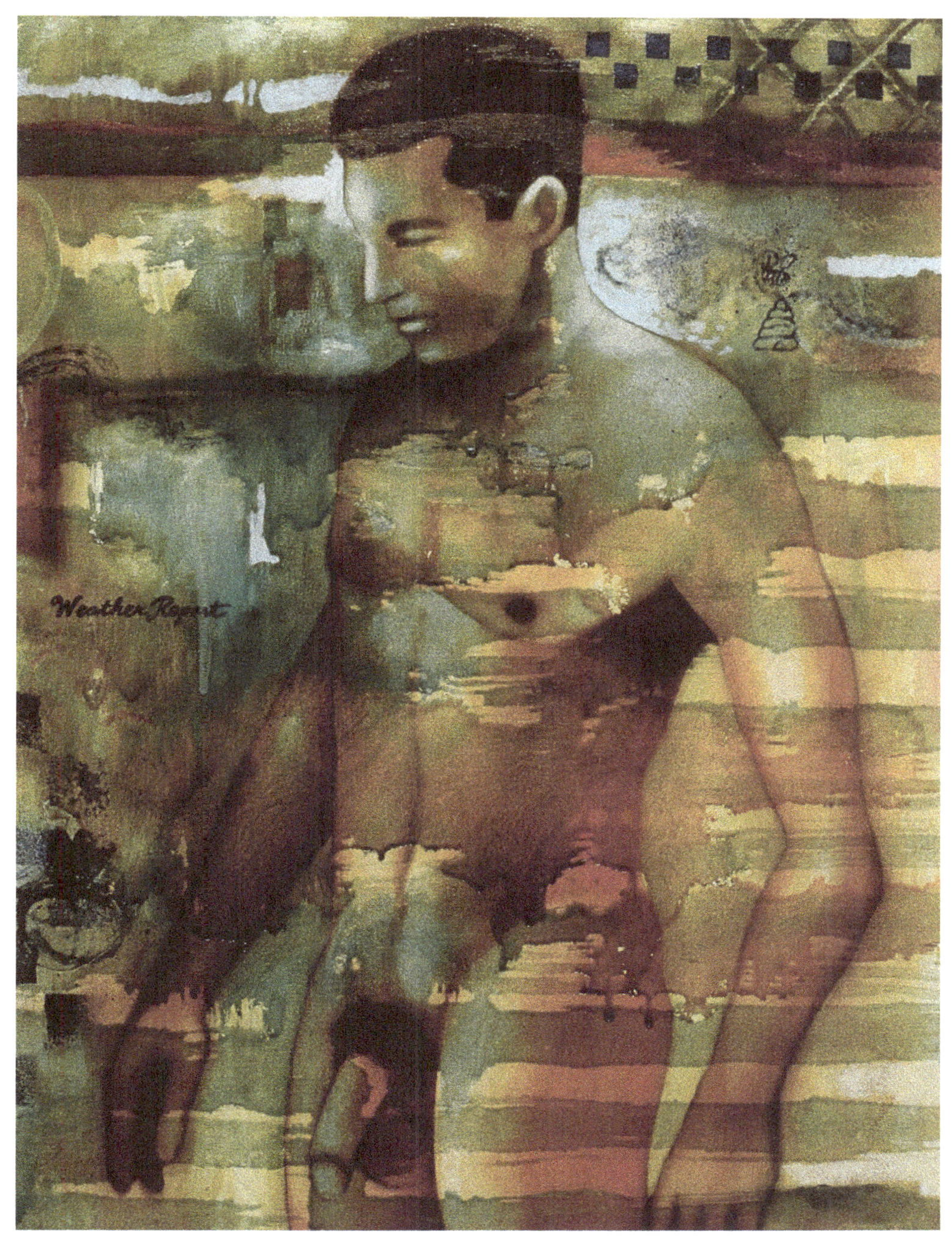

Weather Report, 2003
Oil on canvas, 24" x 18"

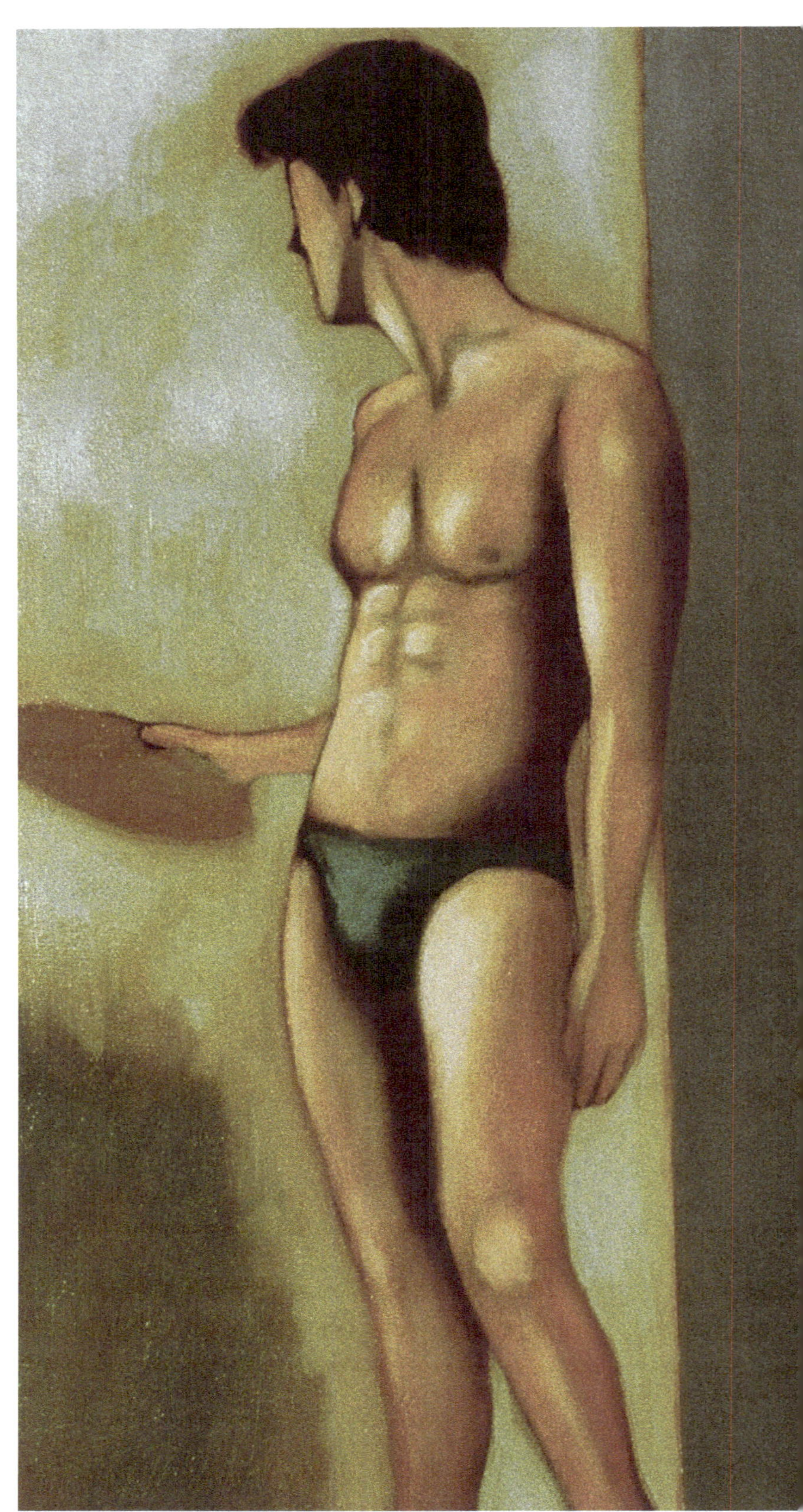

Chance Meeting, 2003
Oil on canvas, 14" x 18"
Private Collection, Montreal, Canada

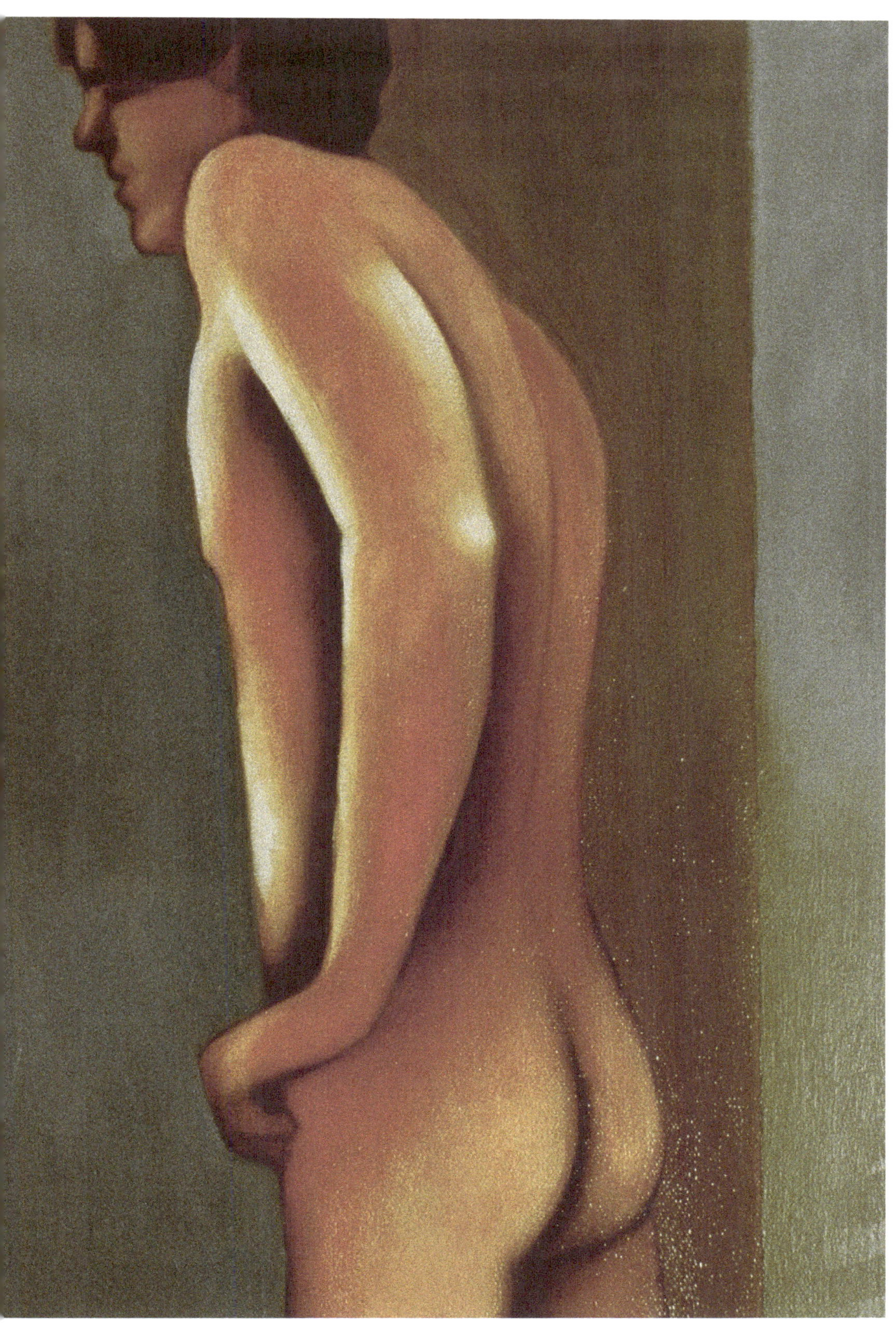

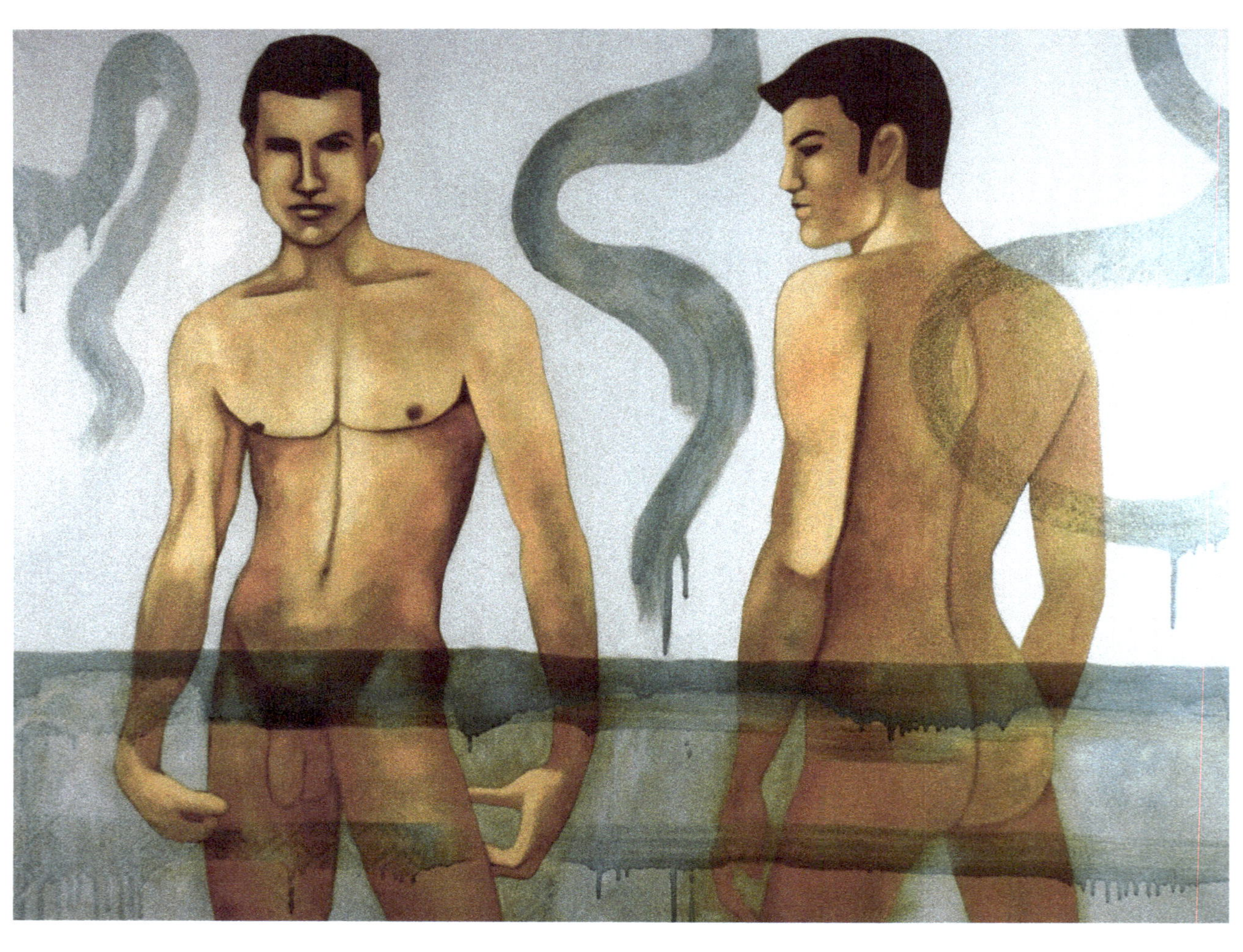

Lives of a Dreamtime, 2004
Oil on canvas, 30" x 40"

94

Some Distant Memory, 2008
Oil on canvas, 24" x 30"

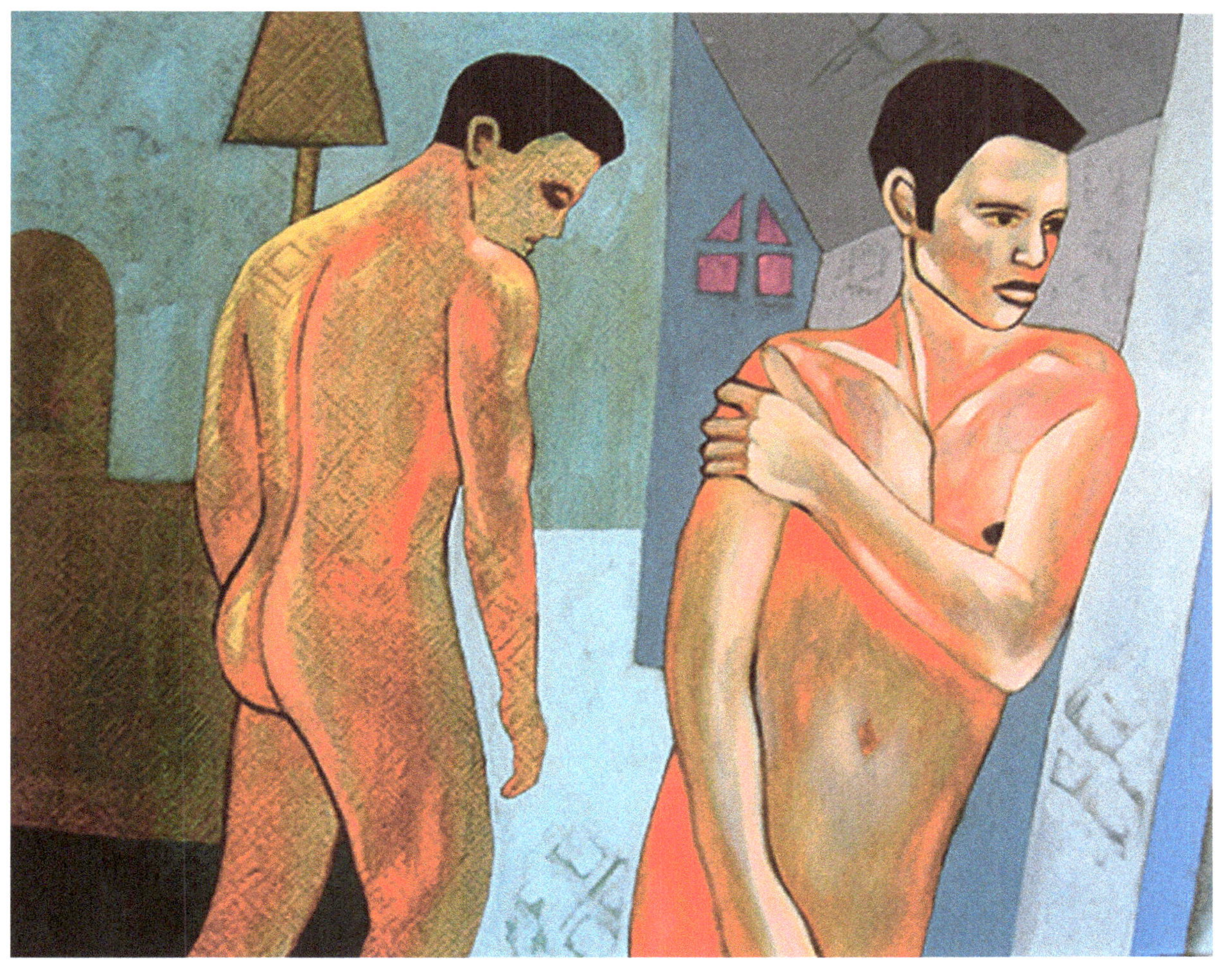

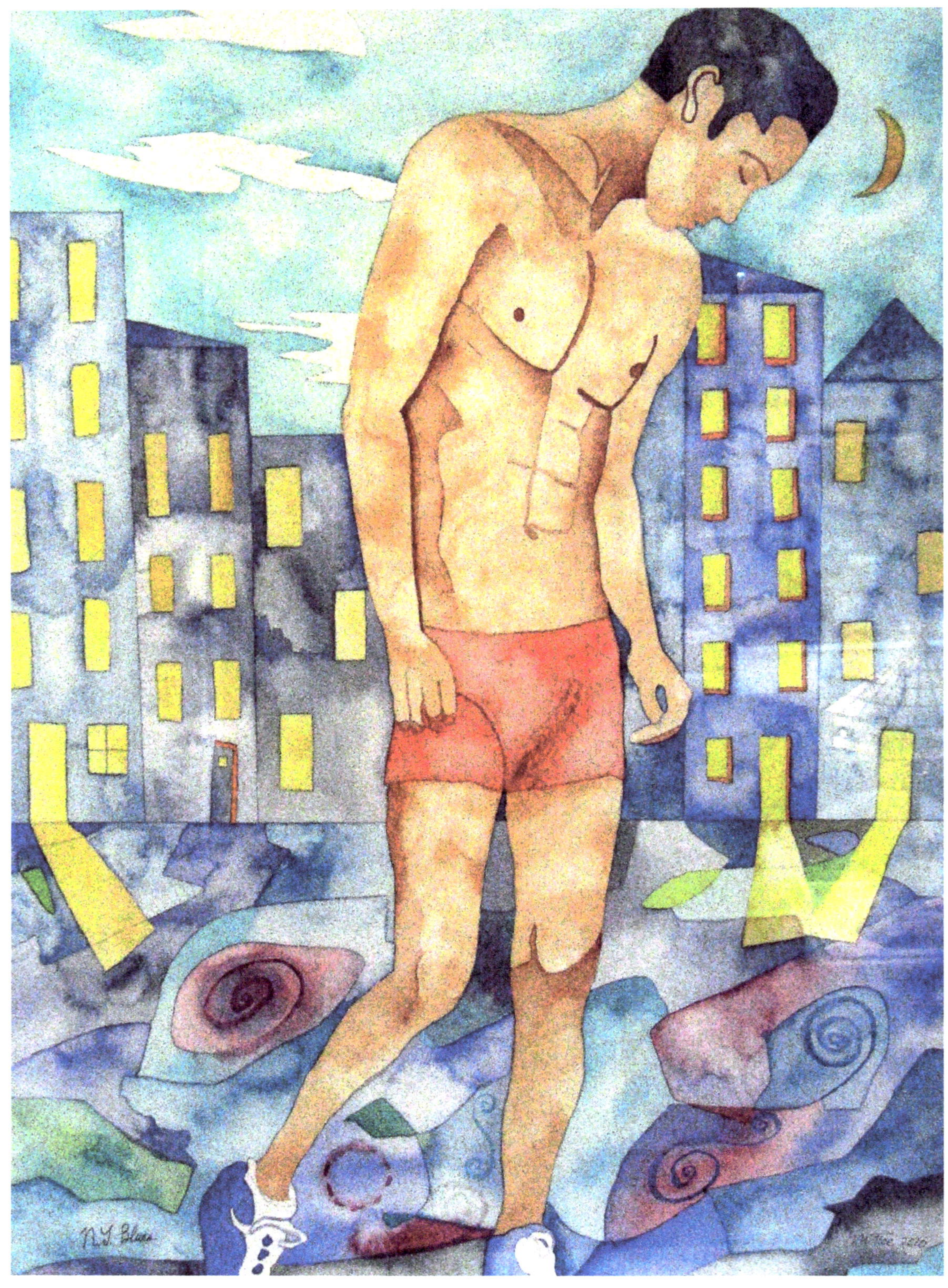

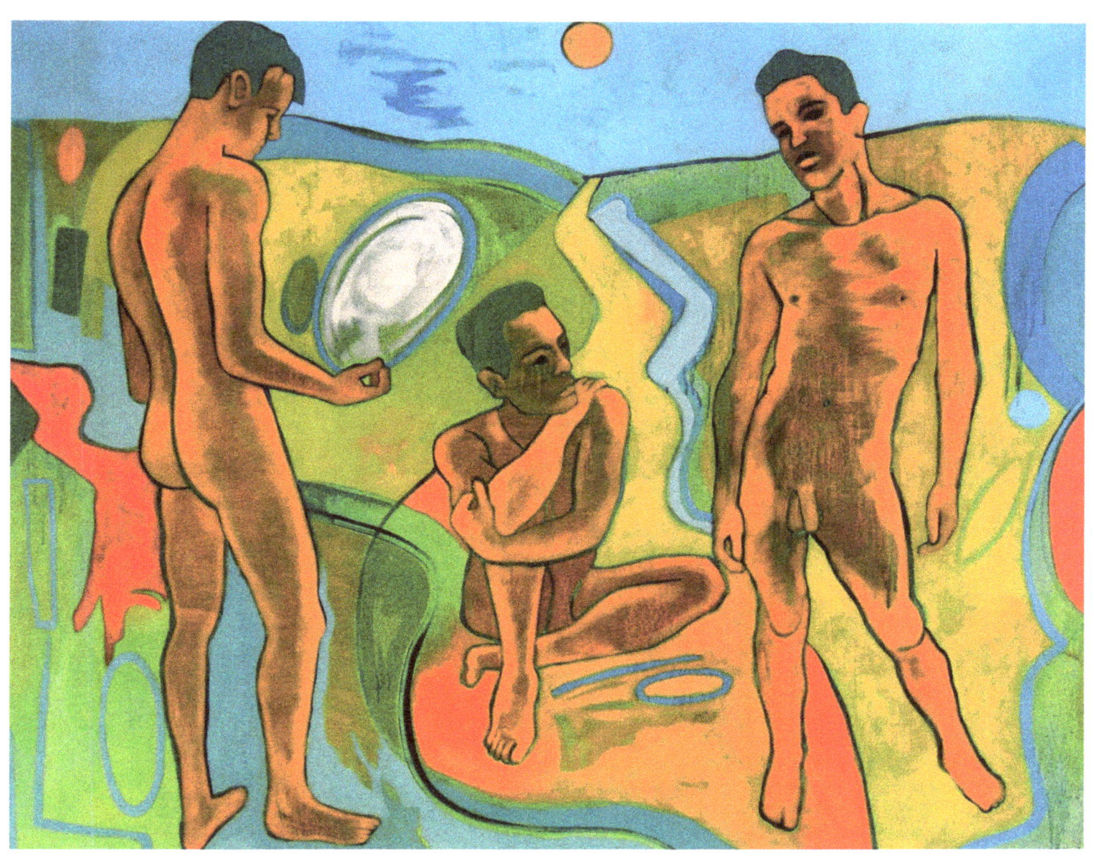

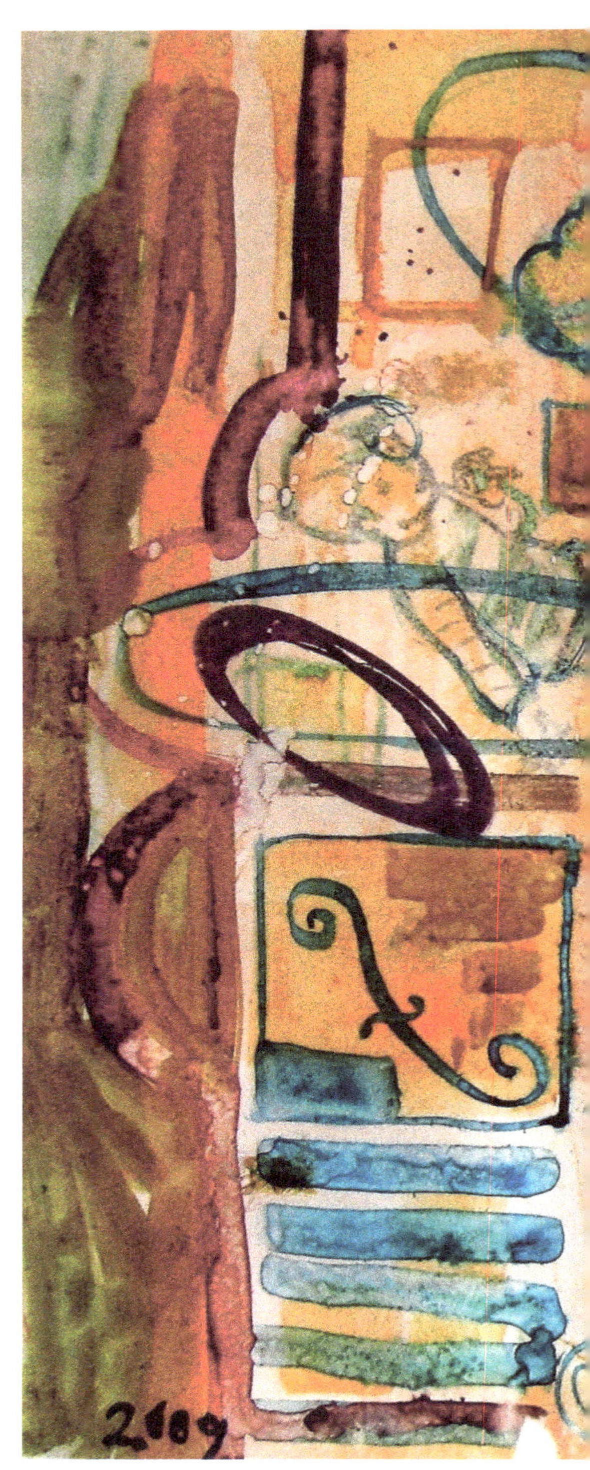

Spiraling Away, 2009
Monotype on paper, 17 1/2” x 24”
Private Collection, New York

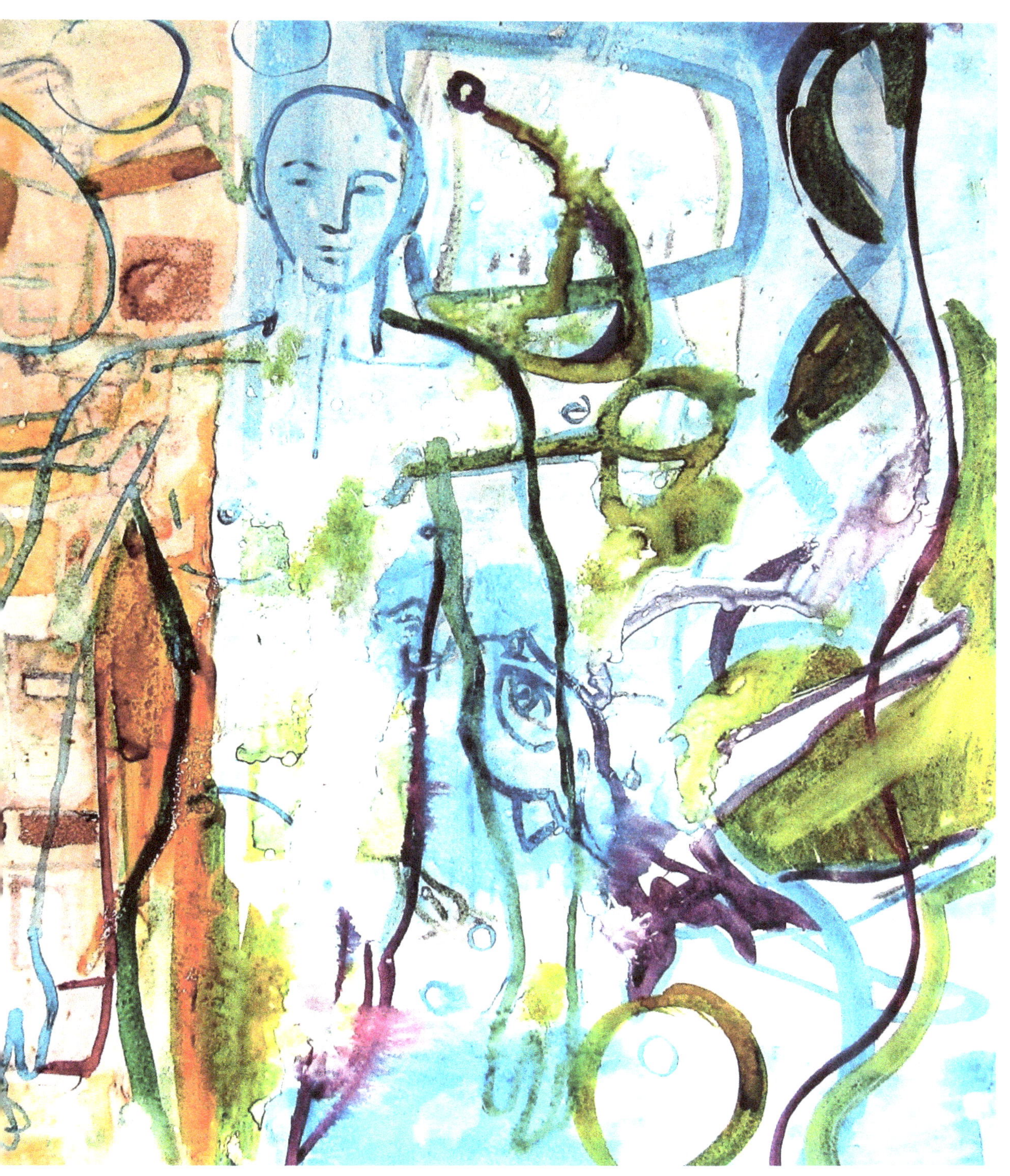

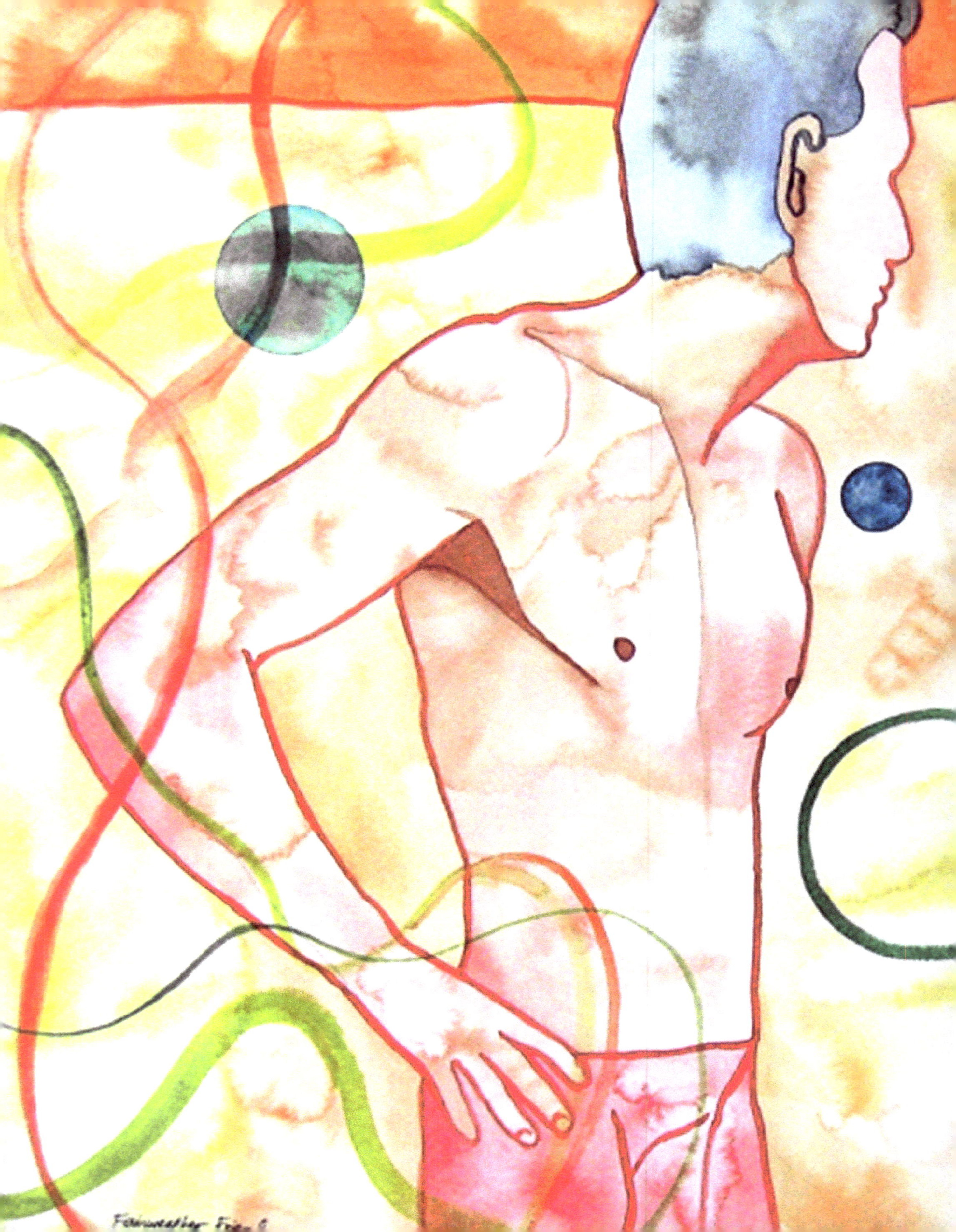

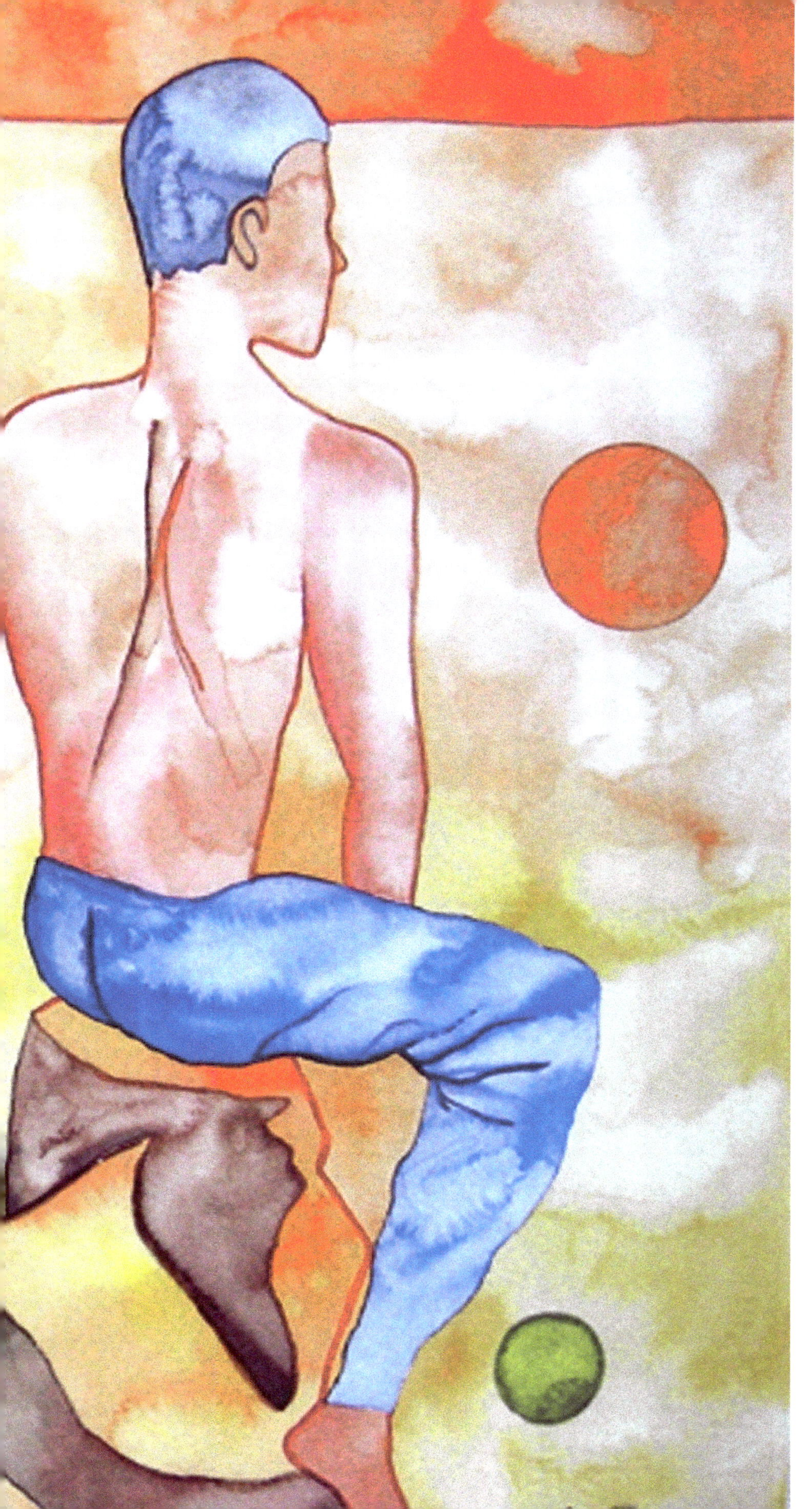

Fairweather Friend, 2010
Watercolor on paper, 22" x 30"

BELOW
Attic, 2012
Oil on canvas, 30" x 24"

OPPOSITE
Invitation, 2012
Oil on canvas, 30" x 24"

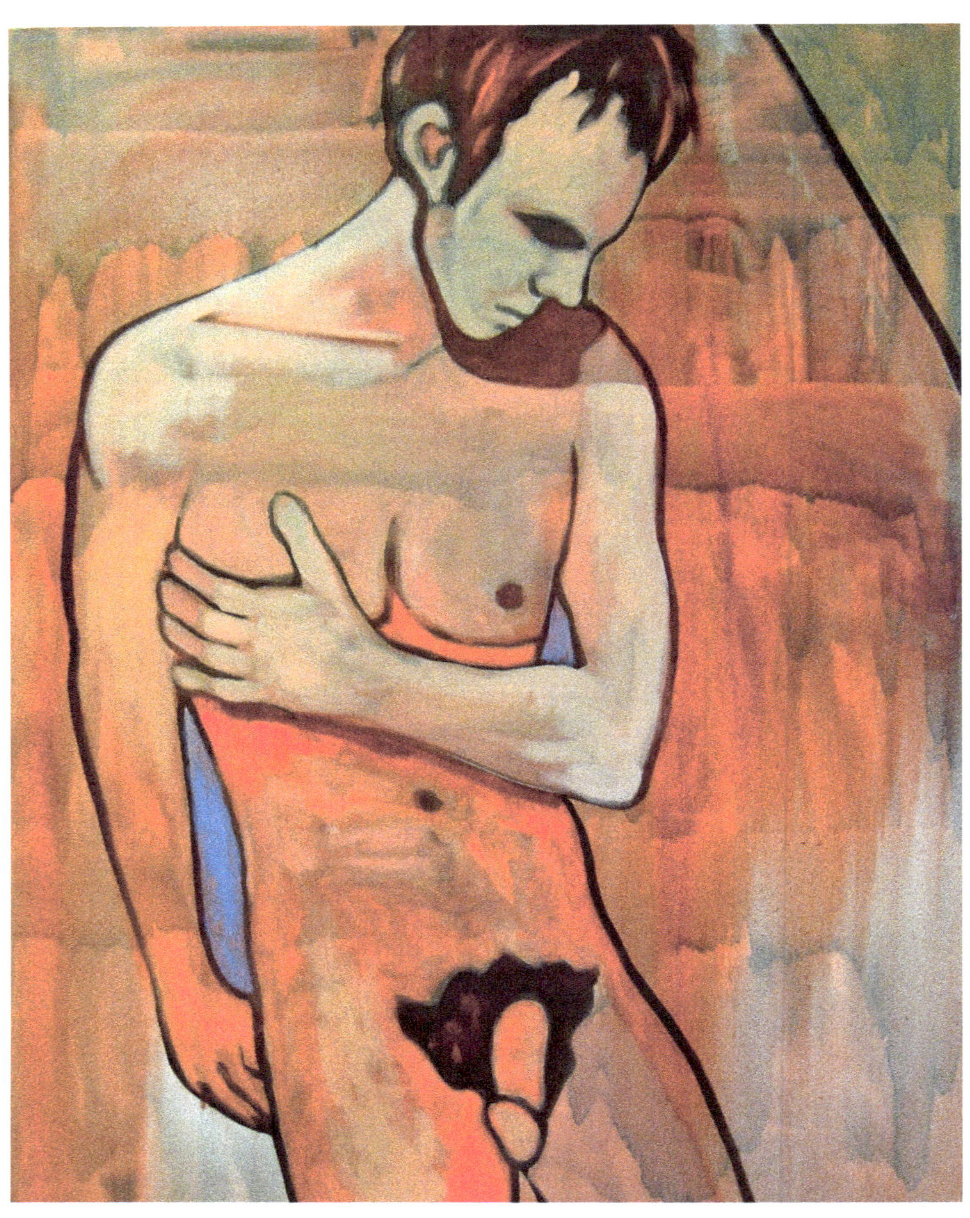

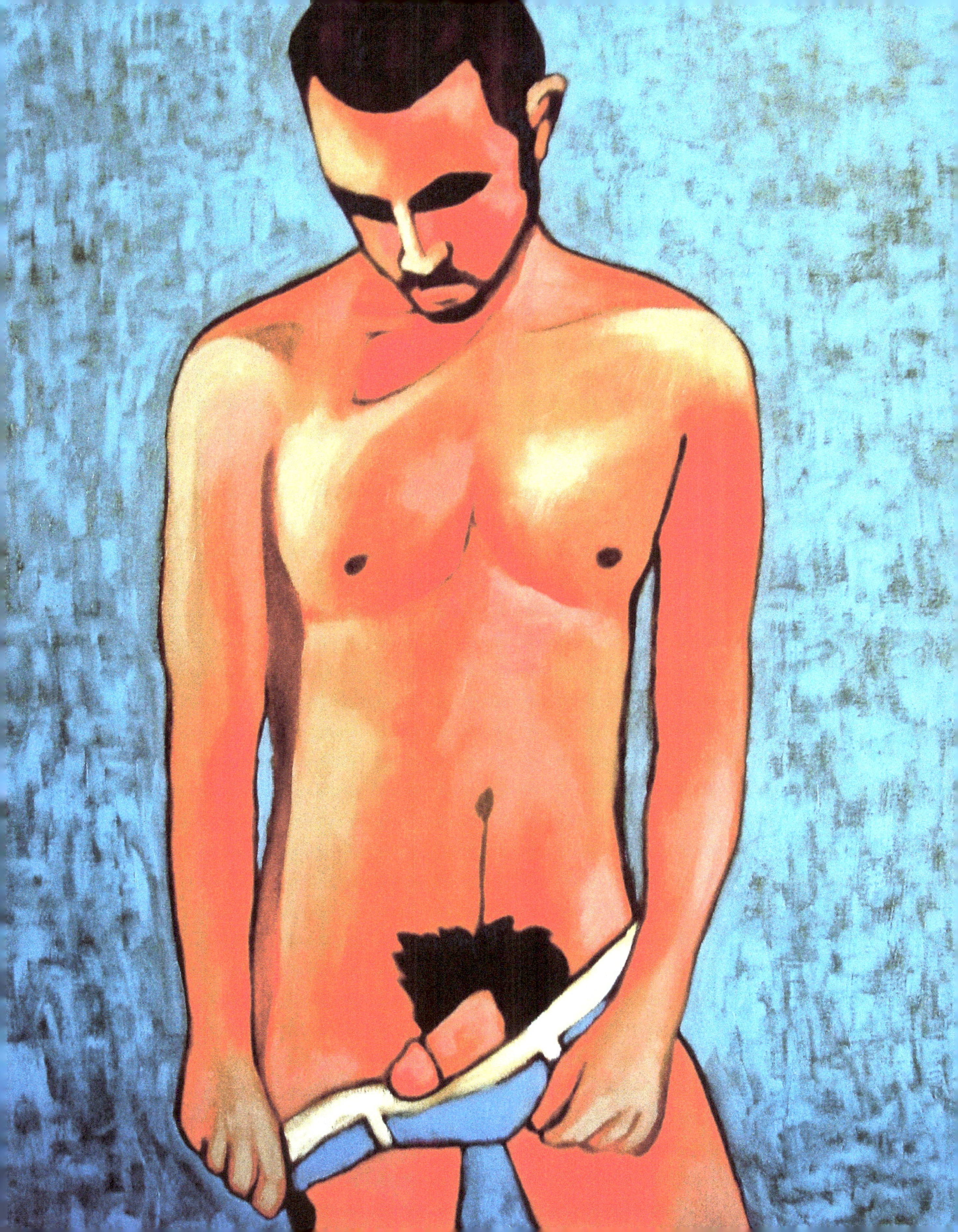

BELOW

Entre Nous, 2008
Watercolor & gouache on paper, 22" x 30"

OPPOSITE

Time Slips Away, 2010
Oil on canvas, 24" x 18"

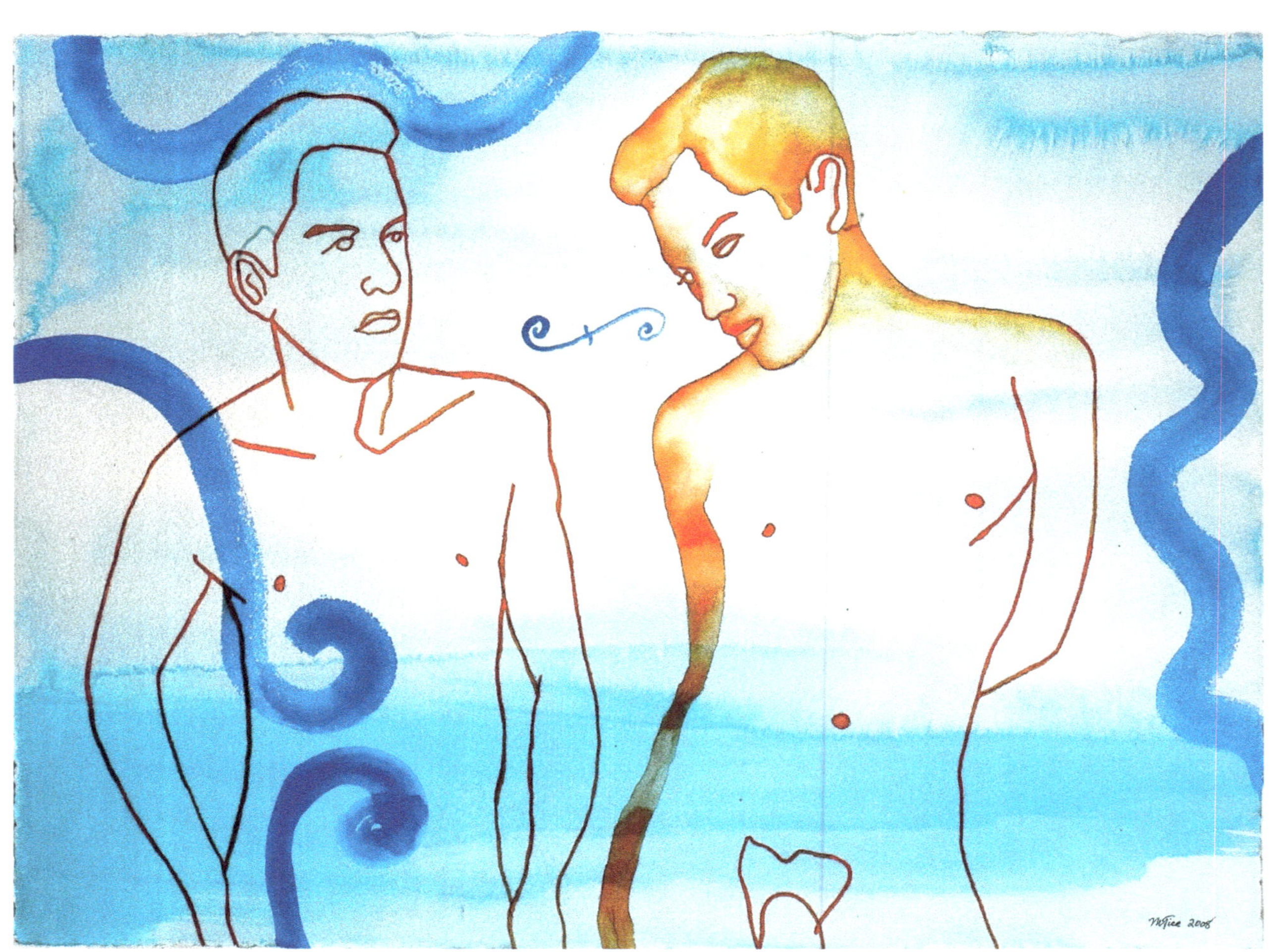

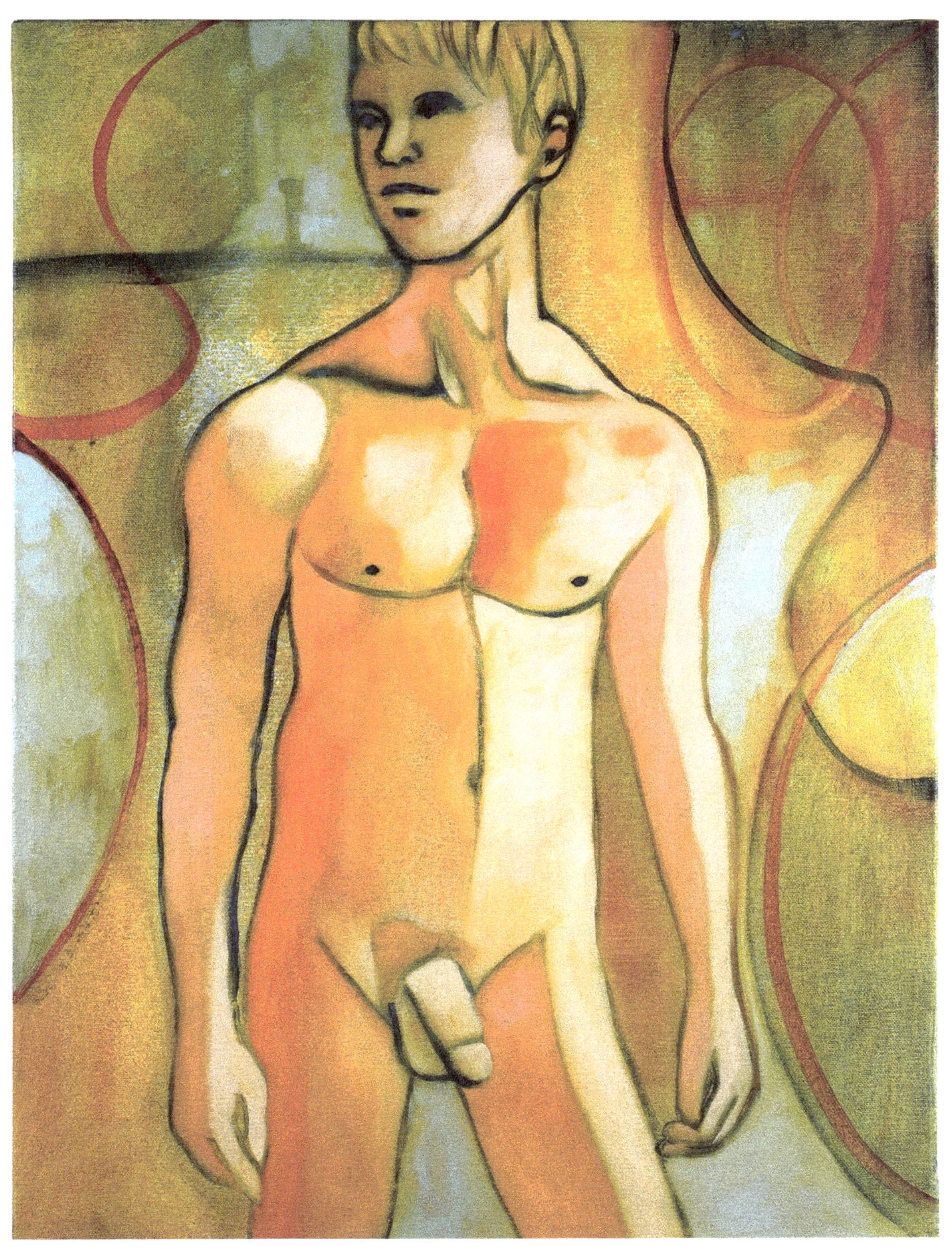

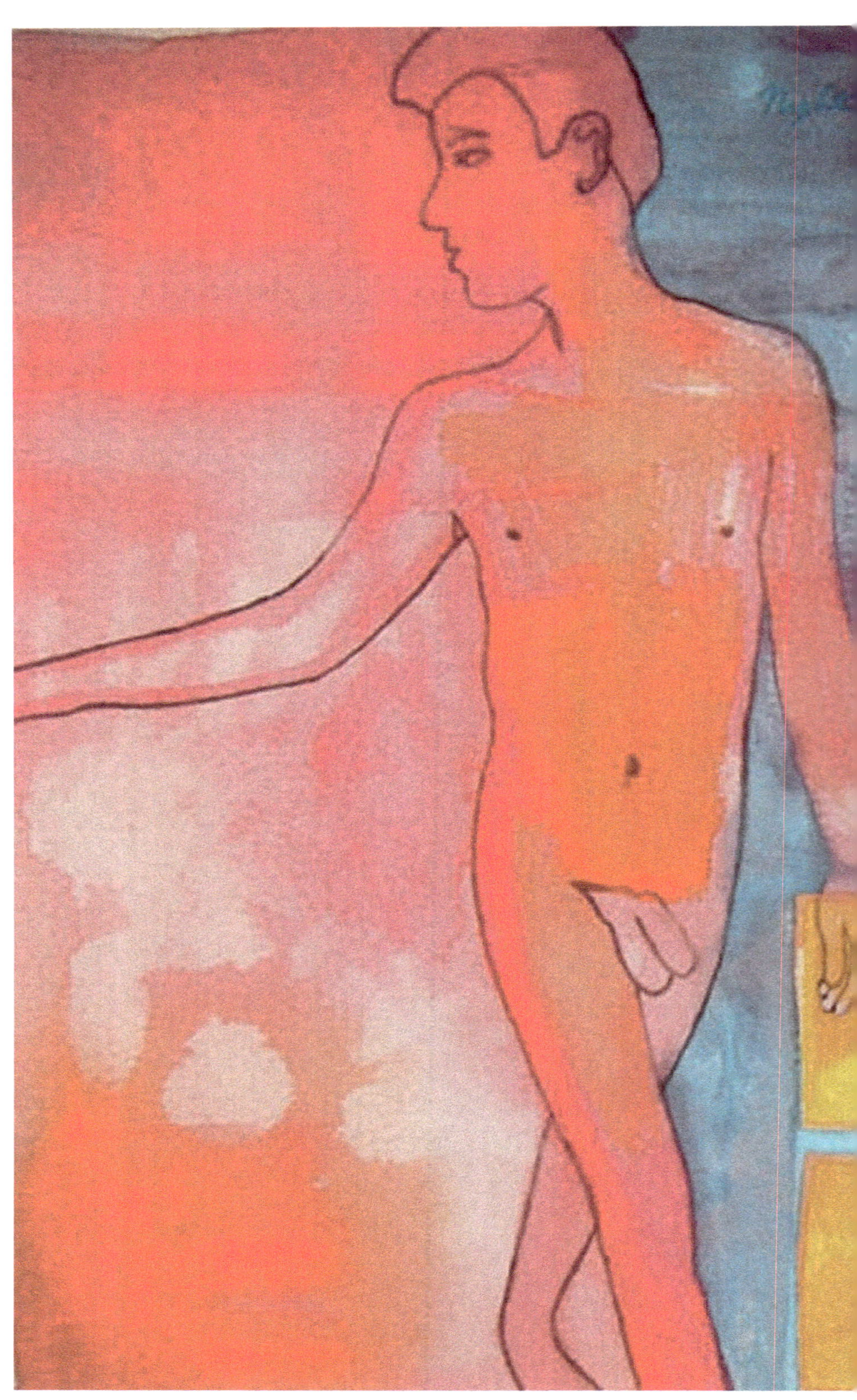

Night & Day, 2008
Watercolor & gouache on paper,
22" x 30"

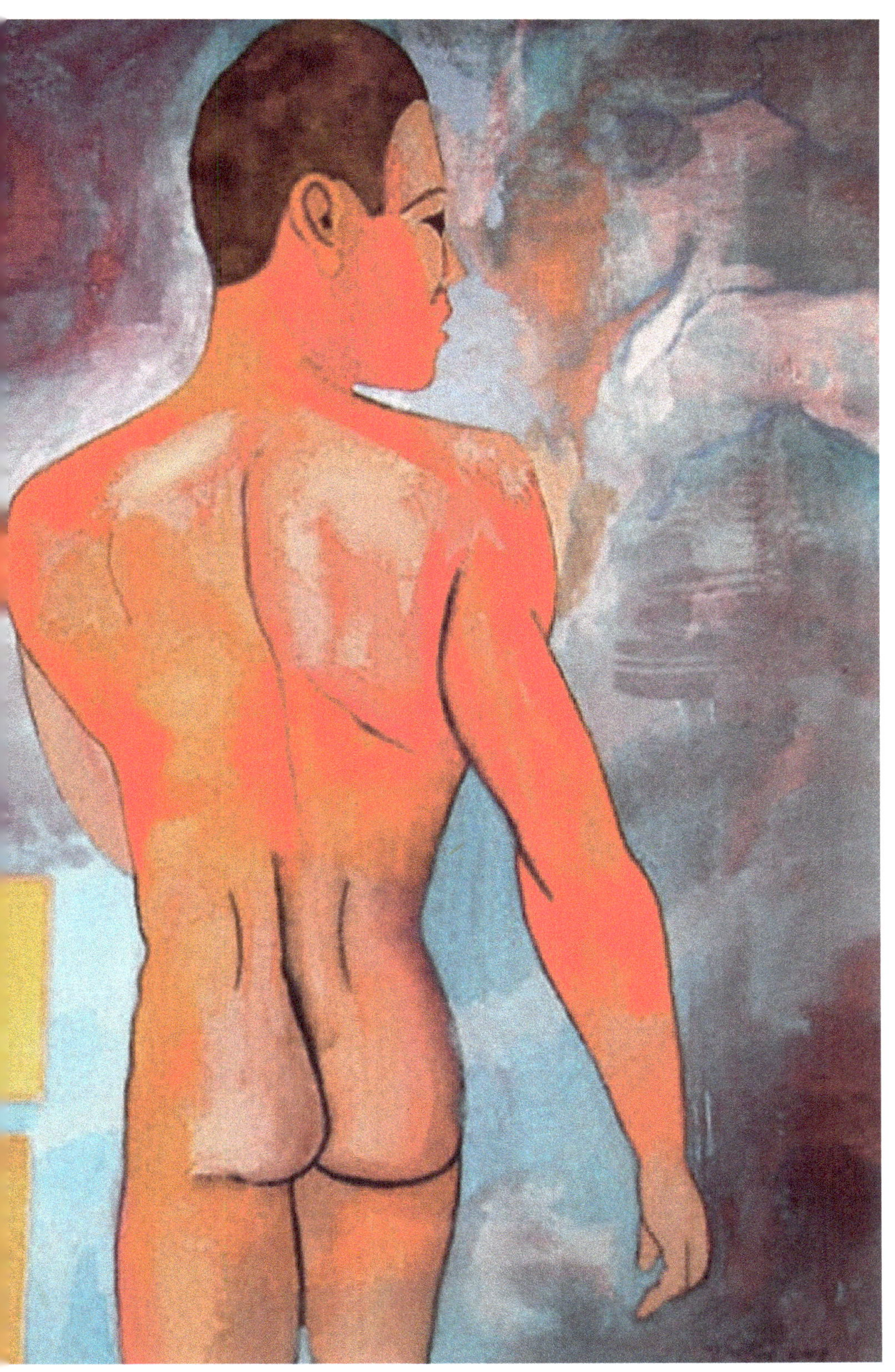

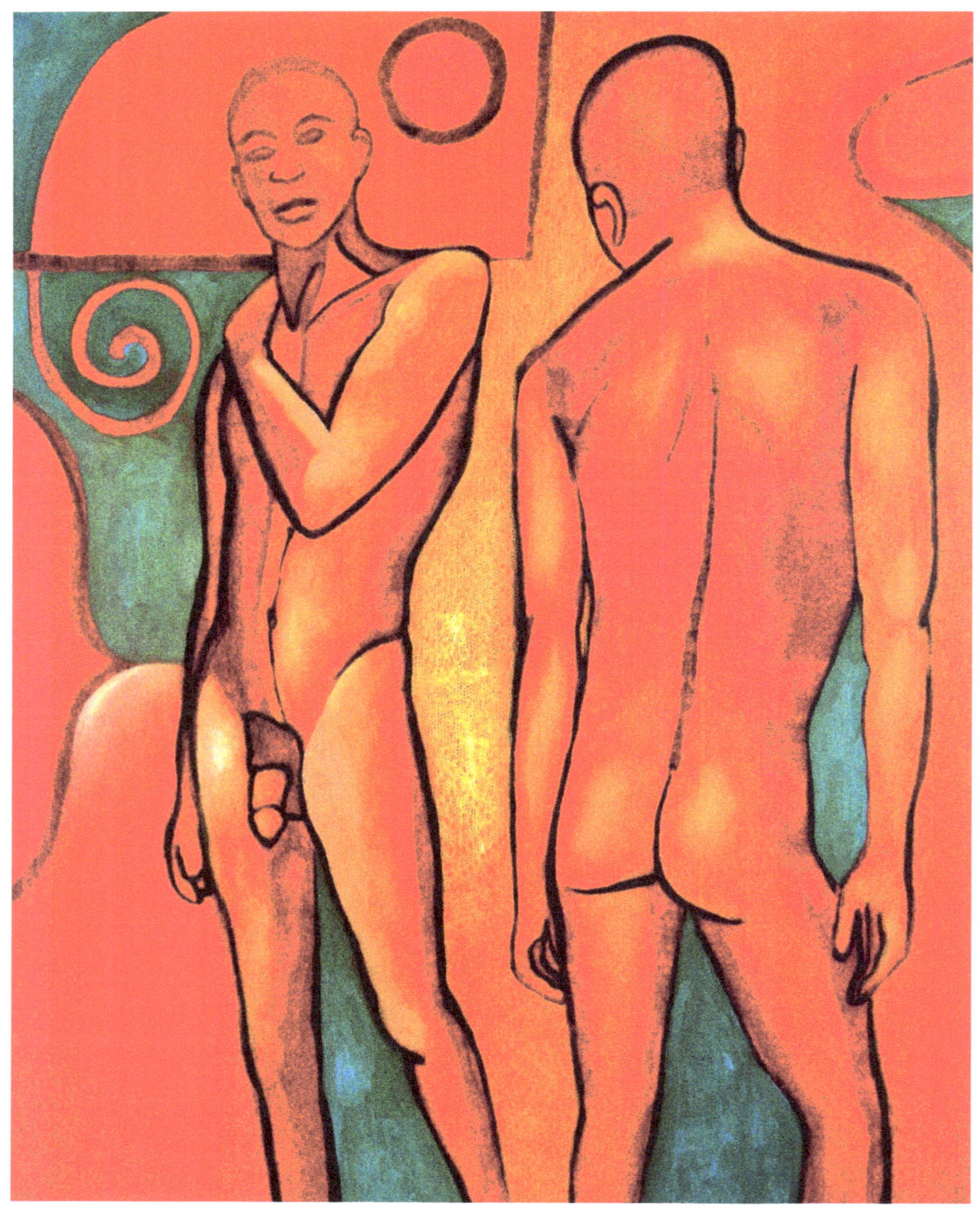

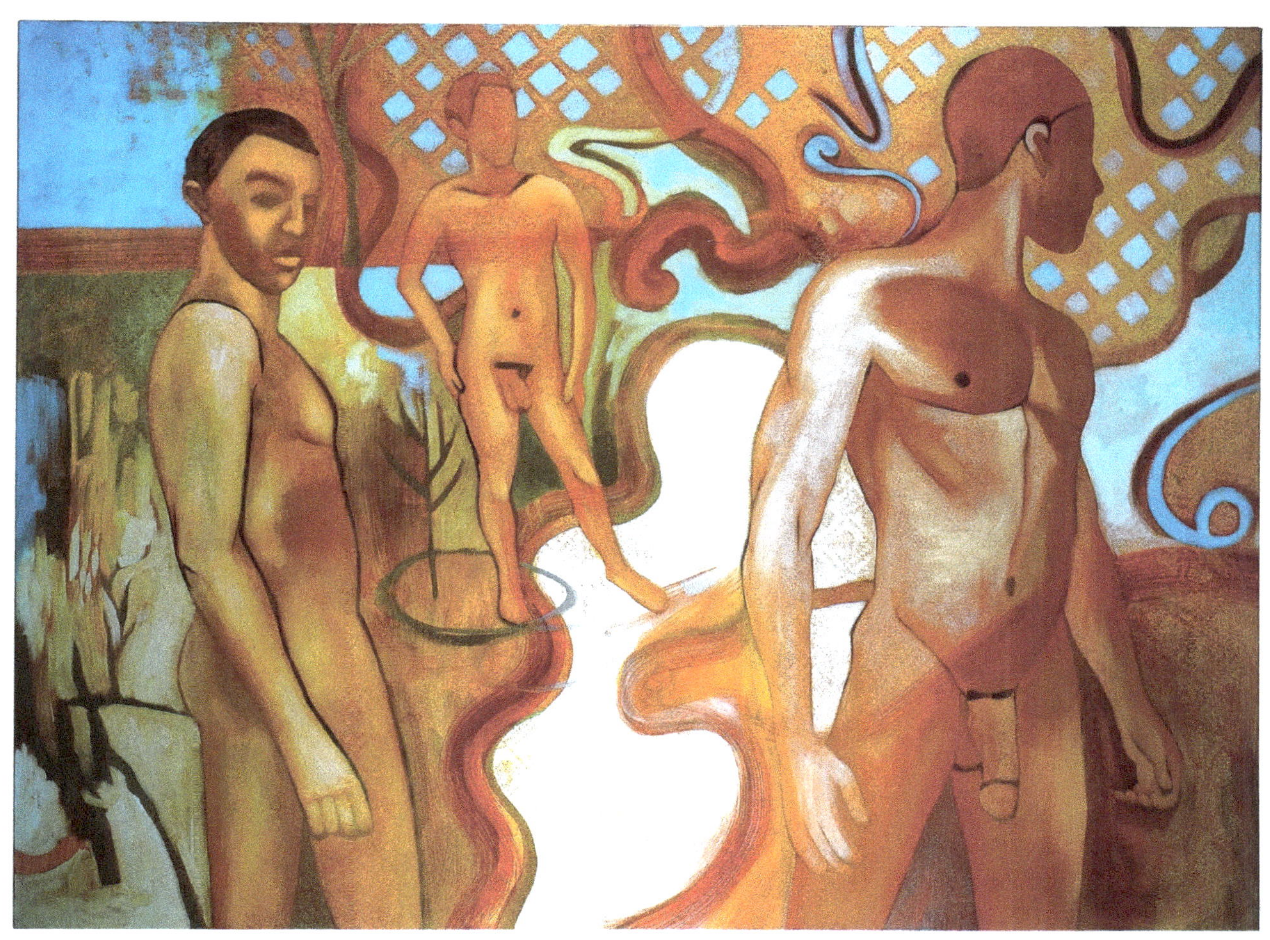

ABOVE

Three Nudes in A Landscape, 2006
Oil on canvas, 30" x 40"

OPPOSITE

October Weekend, 2010
Oil on canvas, 30" x 24"

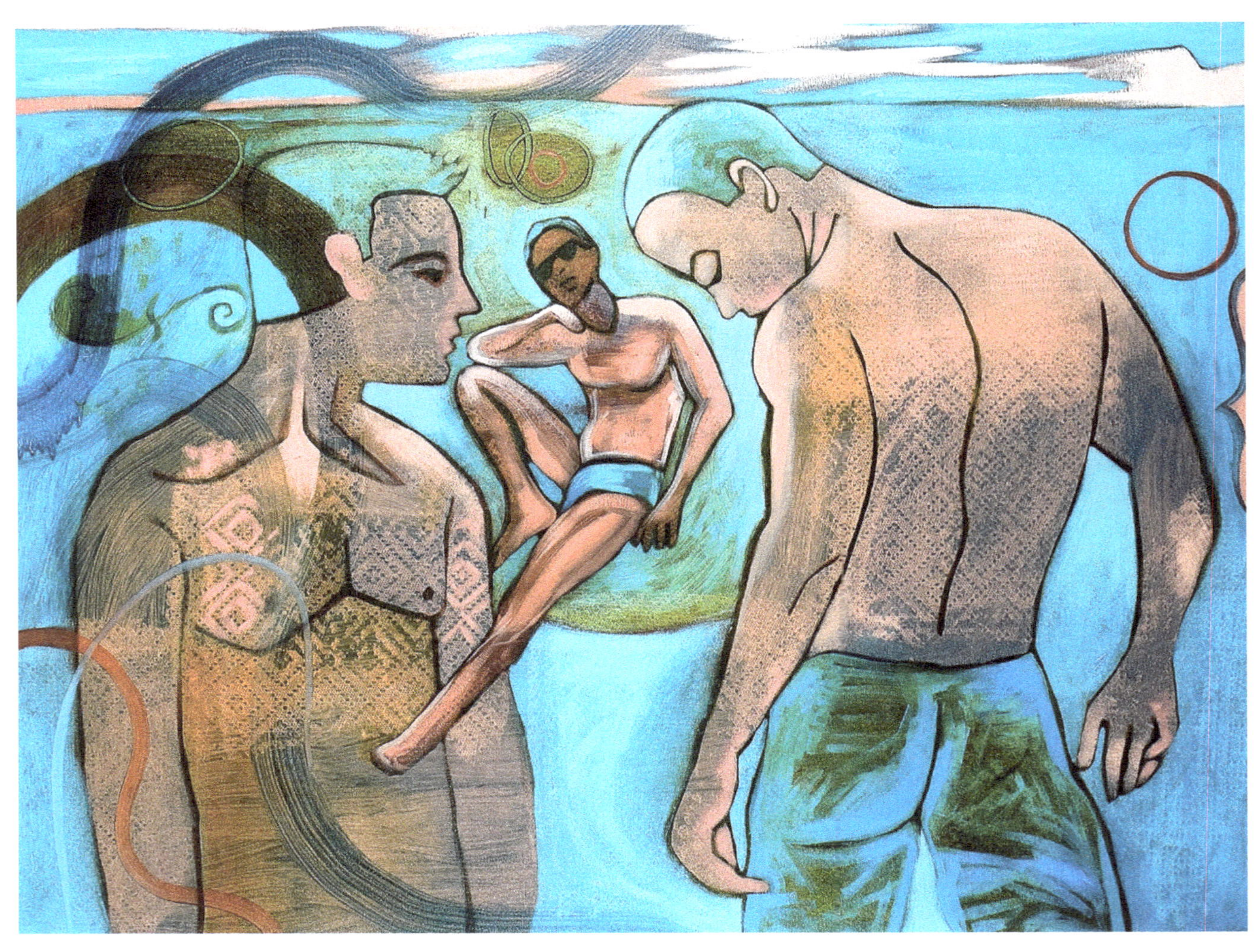

Curiosity, 2009
Oil on canvas, 30" x 40"

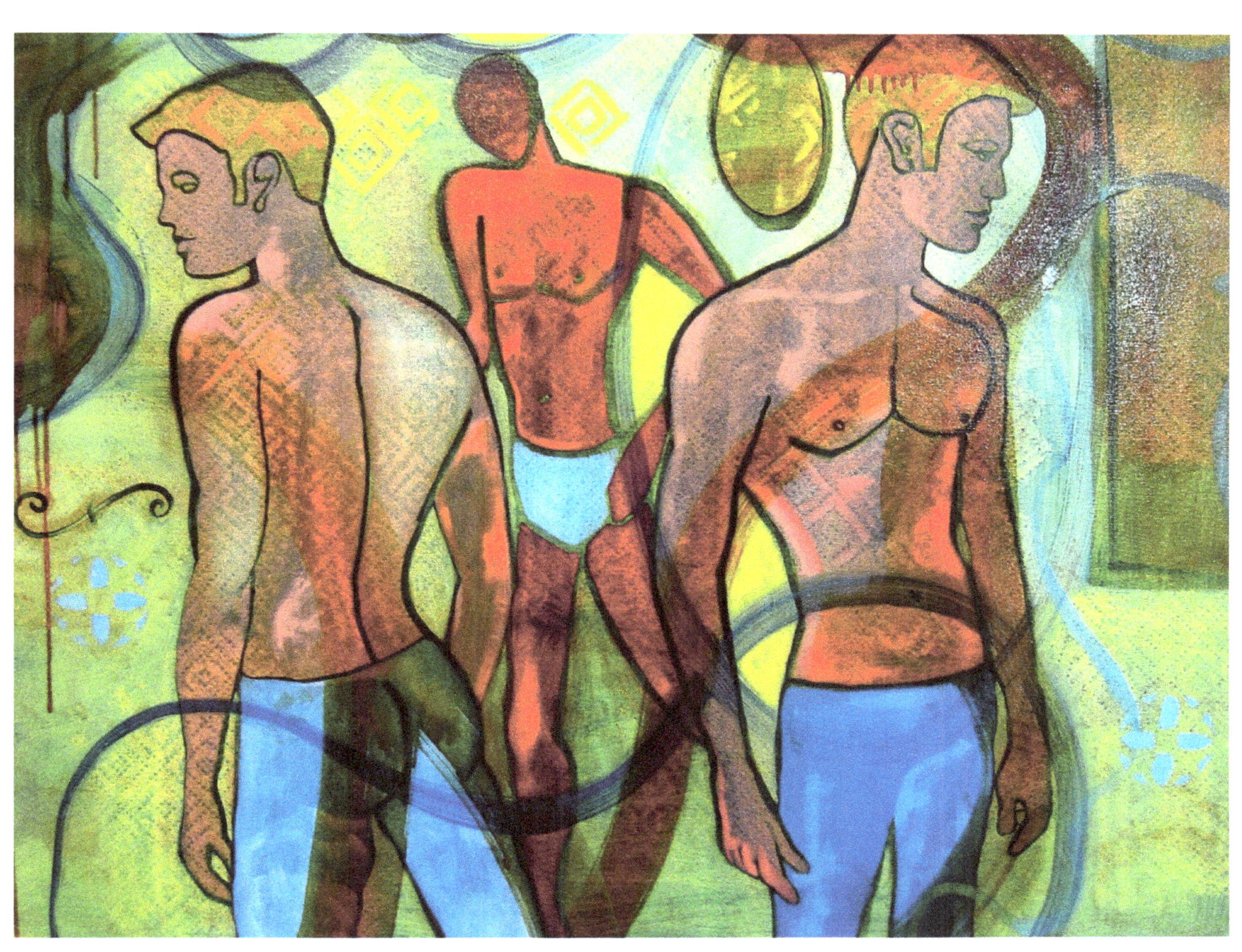

Curiosity, II, 2009
Oil on canvas, 30” x 40”

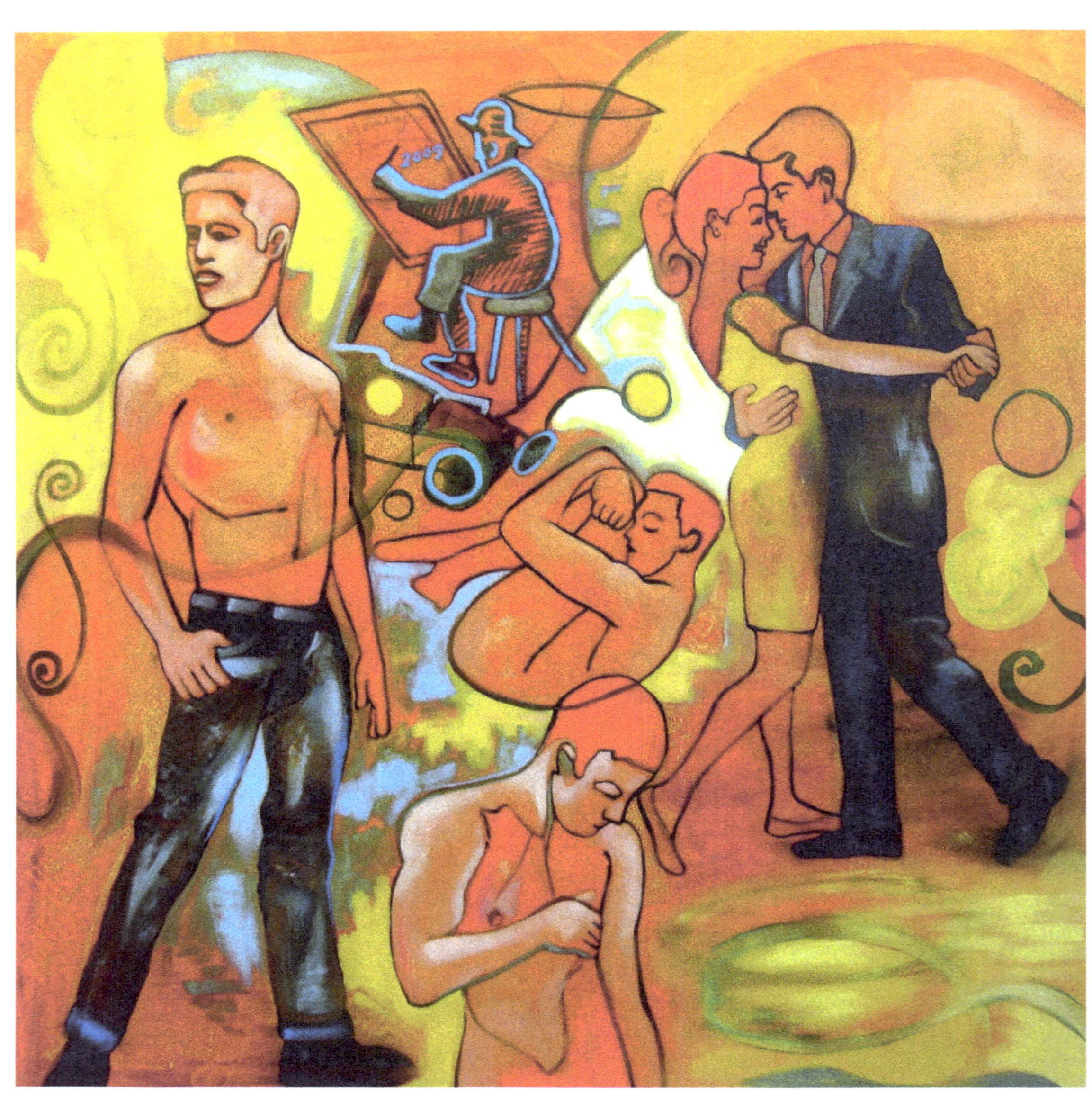

Memory Lain, 2009
Oil on canvas, 48" x 48"

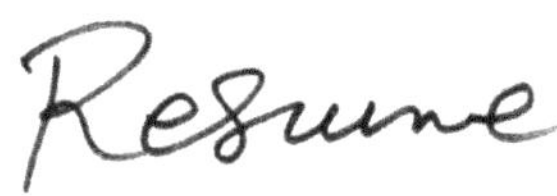

Born October 4, 1953, Augusta, Georgia
Lives in New York, New York
www.michaeltice.com

Michael Tice has had solo exhibitions in Manhattan at the 55 Mercer Gallery, Sensory Evolution Gallery, the Gallery at Flamingo East, and also at the Time & Space, Ltd. Gallery in Hudson, N.Y. He has had solo exhibitions outside New York at the University of Alabama, Huntsville, AL, the Aiken Center for the Arts, Aiken, SC, and the Durham Arts Council, Durham, NC, among others. He has shown his work frequently in New York since the early 1980s, and has been featured in several curated exhibitions in New York at The Painting Center, Fashion Institute of Technology, The Durst Organization, Margaret Bodell Gallery, George Billis Gallery and in other group shows at Exit Art, Sara Meltzer Gallery, PS 122, and numerous other galleries and alternative spaces.

Mr. Tice's work has appeared nationally in group exhibitions at the Stroud Foundation, Philadelphia, PA, the Greenville County Museum of Art, Greenville, SC, the Weatherspoon Gallery at UNC, Winston-Salem, NC, the French Library and Cultural Institute, Boston, MA, the North Carolina Museum of Art, Raleigh, NC, the Stamford Museum of Art, Stamford, CT, and the Minnesota Museum of Art in St. Paul, MN, among others.

Mr. Tice received a BFA from the University of South Carolina, a two-month fellowship to the MacDowell Colony in Peterborough, NH, and has done graduate work at the University of North Carolina and New York University. He lives and works in New York.

SELECTED SOLO EXHIBITIONS

- *Small Paintings*, Christopher 19, New York, NY **2011**

- *Human Tableaux*, Uzi N.Y. Gallery, New York, NY **2004**

- *New Paintings and Works on Paper*, Pegasus, New York, NY **2003**

- *Friends and Neighbors,* Recent Paintings and Works on Paper, 55 Mercer Gallery, New York, NY **2001**

- *Selected Paintings, 1991-2001*, Aiken Center for the Arts, Aiken, SC **2001**

- *Family Life,* Magnolia Grill, Durham, NC **2001**

- *Recent Paintings & Works on Paper*, Rivertown Lounge, New York, NY **1999**

- *Made for Each Other*, Pegasus, New York, NY, **1999**

- *Liquid Evidence*, Time and Space Gallery, Hudson, NY, **1994**

- *Perfect Moments & Other Disturbances*, The Gallery at Flamingo East, New York, NY **1993**

- *New Paintings*, University of Alabama, University Galleries, Huntsville, AL **1988**

- Sensory Evolution Gallery, New York, NY **1986**

- Lucky Strike Gallery, New York, NY **1984**

- Sensory Evolution Gallery, New York, NY **1984**

- Durham Arts Council, Durham, NC **1982**

- Carrboro Center for the Arts, Carrboro, NC **1982**

- University of South Carolina-Aiken, Aiken, SC **1980**

- Lyle Gallery, Augusta, GA **1979**

- AE Gallery, Aiken, SC **1979**

- Francis Marion College, Orangeburg, SC **1979**

- Columbia College, Columbia, SC **1978**

- University of South Carolina, Columbia, SC **1975**

SELECTED GROUP EXHIBITIONS

- *Floating in the Absence of Reason 2*, MH Gallery, New York, NY **2012**

- *Chromatogenous Conversations*, Three Person Show, MH Gallery, New York, NY **2011**

- *Union*, MH Gallery, New York, NY **2011**

- *Floating in the Absence of Reason*, MH Gallery, New York, NY **2010**

- *Collective*, Kimmel Center, New York University, New York, NY **2009-10** (Catalog)

- *Room to Room*, 20 West Gallery, Danbury, CT **2009**

- *Universal Diversity 15*, LGBT Community Center, New York, NY **2009**

- *Universal Diversity 14*, LGBT Community Center, New York, NY **2008**

- *Alumni Exhibition*, University of South Carolina, McMaster Gallery, Columbia, SC **2006**

- *Go Figure*, George Billis Gallery, New York, NY **2005**

- *Best of 2003*, Uzi N.Y. Gallery, New York, NY **2004**

- *Putting the X Back in Xmas*, Uzi N.Y. Gallery, New York, NY **2003**

- *Postcards from the Edge*, Galerie Lelong, New York, NY **2003**

- *October Projekt 30 Exhibition*, Bi-monthly online juried exhibition, www.projekt30.com **2003**

- *Translations: Dialogues on Life*, G2 Greeley Square Gallery, New York, NY **2003**

- *Douglas Dibble Memorial Art Auction*, Hunter College Times Square Gallery, (Invitational), **2003**

- *Summer Group Show*, SK417 Gallery, New York , NY **2003**

- *The Naked Truth, III.*, Pegasus, New York, NY **2003**

- *Universal Diversity 10*, LGBT Community Center, New York, NY **2003**

- *Nurturing the New*, NurtureArt Chelsea Gallery, New York, NY **2003**

- *Holiday Invitational*, Ceres Gallery, New York, NY **2002**

- *Small Works*, Four 53 Gallery, Brooklyn, NY **2002**

- *Benefit Print Sale*, Lower East Side Printshop, New York, NY **2002**

- *Feast of Desire - Painting & Drawing Invitational*, Leslie-Lohman Gay Art Foundation, New York, NY **2002**

- *Witness and Response: September 11th Acquisitions*, The Library of Congress, Washington, DC (Curated by Jeremy Adams and Harry Katz) **2002**

- *Synthesis of Style*, Cork Gallery, Lincoln Center, New York, NY **2002**

- *Postcards from the Edge*, Sperone Westwater Gallery, New York, NY **2002**

- *The Naked Truth, II.*, Pegasus, New York, NY **2002**

- *Recent Figurative Work*, The French Library and Cultural Center, Boston, MA **2002**

- *Winter Invitational*, The Painting Center, (Curated by Christina Chow), New York, NY **2002**

- *Figurative Expressive Work*, Nexus Gallery, New York, NY **2002**

- *Reactions*, Exit Art, New York, NY **2002**

- *Universal Diversity 9*, LBGT Community Center, New York, NY **2002**

- *Postcards from the Edge*, Sara Meltzer Gallery, New York, NY **2001**

- *The Square Show*, Ceres Gallery, New York, NY **2001**

- *Night of a 1000 Drawings*, Artist's Space, New York, NY **2001**

- *WTC Art & Music Benefit*, Arlene Grocery, New York, NY **2001**

- *Offspring*, BHMS Gallery, Brooklyn Heights Montessori School, Brooklyn, NY Curated by Charlotta Kotik, Tom Eccles, Linda Marchisotto, Janet Riker and Wendy Olsoff **2001**

- *Artists Collect Art*, Work from the collections of Philip Mullen, Syd Cross, and Diane Buck, Columbia College Gallery, Columbia, SC **2001**

- *Figurative & Portraiture - Realism to Abstraction 2001*, West Side Arts Coalition, New York, NY **2001**

- *Benefit Auction for NurtureArt*, Margaret Bodell Gallery, New York, NY **2000**

- *Night of 1000 Drawings*, Artists Space, New York, NY **2000**

- *Three Figurative Painters*, The Lobby Gallery, Durst Organization, New York, NY **2000**

- *Patterned Flowers*, George Billis Gallery, New York, NY **2000**

- *Pier Show 8*, Brooklyn Working Artists Coalition, Brooklyn, NY **2000**

- *Salon 2000*, Limner Gallery, New York, NY **2000**

- *Artists Celebrate the Child*, Brooklyn Heights Montessori School Brooklyn, NY Curated by Sarah Greer and Meredith Bergman **2000**

- *1999 Night of a 1000 Drawings*, Artists Space, New York, NY **1999**

- *Print Fair & Open House*, Lower East Side Printshop, New York, NY **1999**

- *Chase Manhattan Holiday Gift Exhibition*, Chase Manhattan Bank, Brooklyn, NY **1999**

- *Universal Diversity 7*, Clemente Soto Velez Cultural Center, New York, NY **1999**

- *Desert Voices Art Auction*, Community Center, Tuczon, AZ **1999**

- *Anniversary Rotation*, Marlen Gallery, New York, NY **1999**

- *Pride 2*, Vincent Louis Gallery, New York, NY **1999**

- *The Freedom to Create*, Chocolate-Milk Gallery, New York, NY **1999**

- *Five Painters*, Pegasus, New York, NY **1999**

- *Plus or Minus 30: Honing the Edge*, Clemente Soto Velez Cultural Center, New York, NY, Curated by Barbara Ann Levy **1999**

- *The Red Show*, Barbara Ann Levy Gallery, New York, NY **1999**

- *Gay Landscape*, Clemente Soto Velez Cultural Center, New York, NY **1999**

- *Salon Show*, Feral Art Gallery, Brooklyn, NY **1999**

- *Art on Artists*, The Times Square Lobby Gallery, New York, NY, Curated by Cyn McLean **1999**

- *Christine Carrier Chiquelin Curates*, George Billis Gallery, New York, NY **1998**

- *SexualityObject*, New Century Artists Gallery, New York, NY. Curated by Scott Holman **1998**

- *A World View*, (World Artists for Tibet) The Times Square Lobby Gallery, New York, NY Curated by Cyn McLean **1998**

- *3rd Annual Small Works Show*, PS 122 Gallery, New York, NY **1998**

- *Media Madness*, Westbeth Gallery, New York, NY **1998**

- *Pride 1998*, Vincent Louis Gallery, New York, NY Curated by Lisa Johnson **1998**

- *Out on the Edge Together*, Clemente Soto Velez Cultural Center, New York, NY (Invitational) **1998**

- *2nd Annual Small Works Show*, PS 122 Gallery, New York, NY (Invitational) **1997**

- *Universal Diversity 5*, La Mama Galleria, New York, NY **1997**

- *A Convocation of Artists*, Leslie-Lohman Gallery, New York, NY. Curated by Wayne Snellen **1996**

- *Emerging Artists*, Harper Gallery, New York, NY (Invitational) **1995**

- *Universal Diversity 3*, Leslie-Lohman Gallery, New York, NY **1995**

- *Organization of Independent Artists Group Show*, 59 Franklin Street Gallery, New York, NY **1993**

- *Figurative Poetics: The Union of Psyche & Myth*, Organization of Independent Artists Gallery, New York, NY. Curated by Matthew Turov **1993**

- *Wall to Wall*, 121 Chambers Street, New York, NY **1993**

- *They Came By Boat: A Celebration of Discovery*, Elsa Mott Ives Gallery, New York, NY. Curated by Paul Bridgewater and Laura Kruger **1992**

- *Salon '92*, Tribeca 148 Gallery, New York, NY **1992**

- *15 Years of Fellowship Awards Artists*, S.C. Arts Commission, South Carolina State Museum, Columbia, SC (catalog) **1990**

- *Tunnel Mural Series Project*, Tunnel Club, New York, NY **1987**

- *The East Village*, Fashion Institute of Technology, New York, NY. Curated by Richard Martin (catalog) **1986**

- *Post-Alabama Contemporary Artists*, Phenix City Gallery, New York, NY, Auburn University, Auburn, AL, and University of Alabama, Birmingham, AL **1986**

- *The Liberty Show*, La Mama Gallery, New York, NY **1986**

- *Jungle Fever*, Sensory Evolution Gallery, New York, NY **1986**

- *Summer Pop Invitational*, Sensory Evolution Gallery, New York, NY **1986**

- *Small Works by Big Thinkers*, Bess Cutler Gallery, New York, NY **1985**

- *Third International Fair of Contemporary Art*, London, England **1985**

- *Pressure Point--East Village , NYC*, Wunsch Arts Center, Glen Cove, NY **1985**

- *The Nude As Painting Subject*, Danceteria, New York, NY **1985**

- *Third Annual Art Auction*, Limbo Lounge Gallery, New York, NY **1985**

- *Micro Show II*, Now Gallery, New York, NY **1985**

- *Breaking Ground*, Sensory Evolution Gallery, New York, NY **1985**

- *Combat Zone*, Sensory Evolution Gallery, New York, NY **1985**

- *Game Show*, Sensory Evolution Gallery, New York, NY **1985**

- *Small Works by East Village Artists*, Stroud Foundation, Philadelphia, PA **1984**

- *The Future Is Now*, Sensory Evolution Gallery, New York, NY **1984**

- *Trade Piece with Claudia de Monte*, Gracie Mansion Gallery, New York, NY **1984**

- *Carnival*, Sensory Evolution Gallery, New York, NY **1984**

- *Second Annual Art Auction*, Limbo Lounge, New York, NY **1984**

- *Friendly Neighbors*, El Pueblo Gallery, New York, NY **1984**

- *Art Forgery*, Public Image Gallery, New York, NY **1984**

- *Black Tie Optional*, Sensory Evolution Gallery, New York, NY **1984**

- *Conspiracies*, Limbo Lounge Gallery, New York, NY **1984**

- *Sneak Preview*, Nico Smith Gallery, New York, NY **1984**

- *The Acid Test*, Ground Zero Gallery, Sensory Evolution, & Kamikaze Klub, New York, NY **1984**

- *Micro Show*, Now Gallery, New York, NY **1984**

- *The East Village Look---Again*, Danceteria, New York, NY **1984**

- *Nativity*, Limbo Lounge Gallery, New York, NY **1984**

- *North Carolina Artists Exhibition*, North Carolina Museum of Art, Raleigh, NC (Curated by Howard N. Fox) (catalog) **1984**

- *The Sixth North Carolina Artists' Invitational*, Waterworks Gallery, Salisbury, NC (catalog) **1983**

- *Art on Paper*, Weatherspoon Art Gallery, Greensboro, NC **1982**

- *Durham Art Guild Show*, Durham Arts Center, Durham, NC **1981, 1982**

- *Miller Plus 80*, Green Hill Art Gallery, Greensboro, NC (catalog) **1982**

- *Bradley National Prints & Drawings*, Bradley University, Peoria, IL (catalogs) **1977, 1979**

- *Connecticut Painters & Sculptors*, Stamford Museum of Art, Stamford, CT **1979**

- *National Drawings & Prints*, Miami University, Oxford, OH (Juried by Nancy Graves) (catalog) **1978**

- *Dulin National Prints & Drawings*, Dulin Gallery of Art, Knoxville, TN **1977**

- *Drawings USA '77*, Minneapolis Museum of Art, St. Paul, MN (Juried by Paul Cumming) (catalog) **1977**

- *Appalachian National Drawing Competition*, Appalachian State University, Boone, NC (Honorable Mention) (catalog) **1977, 1978**

- *Springs Mills Traveling Show*, Lancaster, SC and Springs Mills Corporation, New York, NY (catalogs) **1975, 1976, 1982**

- *South Carolina Arts Commission Exhibition*, Columbia, SC **1974, 1975, 1976, 1978**

- *South Carolina Art Guild Exhibition*, Columbia, SC **1973, 1974, 1975, 1976, 1978**

SELECTED AWARDS

- South Carolina Arts Commission, Individual Artist's Fellowship, **1979-1980**

- MacDowell Colony Fellowship, Peterborough, NH, **1979**

- Durham Art Guild, Best in Show & One Person Show Award, **1982**

- First Place Drawing Award, National Drawings & Prints, Miami

- University, Oxford, OH (Nancy Graves, Juror) (catalog), **1978**

- First Place Painting Award, South Carolina Art Guild Exhibition, Columbia, SC (Linda Shearer, Juror) **1978**

PERMANENT COLLECTIONS

- South Carolina State Museum, Columbia, SC
- The Library of Congress, Washington, DC
- Miami University, Oxford, OH
- University of South Carolina, Columbia, SC
- Greenville County Museum of Art, Greenville, SC
- Springs Mills, Inc., New York, NY
- The Miller Brewing Company, Edenton, NC
- University of South Carolina, Aiken, SC
- South Carolina Arts Commission
- Hallmark Corporation, New York, NY
- The MacDowell Colony, Peterborough, NH

SELECTED BIBLIOGRAPHY

- Gibbons, E., *100 Artists of the Male Figure*, **Schiffer Publishing**, 2011.
- McDermott, Stephen W., "ArtGroup's Emerging Legacy--Important mid-summer shows at SK417 and Pegasus," ***Gay City News***, p. 25, July 25-31, 2003.
- McDermott, Stephen W., "Happy Meals--Artists explore and inspire carnal appetites in paint," ***Gay City News***, p. 16, December 6-12, 2002.
- Cotter, Holland, "Amid the Ashes, Creativity," ***The New York Times***, p.E33, February1, 2002.
- Mack, Dr. Tom. "Local Artist Michael Tice comes full circle," ***The Aiken Standard***, October 14, 2001.
- Combs, Whitney, "Michael Tice," ***NYArts Magazine***, September 2001.
- Pagano, Marie R., "Figurative and Portraiture," ***Gallery & Studio*** magazine, March/April 2001.
- "The East Village Show," Voice Choices, Galleries, ***The Village Voice,*** March 26, 1986.
- Wallach, Amei, "Abstract Power," ***Newsday***, February 22, 1985.
- "Cutting Edge of Art Travels to Glen Cove," Galleries, ***Sun Storm***, February 1985.
- Byrd-Platt, Ann, "The Art Scene Moves to the East Village," ***The Wall Street Journal***, May 2, 1984.
- "The Class of 1984," Galleries, ***New York Talk***, October 1984.
- Horton, Charles, "Local Art Shines in North Carolina Show," ***The Chapel Hill Newspaper***, April 22, 1984.
- Ermutlu, Karen, "Marcia Tucker Curates South Carolina Arts Commission Exhibition," ***Art Voices/South,*** July/August 1978.

EDUCATION

- University of South Carolina, BFA in Printmaking & Drawing, 1975
- University of North Carolina, Chapel Hill, NC, Painting,1982
- New York University, Painting, 1991-93

Other titles published by bd-studios.com

Tentative Armor by Michael Harren
Angkor Wat by luke kurtis
INTERSECTION by luke kurtis
The Language of History by luke kurtis
Visions of the Beyond by Stefanie Masciandaro
Puertas Españolas by Josemaria Mejorada & May Gañán
Jordan's Journey by Jordan M. Scoggins
Just One More by Jonathan David Smyth